Globalization or Empire?

Jan Nederveen Pieterse

ROUTLEDGE

NEW YORK AND LONDON

Published in 2004 by
Routledge
29 West 35th Street
New York, NY 10001
www.routledge-ny.com

Published in Great Britain by
Routledge
11 New Fetter Lane
London EC4P 4EE
www.routledge.co.uk

Routledge is an imprint of the Taylor and Francis Group.

Printed in the United Stated of America on acid-free paper.
Typesetting: BookType

10 9 8 7 6 5 4 3 2 1

Library of Congress Cataloging-in-Publication Data

Nederveen Pieterse, Jan.
  Globalization or empire? / Jan Nederveen Pieterse.
    p. cm.
Includes bibliographical references and index.
  ISBN 0-415-94848-7 (acid-free paper) — ISBN 0-415-94849-5 (pbk. :
acid-free paper)
  1. United States—Foreign relations—2001- 2. Balance of power. 3. Imperialism.
4. United States—Foreign economic relations. 5. Globalization—Political aspects—
United States. 6. World politics—1989– I. Title.
  E902.N43 2004
  327.73'009'0511—dc22
                                                              2003021147

Contents

iii

Introduction

Through the 1990s, the leading topic of debate in social science and policy was globalization. The theme emerging in the 2000s is imperialism. The obvious question is how does globalization relate to empire? Should we consider imperialism as a phase or a modality of globalization, or as a fundamentally different dynamic? In my view globalization is a dynamic of far greater moment and historical duration than empire. Globalization refers to the long-term historical trend of greater worldwide interconnectedness; imperial episodes are part of this trend, so empire is part of globalization. Globalization also serves as a flag word for concurrent changes that unfold amid unequal relations of power, and imperialism is but one form that unequal power relations take. Empires come and go, globalization continues.

But if globalization stays, the question is what kind of globalization? American capitalism has played a large part in shaping contemporary globalization in its own image, as neoliberal globalization, and this impact may be more significant than specific imperial interventions. To understand the present we must revisit the past and to understand empire we must revisit globalization. The most recent globalization project, neoliberal globalization, is the deluxe model of Pax Americana that combined economic unilateralism with political multilateralism.

Is the recent belligerent unilateralism in American policy just an extension of past policies or a fundamental change of dynamics? It's intriguing that imperialism should make a comeback in the twenty-first century.

Although many developments in the United States have built up to this, it's not obvious that this avenue should have been taken or that it will endure. I spent years studying imperialism, and I have been glad to give it up for "globalization." Returning to empire feels like time travel. Empire in my view is part of the emerging configuration but not a necessary part. Given the still available instruments of neoliberal globalization—financial and economic discipline—and the massive costs and risks of empire, recourse to territorial imperialism is likely to be exceptional.

Globalization and imperialism are multidimensional and kaleidoscopic, so they should be understood in a kaleidoscopic fashion. The segmented approach to globalization (globalization *and* the state, culture, political economy, development, the South, etc.) reflects the disciplinary dispersion in social science, which is understandable but old-fashioned. I try to overcome this segmentation by merging and mixing perspectives and themes. Looking at globalization and American policies not just from the point of view of political science and international relations, but also in light of economic dynamics and global inequality, technological changes and military affairs, and cultural attitudes and discourses, is more realistic than a single disciplinary perspective. Understanding real globalization requires both depth, including historical depth, and breadth. Another sensibility that informs this book is looking beyond the North to the global South; these inquiries are inspired by conversations on globalization in many countries and continents.

The first chapter examines neoliberal globalization and focuses in particular on the role of the American South in reshaping American capitalism and on the cold war setting in the making of real neoliberalism.

Chapter 2 probes the scenarios that shape the policies of the Bush II administration and various ways of understanding them. If these policies are imperial, is it an imperial moment, or an imperial episode?

Chapter 3 is an analytical intermezzo that discusses the differences between globalization and empire. This is a controversial question in view of many arguments that view contemporary globalization as imperialism all along.

Chapter 4 asks, if present American policies are imperial, what kind of empire is it? Is American economic unilateralism, which characterized neoliberal globalization, now being combined with political-military unilateralism? I propose neoliberal empire as a novel historical formation and a hybrid that attempts to merge the logics of business and war.

Chapters 2 and 4 (and part of Chapter 9) focus on policies of the Bush II administration. Other chapters probe more deeply the underlying tendencies of neoliberal globalization and address dynamics that matter more or less regardless of how the recent projects of power unfold. Chapter 5 considers global inequality and the economic ramifications of neoliberal globalization for the world majority. The international policy focus on poverty alleviation coexists with neoliberal policies that widen inequality domestically and internationally. This chapter examines where the data depart from the conventional wisdom. The belief that the risks global inequality poses can be contained in the global margins is contradicted by the crossborder effects of environmental degradation, migration, transnational crime, and terrorism. The interacting policies of developmental and financial discipline, marginalization, and containment may be viewed as part of a process of *hierarchical integration*, which has turbulence built in.

Chapter 6 looks at conflict and security from the point of view of technological changes that unfold in the worlds of production, war, and politics. This chapter concentrates on the background role of technology, asymmetric conflict, and the geopolitics of globalization. Focusing on technology serves to shift the attention from globalization events to the infrastructure of globalization. Considering violence means zeroing in on the dark side of globalization: how is it that accelerated globalization is so deeply mired in containment politics? Focusing on conflict and security shows the Janus faces of globalization. A point where key dimensions—technologies, the political economy of conflict and security, and geopolitics—intersect is asymmetric conflict.

Technological changes enhance capabilities for conflict, but these capacities are meaningless outside a cultural context. It requires cultural attitudes and narratives to produce the will to power or the will to transformation. Chapter 7 discusses cultural perspectives on globalization North and South. Existing analytical frameworks and narratives—such as dependency, imperialism, social exclusion, conspiracy theories, clash of civilizations, fundamentalism—are not adequate for dealing with uneven globalization. Several layers of attitudes shield the "chauvinism of prosperity." It is one thing to diagnose different conditions North and South, but equally important is the relationship between these differences, the articulations across different conditions.

Chapter 8 asks, if we take seriously the claim to American exceptionalism, what does this imply for United States hegemony? What does it mean when a country that by its own account is a historical exception and a special case sets rules for the world? Key dimensions of American exceptionalism are free enterprise, political conservatism, Americanism, social inequality, the large role of the military, and hyperpower status; what do they imply for American world leadership? Globalization the American way reproduces the American winner-takes-all pattern on a world scale, producing growing inequality globally and within societies. American exceptionalism is a self-caricature and we must consider several counterpoints; yet the present rapports of force do not enable major changes from within.

What is the scope for changes from without? The closing chapter probes alternative options by looking at different capitalisms in Asia and Europe. In light of the Enron episode in the United States and American belligerence, can greater Asian-European dialogue and rapport contribute to shaping a global alternative? The focus is on Asia and Europe but the question resonates worldwide and concerns the overall direction of contemporary globalization.

Acknowledgments

My thanks to Lisa Chason for her help in editing this book and to Emin
Adas and Carlos Zeisel for their research assistance.

Most chapters have been presented in seminars, lectures, or conferences
and I thank all participants for their comments. Several chapters have been
published earlier as articles and are reworked here. Versions of Chapters 3
and 4 were presented at the Unit for Criticism, University of Illinois
Urbana-Champaign, Queen's University in Belfast, Binghamton University,
the Institute of Social Studies in The Hague, at conferences at NYU, the
CUNY Graduate Center, and the British Association of International
Studies in London, in 2002 and 2003. A version of Chapter 4 appears in
Theory, Culture and Society in 2004, and I acknowledge permission of Sage
to use a version of the article here. An earlier version of Chapter 5 on global
inequality appeared in *Third World Quarterly*. I thank Keith Griffin and
Howard Wachtel for their comments. Chapter 6 originates in a conference
on globalization, state, and violence at University of Sussex, 1998. An earlier
version appeared in the *Review of International Political Economy* (9, 1). For
their comments I thank Michael Humphrey, Ananta Giri, seminar participants at the Centre for the Study of Globalisation and Regionalisation,
University of Warwick, the Sociology Department of University of Illinois
Urbana-Champaign, and reviewers. An earlier version of Chapter 7 was
published in *Theory, Culture and Society* in 2000. Chapter 8 was originally
presented at a conference on globalization and Americanization in Munich,

2000; it appears in *New Political Economy* and in a volume edited by Ulrich Beck, Nathan Sznaider, and Rainer Winter. I thank Jeff Powell and Joost Smiers for their comments. Chapter 9 was presented at the conference Identités et Démocratie in Rennes, 2002; it appears in the *Asian Social Science Journal* and in a French translation. I thank Emin Adas, Ruth Aguilera, Walden Bello, and Amit Prasad for their comments. Several chapters were also presented as lectures at Chulalongkorn University and Thammasat University in Bangkok, 2003.

References

Full references are given in the Bibliography and short references are in the endnotes after each chapter. References to newspapers, weeklies and websites are only given in the endnotes (and not repeated in the Bibliography). Abbreviations in references:

New York Times	NYT
Financial Times	FT
Guardian Weekly	GW
International Herald Tribune	IHT
Los Angeles Times	LAT
Wall Street Journal	WSJ

Abbreviations in references and text:

Central Intelligence Agency	CIA
European Union	EU
Human Development Report	HDR
International Monetary Fund	IMF
United Nations	UN
United Nations Development Program	UNDP
World Trade Organization	WTO

CHAPTER **1**

Neoliberal Globalization

During the past two decades the dominant approach in policy has been neoliberal globalization, not in the sense that it is all there is to globalization, but in the sense that it became a global regime. Most protest against globalization concerns neoliberal globalization, and arguably this is the actual problem, rather than globalization per se. Contemporary globalization can be described as a package deal that includes informatization (applications of information technology), flexibilization (destandardization in the organization of production and labor), and various changes such as regionalization and the reconfiguration of states. Since the 1980s, the growing impact of neoliberal policies add to the globalization package, deregulation (liberalization, privatization), marketization (unleashing market forces), financialization and securitization (conversion of assets into tradable financial instruments), and the ideology of lean government. This chapter considers how this has come about and focuses on the economic and political shift within the United States to the South, the connection between the cold war and neoliberalism, and the Washington consensus.

Studies generally explain the onset of neoliberalism as the confluence of the economic ideas of the Chicago school and the policies of Ronald Reagan and Margaret Thatcher. A further strand is the Washington consensus, the economic orthodoxy that guided the IMF and World Bank in their policies through the 1990s and turned neoliberalism into global policy.

Adding detail to this account, Adam Tickell and Jamie Peck discuss the development of neoliberalism in three phases: an early phase of *proto-*

1

neoliberalism from the 1940s to the 70s in which the main ideas took shape; a phase of *roll-back neoliberalism* in the 1980s when it became government policy in the United States and United Kingdom; and *roll-out neoliberalism* in the 1990s when it became hegemonic in multilateral institutions.[1]

Like many accounts this focuses on economic ideas (of the Mont Pèlerin Society, Friedrich von Hayek, and Milton Friedman) and the policies of Reagan and Thatcher. But by locating the origins of neoliberalism in the realm of ideas and the theories of the Chicago school, this overlooks the actual economic policies that shaped "real neoliberalism" already before the Reagan era. The low-taxes, low-services regime envisioned by free market advocates already existed in the American South. Real neoliberalism in the United States in the 1970s and 80s meant the implementation of the low-wage, low-tax model of Southern economics. The political muscle of the Southern conservatives and the welcome mat of the anti-union South for corporations fleeing the Northeast is what gave the "Reagan revolution" its depth and punch. Eventually this led to the rollback of the regulatory and social functions of the state as a national trend.

The material matrix of real neoliberalism is the American South. This is worth considering for several reasons. Just as we don't analyze Soviet society by reading the texts of Marx but by examining real existing socialism, we should look at the material political economy of neoliberalism and not just its theoretical claims. Had the American South with its low wages, high exploitation, and reactionary culture been upheld as the model of economic growth, it would never have exercised the glossy appeal that the "free market" did in theory. The Chicago school provided an economic rationale and intellectual gloss to what was, and remains for the majority, a backward, conservative and impoverished economic condition. Revisiting Chicago economics in order to understand neoliberalism is, in effect, revisiting smoke and mirrors (though neoclassical economists would not agree). A further omission in most accounts of neoliberalism is that it ignores the setting of the cold war and glosses over the affinities between neoliberalism and cold war strategies. Both these elements are fundamental to understanding the actual character of neoliberal globalization and its subsequent metamorphoses.

Dixie Capitalism

American politics has undergone a long conservative trend that has recently taken an aggressive turn; to understand this trend we must go back several decades in American history. When in response to stagflation in the 1970s the U.S. Federal Reserve raised interest rates, it prompted the onset of the debt crisis in the global South, which led to the IMF imposing its financial discipline and eventually the regime of structural reform. Meanwhile in the United States, corporations sought to retain their profitability by moving to low-wage areas of operation, which they found first in the American South.

The economic strategy of the American South was "based on low-wage, labor-intensive, high-exploitation production, and hostility to unions" and has its roots in the period after Reconstruction. During the New Deal the agricultural South and West had been modernized through vast state-capitalist projects of which the Tennessee Valley Authority is best known. But its tax structures, labor laws, and institutions did not change and remained as conservative and illiberal as during the days of post-Reconstruction. In the 1970s its industrial policy consisted of providing "a safe haven for 'footloose' capital seeking refuge from the regulatory and industrial relations regime and tax structures of the Northeast and Midwest." The South was committed to low taxes on capital and limited social services and also had "a long tradition of using the law as a tool to build and protect a racialized political and economic order."[2]

During the liberal sixties and in the wake of the 1964 Civil Rights Act, the expectation was that Fordism would spread southward and this would result in the "Americanization of Dixie." What happened instead was the "Dixiefication of America." The Southern model not only survived but became the way out of the 1970s economic crisis and the template for the Reagan revolution: "the economic development policies that we have implemented in the United States over the past three decades have taken on the characteristics of an up-to-date, modified version of those that have been in effect in the American South for decades."[3] Southern economics has its roots in plantation economics with rural oligarchies and a low-cost workforce that performs manual labor—slaves, segregated blacks, rightless migrant workers from Mexico under the Bracero program, and after 1964, many illegal immigrants. According to the economist Stephen Cummings, it is "the export of Southern and Republican conservative economic values to the nation that replaced the northern liberal values of the New Deal and the Great Society programs that set the country on the path to economic insecurity." "The South has been a political greenhouse for conservative economic ideas from colonial times."[4]

The Reagan reforms attacked the labor and civil rights movements, weakened workplace and environmental regulations, and cut back public services. This economic restructuring came with an antidemocratic cultural and racial backlash that had its beginnings in the 1960s with George Wallace in the South: "it was no accident that the groups Wallace attacked were the least powerful in society, such as welfare mothers and aliens—easy targets to scapegoat."[5] In 1971 the prison population in the South was 220 percent higher than in the Northeast; now nationwide incarceration rates began to approximate those that had long prevailed in the South. Within corporations management became punitive—all elements that feed into a low-wage, high-exploitation accumulation strategy. Adopting these strategies offered a way out of economic crisis and over time became the U.S. standard.

If the American South provided the material template, Chicago school economics provided the intellectual sheen. At a time of rapid technological change, a return to neoclassical economics offered a gloss of modernist minimalism. Hayek added a cybernetic twist by claiming that market forces provide superior circulation of information. Friedman's monetarism attacked Fordism and New Deal capitalism. The Laffer curve (fewer taxes stimulate the economy and will yield more tax revenue) provided a rationale for rolling back government. Deregulation and tax cuts became bywords for achieving "competitiveness" and "flexibility," while in effect these changes converged on creating a low-wage, high-exploitation regime.

The period from 1921 to 1933 may be considered as "the first conservative era" in the United States: "a period like the present characterized by the neo-liberal model that dominated the South: tax cuts, anti-unionism, income polarization, and so on. . . . A combination of democratic rebellion, economic crisis and globalization in the last three decades of the twentieth century created the conditions that permitted the nationalization of the Southern accumulation strategy and its associated racial political ideology and reasserted the neo-liberal nexus of 'free economy, strong state.' "[6] As the British economist Will Hutton points out, the origin of what became the Washington consensus lies in a Southern conservative campaign.

> By 1979, when the Business Roundtable published its manifesto, essentially arguing for what was later to be dubbed the 'Washington consensus' (balanced budgets, tax cuts, tight money, deregulation, anti-union laws), with the Moral Majority and the NRA campaigning hard on conservative social issues, the conservatives . . . were on the move. . . . The center of political and economic gravity was moving to the south and west.[7]

While this goes some way to explain the profound conservative turn in American capitalism and society, another variable is Wall Street, which had played a destructive role in the 1920s, leading to the 1929 crash. The Reagan administration dismantled the New Deal regulatory structure that had been put in place precisely to counteract the speculative financial practices of the 1920s, and unleashed the financial sector. As Will Hutton explains in a detailed study comparing American and European capitalisms, with the institutional restraints gone, the Wall Street–driven preoccupation with short-term stock value gradually transformed the character of American corporations. Since corporations needed to show profits at the end of each quarter, the organizational weight within firms shifted to the financial department and elevated the status of financial over productive operations. The obsession with earnings led to fraud and eventually culminated in Enron and the cascade of related scandals.[8] Both forms of capitalism, the high-exploitation capitalism of the South and Wall Street financial engineering, are essentially predatory and profoundly different from the productive capitalism that had been the basis of American economic success.

The Bush II administration adds a Texan chapter to the Southern magnolia model and reflects an ethos unlike any previous administration. The Texan approach is an aggressive strain of Southern conservatism; backed by oil wealth, it has more swagger than generic Southern conservatism. George W. Bush is the first Southern conservative and the first Texan conservative to be elected president: "thanks to rural over-representation in the electoral college, the alliance of the country church and the country club had captured Washington, D.C." Michael Lind further describes this culture thus:

> Although Bush's ancestors were Northeastern, the culture that shaped him was made in Texas—a culture that combines Protestant fundamentalism and Southern militarism with an approach to economics that favors primitive commodity capitalist enterprises like cotton and oil production over high-tech manufacturing and scientific R&D. . . .[9]

While this sheds light on the Bush II administration, Lind easily lapses into schematic judgments, at times essentializes the South, assumes sweeping continuities over time, dichotomizes Texas elites into modern and premodern factions, and treats the attitude of part of the Southern elite as premodern (for instance, "the mentality of the traditional Texan businessman is that of the premodern 'seigneurial' elite"[10]). The historian Peter Applebome notes that "the South's stock in trade has been the myth and reality of its distinctiveness: the only part of the nation with institutionalized apartheid; the only part of the nation to know the crushing burden of losing a war."[11]

There is an American "Dixie industry" that produces a "Southern mystique," which operates as an "internal orientalism" within the United States. This comes with the usual North-South dichotomies of modern-traditional, rational-irrational, secular-fundamentalist, urban-rural, tolerant-racist that are familiar from other regions of the world.[12] So while there is a "Southern exceptionalism" tucked within American exceptionalism, this is not a straightforward matter. The South is internally differentiated and quite dynamic; for decades it has led the United States in population and economic growth. ("Between 1950 and 1970, the share of traditional manufacturing activity in the Northeastern core declined by 3 percent and grew in the Sunbelt by a factor of 56 percent.")[13]

Traditional Southern elites represent a different political economy, but to classify it as "premodern," as Lind does, is too easy; it may well be considered an alternative modernity. This means to acknowledge that it has dynamics of its own and is not simply locked in a premodern pattern. So assessing the significance of the American South is not simply a matter of adding up stereotypes and indicators of uneven regional development, but a matter of navigating representations and deciding what kernels to keep.

While avoiding the trap of "internal orientalism," a few points stand out when we seek to understand the ongoing changes in American policies. One is the empirical circumstance of the American South as a low-tax zone; as in the boast of a Texan politician, "We are a low-tax, low-service state."[14] The second is the leadership of Southern conservatives in American politics virtually since the 1970s. While Republicans also lead in the West and Northwest, the demographic center of the GOP is the much more densely populated South. The third circumstance is that over a long period Southern conservatives have consistently resisted the politics of the New Deal; they resisted the New Deal, the Fair Deal, and the Great Society, and their current politics should be seen in this light. "The Bush II administration," notes Lind, "was also the culmination of seventy years of a counter-revolution against the New Deal, in both domestic policy and foreign policy."[15]

It may be an essentializing exaggeration to say, as Lind does, that the Southern view of economic progress is rooted in the late-medieval plantation economies of Britain and Spain. Yet today the American South "has the largest concentration of low-wage jobs, its economy is dominated by externally owned branch plants ... and is still dependent on natural resources, particularly oil and gas, just as it was a century ago."[16] According to Lind, "What might be called 'Southernomics' is based, like pre-industrial agrarian economics, on extensive development, not intensive development."[17] This is an economy geared to ample resources and cheap surplus labor, and its traditional response to crisis, rather than innovation or improving production methods, is to add either resources or manpower.

The United States has been subject to three decades of nonstop conservative onslaught coming from multiple sources. Southern conservatives pushed for dismantling social government and the New Deal, bringing the country to the low-taxes, low-wages, and low productivity level of the South. Chicago economics advocated the virtues of free markets and deregulation. Both agree on the conservative equation that "less regulation = more growth = more employment."[18] These socially reactionary changes were pushed through at a time of rapid technological change and presented as progressive measures, in keeping with the information society. New technologies were harnessed to achieve a fundamental change in the balance of forces between capital and labor, duly amplified by the spin of business media, *The Economist* and *The Wall Street Journal.*

In Britain during the Thatcher years, the neoliberal package was welcomed as an attack on trade union power, and New Labor continued this realignment. New Democrats in the United States accepted the tenets of the postindustrial and information society, flexibility and the new economy, abandoned the commitment to Fordism and the New Deal and went post-Fordist.[19] The Democratic Party moved to the center right and, albeit for different reasons than the Southern conservatives, accepted major parts of Reaganomics. The Clinton administration institutionalized strands of Reaganomics as a bipartisan agenda—business deregulation, welfare reform, the punitive "three strikes and out" regime—and exported it on an international scale. Instead of a democratic approach of stakeholder capitalism, New Democrats and New Labor adopted a right-wing, authoritarian version of "flexibility."[20]

American liberalism by this account plays a leading role from 1933 and the New Deal onward and experiences its high tide in the period from the 1964 civil rights act to the Roe versus Wade decision that legalized abortion in 1973. This also identifies three major American progressive movements: labor, civil rights, and the women's movement.

How does Southern economics travel? The low-wage model increased the number of American families with two wage earners and lengthened working hours without a proportional increase of incomes. The single-minded pursuit of short term profits and shareholder revenue eroded economic capacities to the extent that the main product of leading American enterprises has become financial engineering or paper entrepreneurialism: making sure that the books show higher numbers at the end of each quarter. The conservatives have been so busy dismantling government and the New Deal that they have paid little attention to the actual American economy, which has experienced a thirty year decline.

Long-term trends in the American economy include massive deindustrialization, decline in research and development, and the growth of service jobs with low productivity, low wages, low job security, and long working hours. ("If service productivity had grown in the United States at the same rate that it grew in Germany between 1972 and 1983, then U.S. service employment would have grown by only 3.6 million workers instead of the 18.7 million that it actually did."[21]) Downsizing corporations has resulted in employee alienation and low morale. Income inequality has grown steadily.

The result of trying to be competitive on the cheap is that American industries have lost international competitiveness in several sectors.[22] This is reflected in the U.S. trade deficit and growing indebtedness at every level of the American economy, in households, corporations, cities, states, and the federal government. The bottom line, in Wall Street language, is a current account deficit that has grown to unsustainable levels.

From time to time various circumstances have boosted the numbers, such as recession or financial crisis in other parts of the world (in part as an effect of American-induced liberalization) and the "new economy" bubble of the Clinton years. What keeps the American economy going in a structural fashion is a combination of expansion, government deficit spending, and the influx of foreign funds. Expansion takes the form of corporations branching into other areas of business (as in conglomerates, frequently leading to business failure), waves of mergers and acquisitions (spinning fortunes in Wall Street while usually leading to less productive combinations), and opening up other markets by means of free trade agreements that liberalize capital markets and export American financial engineering overseas. The main form of government funding is the military-industrial complex. The inflow of foreign funds is a major cornerstone of the American economy (discussed in Chapter 9). The influx of low-priced goods from China and Asia (and increasingly also services) keeps prices low as American incomes stagnate; also significant is the steady inflow of cheap migrant and immigrant labor, in particular from Mexico.

The Cold War and Neoliberalism

The postwar period of "proto-neoliberalism" coincides with the cold war era; during these years the infrastructure of neoliberalism was built in economic thinking and ideology (free market), think tanks (Heritage Foundation, Cato Institute, American Enterprise Institute, Rand Corporation, Adam Smith Institute, etc.), and economic policy (the "Chicago boys" in Chile and Indonesia). In fact, could we consider neoliberalism as the sequel to the cold war?

Founding texts such as Friedrich von Hayek's *From Serfdom to Slavery* and Walt Rostow's *Take-off to Economic Growth* (subtitled *An Anti-Communist Manifesto*) were originally anticommunist tracts. Over time anticommunist critique became "Free World" policy, cold war geopolitics was converted into a global financial regime, and the erstwhile anti-communist alliance morphed into a free-market hegemonic compromise. Since the spoils come to the victor, the kind of capitalism that triumphed was Anglo-American "free enterprise" capitalism. As part of anticommunism the United States actively undermined socialist forces throughout the world, pressured international labor unions, and blocked global alternatives such as a new international economic order. European social democracy and Asian state-assisted capitalism were similarly disparaged.

The affinities between the cold war and neoliberalism take several forms. The postwar modernization of Dixie capitalism in the non-union Sunbelt was made possible by military tax dollars, so Dixiefication and the cold war were tandem projects. The Sunbelt is now the most dependent on military contracts. The overseas network of security alliances built during the cold war was reproduced under the neoliberal dispensation with a new inflection. From the "Washington connection" it was a small step to the Washington consensus. Now IMF conditionalities disciplined unruly states. Applied to the USSR, Fred Halliday refers to this process as the "second cold war."[23] By undermining trade unions and nationalist governments in much of the global South, U.S. foreign policy helped create a favorable investment climate for American capital. American capital flight in turn weakened the hold of the New Deal within the United States, thus establishing an elective affinity between domestic and transnational hegemony.

During the cold war, economic and security interests mingled in the military-industrial complex. If the Soviet Union had been economically exhausted by the arms race, so arguably was the United States, though this was masked by economic achievements. For the United States the real burden of the superpower arms race was its growing path dependence on the military-industrial complex. American economics, politics, and institutions have been huddled around the military-industrial complex for so long that it has become a functionally autonomous logic. American militarism has become entrenched in policy; as Chalmers Johnson notes, this entails the formation of a professional military class, the preponderance of the military and the arms industry in administration policy, and military preparedness as the main priority of government policy.[24] The end of the cold war, then, created an "enemy deficit" for how to sustain this gargantuan apparatus in the absence of a threat?

With the waning of the cold war, security interests slipped into the background and the Treasury and Commerce departments became the most salient government agencies, in cooperation with the international financial institutions based in Washington. So in the shift from the cold war to neoliberalism some elements remained constant—such as a strong U.S. military and support for strategic allies such as Israel—while in other respects there were marked shifts of emphasis (see table 1.1).

The Washington Consensus

Postwar American development policies in the global South favored nation building, "betting on the strong," Community Development that matched the American voluntary sector, and instilling achievement orientation—all

Table 1.1   Continuities/Discontinuities between Cold War and Neoliberal Globalization

Dimensions	Cold War	Neoliberalism
Ideology	Free world Open door Anti-communism	Free market Free trade Pro-American capitalism
Key state agencies	Pentagon, CIA	Treasury, Commerce
Economic center	Military-industrial complex, MNCs	MNCs, banks, Silicon Valley, telecommunications, media
Pressure on developing countries	Join Free World	Structural adjustment
Means of pressure	National security and economic incentives	Financial discipline and economic incentives
Agents of pressure	U.S. government, Pentagon	IMF, World Bank, WTO
Investments	Sunbelt	Third World made safe
Security	Strong U.S. military	Strong U.S. military
Politics of containment	Military intervention, covert operations	Humanitarian intervention, nation building
Allies	NATO, Israel, etc. Religious movements (Mujahideen, Hamas, etc.)	NATO, Israel, etc. "Clash of civilizations": Islam as opponent

strands of modernization theory in which modernization equals westernization equals Americanization.[25] Policies such as the Alliance for Progress interacted with cold war strategies and the "Washington connection."

The Washington consensus that took shape in the late 1980s as a set of economic prescriptions for developing countries echoes the core claim of cold war ideology: the free market and democracy go together. The main tenets of the Washington consensus are monetarism, reduction of government spending and regulation, privatization, liberalization of trade and financial markets, and the promotion of export-led growth. A difference is that postwar modernization was a *rival* project, a contender in the cold war, while the Washington consensus no longer looks to national security states to withstand communist pressure or insurgency; at the "end of history" there was little need for national security states. Hence if modernization theory was state-centered and part of the postwar governmental Keynesian consensus in development thinking, the Washington consensus turns another leaf, to government rollback and deregulation, now elevated from domestic policy to international program. In this sense the Reagan era was a foretaste and then consummation of American cold war victory, acknowledging no rival, no competition. This imprint shows in the policies of the international financial institutions: "the end of the Cold War has been associated with the increasing politicization of the IMF by the US. There is evidence that the US has been willing to reward friends and punish enemies only since 1990."[26]

The Washington consensus was implemented through IMF stabilization lending and World Bank structural adjustment programs. "The IMF and the World Bank were agreed at Bretton Woods largely as a result of the U.S. Treasury: the forms were international, the substance was dictated by a single country."[27] These policies resulted in a rollback of developing country government spending and the growth of NGOs. The Washington institutions have been governed by the Wall Street-Treasury-IMF complex in accordance with American economic orthodoxy, so a shorthand account of neoliberal globalization is American economic unilateralism.[28]

The 1990s have been described as a time of contestation between American and Asian capitalism, and American capitalism won.[29] Speculative capital and hedge funds unleashed by Reagan deregulation played a major part in the Asian crisis of 1997 and subsequent financial crises. In the United States the Asian crisis was hailed as an opportunity for the further Americanization of Asian economies.[30] The export-oriented growth path promoted by the United States makes emerging markets dependent on American market access and trade policies. While the Washington consensus proclaims free trade and export-oriented growth, the actual policies underneath the free trade banner range from using trade as a foreign policy instrument (lifting or imposing tariffs, granting most-favored trading nation status) to influencing countries' exchange rates (as in the 1985 Plaza Accord and the appreciation of the yen), prying open markets, and introducing legalism into world trade rules via the WTO.

Amid all the criticism of neoliberalism, little attention is given to the counterrevolution in the United States that prefigured the "counterrevolution in development."[31] Changes in the United States predate and prefigure those undertaken in the global South in the name of structural reform; in both, there is an attempt to dismantle the regulatory state. In the United States government cutbacks were implemented through Reaganism; on a world scale the drive to liberalize and privatize economies was implemented by means of IMF stability lending and World Bank structural adjustment.

Through structural reform the combination of Dixie capitalism and Wall Street financial engineering has been extrapolated on a global scale. Southern economics and its depth structure of plantation economics sheds light on the realities of structural adjustment in the global South. Real neoliberalism, on display in the American South, is also known as "the Haitian road of development." So it's no wonder that during neoliberal globalization, development was a paradox, which is politely referred to as "policy incoherence": institutions matter, but governments are rolled back; capacity building is key, but existing public capacities are defunded; accountability is essential, but privatization eliminates accountability; the aim is "building democracy by strengthening civil society," but NGOs are professionalized and depoliticized.

The aim of neoliberalism was to do away with "development economics" and the idea that developing countries are a "special case"; in its stead came the unfettered market as the answer to all economic questions. If we would only consider the economic theories of the free market advocates, there might be a rationale to this, even if at best half true; enough of a rationale to serve for a while as the basis of a transnational hegemonic compromise. During the Clinton years, the WTO became the overarching framework of neoliberal globalization. But neither structural reform nor multilateral trade would conceal the actual character of neoliberalism as a high-exploitation regime. Stepping in as a debt collector for western lenders and investors, the IMF weakened states in the South. This is frontier capitalism that thrives on low wages and high exploitation. When neoliberalism in the global South fails to bring development and produces income polarization, it's not because of the failure of neoliberalism but because of its success. It's not because of the "politics of structural reform," but because of structural reform itself.

While neoliberal globalization means "cheap government" and a weak public sector, in some respects states remained strong all along: in implementing IMF conditionalities and reforms, imposing cutbacks, and suppressing popular resistance; but they are weak in economic policy and in contending with multinational corporations.

Commenting on 9/11, the sociologist Ulrich Beck observes that "The terrorist attacks on America were the Chernobyl of globalization. Suddenly, the seemingly irrefutable tenets of neoliberalism—that economics will supersede politics, that the role of the state will diminish—lose their force in a world of global risks. . . . America's vulnerability is indeed much related to its political philosophy. . . . Neoliberalism has always been a fair-weather philosophy, one that works only when there are no serious conflicts and crises." Naomi Klein makes a similar point: "Americans are finding out fast what it means to have a public health system so overburdened it cannot handle the flu season, let alone an anthrax outbreak. . . . In this "new kind of war," it becomes clear that terrorists are finding their weapons in our tattered public infrastructures.'[32]

The 9/11 crisis has shaken the "animal spirits" of late capitalism. An economy driven by replacement demand and consumer spending on status goods and kept going by marketing mood making, comes tumbling down like a house of cards once consumer confidence fades. "Hundreds of thousands of jobs disappear in a month. Confidence—and stock market gains—evaporate in a blink. Companies whose strategies appeared brilliant are exposed as overreaching, or even fraudulent, the moment times get tough.'[33] Aviation, tourism, retail, stocks, banks, insurance, advertising, Hollywood, fashion, media—all sectors have been trembling and repositioning under the impact of 9/11. Global capitalism turns out to be as interconnected as network analysis has suggested and as vulnerable. To do their share, Americans have been urged to go shopping. With the exception of insurance rates, the economic impact of 9/11 has been temporary; the impact of the Enron episode is probably far more significant.

That neoliberalism is crisis-prone rather than crisis-proof is no news to most of the world but a novel experience for the United States. There is glaring inconsistency between federal government support for sectors hit by the 9/11 crisis—especially airlines and insurance (which incurred a $50 billion loss)—and the Washington consensus, which has been urging all governments, crisis or no, to liberalize economies and cutback spending. If the insurance industry would not receive government support, rates would increase, delaying economic recovery. Countries that have been lectured by Washington and the IMF on economic sanity may be surprised to learn that the United States does not follow its own counsel.

This raises the wider question whether the Washington consensus applies to Washington. The economist John Williamson formulated the Washington orthodoxy in ten points.[34] The first is *fiscal discipline*. In Washington this applied during the 1990s but not before or after. (In 2003 Congress raised the ceiling on government debt by $1 trillion to $7.3 trillion.) The second point is *reordering public expenditure priorities in a pro-poor way*. This has not been a Washington priority since the New Deal. Like the Reagan administration, the Bush II government uses deficit spending as a political instrument to cutback social spending. The third point is *tax reform towards a system that combines a broad tax base with moderate marginal tax rates*. The Bush II administration scrapped estate and dividend taxes and gives tax cuts disproportionally to the very affluent. States and cities are in financial crisis, and thus cut support for education and services and raise taxes. And so forth. Of the ten points of Washington orthodoxy, it is practically only in privatization and deregulation that Washington follows the Washington consensus.

For some time the neoliberal project has been unraveling and the Washington consensus faces mounting problems. The IMF handling of financial crises has lost credibility even in Washington and on Wall Street.[35] Its reputation is now that of a "Master of Disaster."[36] Congress has pressed the IMF for reforms of its operations since its failures in crisis management, from the Mexican peso crisis in 1995 to the Asian crisis in 1997. A report of the General Accounting Office to Congress observes that IMF forecasting in its World Economic Outlook has been off the mark more often than not, confirming the critics in their views.[37] In 2000, the Meltzer Commission examined the World Bank on behalf of the U.S. Congress and found that most of its projects have been unsuccessful and the bulk of its lending has gone to higher-income developing countries (which ensure a higher return on investment), so its impact on global poverty has been close to nil.[38] Subsequently the World Bank made combating poverty its priority, but this does not sit well with the neoclassical orthodoxies of the Treasury, which has pressured the World Bank to the point of weakening its credibility.[39]

The WTO is stalled by mounting public criticism and zigzagging American policies. It is no longer merely a tool of American power but also monitors the United States (on tax breaks, steel tariffs and farm subsidies). Growing worldwide mobilization against the WTO, from the battle of Seattle to the World Social Forum, has made this an increasingly difficult and high-risk option. Earlier international NGOs blocked the Multilateral Agreement on Investments.

Arguably there is no more Washington consensus; what remains is a disparate set of ad hoc Washington agendas. In view of the disarray of the international financial institutions, the idea of a "post–Washington consensus" papers over incoherence and improvization.[40] In economics, the neoliberal orthodoxies are no longer broadly accepted; attention has long shifted from state failure to market failure, the importance of institutions and themes such as social capital. As a development policy neoliberalism has been an utter failure—not surprisingly because it is a regime of financial discipline. After decades of structural adjustment, most developing countries are worse off (the economic ramifications of neoliberal globalization are discussed in Chapter 5 below).

Since the Washington consensus followed the compass of American neoliberalism, its status rises and falls with the success or failure of the American economy, which has been losing points in its own right. Signals of failure are the collapse of the new economy followed by the Enron series of corporate scandals, Wall Street decline, and recession. A reorientation of U.S. policies would be in the cards at any rate. The decomposition of the neoliberal order sheds light on the subsequent American turn to "permanent war," which is taken up in the subsequent chapters.

Twenty years of rampant neoliberalism created a culture and habitus of neoliberalism. An anthropological study of the "meanings of the market" in western culture finds as the basic assumptions of the market model that the world consists of free individuals who are instrumentally rational and operate in a world that consists only of buyers and sellers.[41] The peculiar ethos of casino capitalism that neoliberal globalization unleashed on the world is ultimately an occidental cargo cult. Its secret rituals include Dixie capitalism, Wall Street wizardry and cold war strategy.

CHAPTER 2

Scenarios of Power

We are the indispensable nation. We stand tall. We see farther
into the future.

—Madeleine Albright, 1998

Power is multidimensional and according to the usual template of global
politics, it unfolds on multiple chessboards—political, economic, and military. Different ways of combining these dimensions yield various scenarios
of power and options in interpreting them. How to interpret the American
regime change from neoliberal globalization to military globalism? Does it
follow from triumph in the cold war or also from the failure of the neoliberal project? Hyperpower status and economic reorientation may both hold
true for different actors. Another obvious question is whether the policies
of the Bush II administration are a blip or a trend; do they represent an
extension of the "unipolar moment" that came in the wake of cold war
victory, or are they part of a long-term imperial episode? Just considering
politics of the moment risks ignoring strategic continuities, while high-
lighting continuities risk essentializing American politics.

Unipolar Moment or Imperial Episode?

The end of the cold war bestowed hyperpower status on the United States,
which inspired triumphalism and a trend toward unilateralism. As soon as

the "unipolar moment" materialized, so did the desire to "preserve the unipolar moment" and turn it into enduring American primacy.

In the course of the 1980s, the United States reorganized its armed forces; to curb interservice rivalries, regional commands were set up, each with their commanders-in-chief (CinCs) (the Defense Department Reorganization Bill, 1986). Over time, the four and later five, regional commands grew into formidable powerhouses, each with considerable resources at their command, the authority to negotiate bases, weapons deliveries, and training. The CinCs became far more powerful than U.S. ambassadors or CIA heads of station and came to be seen as "Pro Consuls of empire." Foreign policy is supposed to be conducted by the State Department, but the CinCs and the Pentagon have far greater resources at their disposal. The Clinton administration's National Security Strategy directed the CinCs to "shape, prepare, respond all over the globe," an open-ended mission that reinforced military role expansion; the military became responsible for "peace time engagement" and at times "foreign internal defense." This story is told in, for instance, Dana Priest's book *The Mission*. The title refers to the twilight status of the military: undergoing vast expansion yet uncertain of its mission.[1]

Thus as the Soviet threat diminished, the United States experienced a creeping militarization of foreign policy. As Nye, a former undersecretary of defense, notes: "While Congress has been willing to spend 16 percent of the national budget on defense, the percentage devoted to international affairs has shrunk from 4 percent in the 1960s to just 1 percent today. Our military strength is important, but it is not sixteen times more important than our diplomacy."[2] The Clinton administration made greater use of force than previous administrations but drew a line between the use of force and war. It combined the liberal interventionism of nation building with liberalizing international trade via NAFTA, APEC, and the WTO in a policy that was termed "enlargement." In trade, "aggressive unilateralism" and aggressive demands for market access had become central to U.S. policy since the mid-1980s.[3]

A Defense Policy Guidance that was leaked in 1992 (under Dick Cheney as defense secretary and drafted by Paul Wolfowitz as undersecretary of defense) revealed a grand strategy of American primacy: "our strategy must now refocus on precluding the emergence of any future global competitor."[4] This principle has since become part of security strategy. In other words, several policies that appear striking under the Bush II administration—the politics of primacy, the militarization of foreign policy, aggressive trade policies—were in place long before. A major difference is that previous administrations combined unilateralism with multilateralism.

The desire to "preserve the unipolar moment" and remain the premier global power was countered by centrists in the Senate and by a growing aversion to bearing the cost of this position. So the practical outcome was unilateralism with a multilateral face. Samuel Huntington characterized international politics at the time as a combination of unipolarity and multipolarity: "a strange hybrid, a *uni-multipolar* system with one superpower and several major powers. The settlement of key international issues requires action by the single superpower but always with some combination of other major states; the single superpower can, however, veto action on key issues by combinations of other states."[5] An in-between diagnosis is American "go-it-alone power" with modular coalitions, a formula that matches Operation Desert Storm, and NATO operations in Kosovo.[6]

But the calculus continues to change. A 2002 article on "American Primacy in Perspective" takes a different perspective on the unipolar moment: "If today's American primacy does not constitute unipolarity, then nothing ever will."[7] Pick any measure and, according to the authors, the United States is dominant: "In the military arena the US spends more than the next 15–20 biggest spenders combined." The United States enjoys "overwhelming nuclear superiority," it is "the world's dominant air force" and "the only truly blue-water navy." In addition, "America's economic dominance ... surpasses that of any great power in modern history." "The United States is the country in the best position to take advantage of globalization," "the world's leading technological power" and "the most popular destination for foreign firms." Thus "the United States has no rival in any critical dimension of power." There are "no balancing rival coalitions." Therefore "A slide back toward multipolarity would actually be the worst of all worlds for the United States." "Now and for the foreseeable future, the United States will have immense power resources it can bring to bear to force or entice others to do its bidding on a case-by-case basis."[8]

In sum, the authors suggest that multilateralism is not in the American interest nor required. In closing, they take a different turn. "But just because the United States is strong enough to act heedlessly does not mean it should do so."[9] In a brief conclusion the authors note that influence matters more than power and that the world's overwhelming problems—poverty and the environment—require international cooperation. Yet the infrastructure of hubris and the brief for unilateralism has been given. And this unprecedented power and capability refers to a window in time that will not last.

This gung-ho assessment doesn't mention downsides, not even obvious American frailties; it seems an exercise in marketing America rather than merely describing it, as if salesmanship will improve the product. The diagnosis is biased or outdated in several respects: it ignores the Enron episode and its ripple effects, it ignores the growing external deficit and trade deficit, it ignores the structural vulnerability of the American economy (deindustrialization, unemployment, failure of the new economy), and makes no mention of growing social inequality. Is a consumption-driven economy capable of handling contraction at a time when deregulation and tax cuts have undercut government tools of intervention? The economy hinges on consumer confidence, but what if consumers and businesses are faced with uncertainty (recession, job insecurity, war)?

The policies of the Bush II administration can be viewed either as the unipolar moment extended (or amplified to an imperial moment), or as an imperial episode. The first argument runs as follows. This administration undertakes an open-ended war on terror, attacks Afghanistan and Iraq, and projects its military presence worldwide. It undertakes a monumental expansion of the military budget.[10] It is not just pro-business but particularly close to energy companies, which are the most territorial and geopolitical of all corporations. With the embrace of energy concerns, then, comes a turn to empire. And just as the administration leapfrogs over ecological concerns and civil liberties in the United States, it has little patience with the niceties of sovereignty, international law, and multilateralism. All this could be scaled back or turned around by a different administration. A different administration could return to multilateralism, renounce preventive strikes, and trim the military budget.

The alternative case, that this is a long-term project, an imperial episode, runs as follows. American unilateralism dates back at least to the end of the cold war. Unilateral demarches such as nonratification of the nuclear proliferation treaty, annulling the antiballistic missile treaty, and opting for a missile defense system are the purview of the legislature and predate the Bush II administration. The congressional committees are bipartisan. American geopolitics implies a long-term horizon; stationing a million soldiers in 350 bases and 130 countries across the world requires the backing of foreign relations, armed services, intelligence, and ways and means committees. Structural parameters of American primacy as perceived by American elites pertain regardless of a change of the party in government. Past administrations combined multilateralism and the pursuit of primacy. A different administration can make tactical adjustments without giving up strategic objectives. American exceptionalism is longstanding (discussed in Chapter 8). A common view is that "Whoever is in power in Washington, unilateralism—or put another way, America first-ism—is here to stay."[11]

The case for an imperial episode may be more plausible than an imperial moment, but still it raises the question of continuity and discontinuity. While the case for strategic continuity is plain, there is no point in essentializing American policy and ignoring its Wilsonian strands. Besides, unilateralism is not necessarily imperial, it can also be isolationist. One interpretation is that until 1941, American foreign policy was stubbornly extremist and Roosevelt brought the United States into the center of liberal internationalism, where it remained through the cold war. With the cold war over, extremist factions again take hold of foreign policy.

The long-term pattern of American expansion and imperialism dates from nineteenth-century Manifest Destiny through postwar U.S. hegemony, but the end of the Bretton Woods system in 1971 initiated an era of multipolarity. Neoliberal globalization, shaped by the Wall Street-Treasury-IMF complex and convergence with the WTO, was unilateralism with a multilateral face.

The two hypotheses, unipolar moment and imperial episode, may combine in that the Bush II administration may view the present constellation (United States as hyperpower, no significant domestic opposition due to 9/11, no major international encumbrances, vast military superiority, no ready rivals or rival coalitions) as a unique window to secure American primacy for the coming decades or more. This is an imperial episode, then, in view of the long-term American *disposition* toward primacy, and an imperial moment in view of the recent perceived *capability* to implement this aim.

Another American Century?

(T)he dominant groups in this Administration have now openly abandoned the underlying strategy and philosophy of the Clinton Administration, which was to integrate the other major states of the world in a rule-based liberal capitalist order, thereby reducing the threat of rivalry between them.

—Anatol Lieven, 2002.

Neoconservative circles such as the Project for a New American Century (PNAC) and the American Enterprise Institute, and their lineage in the conservative thought of Leo Strauss have been extensively investigated,[12] so this discussion deals only with essentials. The PNAC, founded in 1997, builds on circles in the Reagan administration such as the Committee on the Present Danger. The PNAC's Statement of Principles of 1997 notes:

We seem to have forgotten the essential elements of the Reagan Administration's success: a military that is strong and ready to meet both present and future challenges; a foreign policy that boldly and purposefully promotes American principles abroad; and national leadership that accepts the United States' global responsibilities.

The objective is "to shape a new century favorable to American principles and interests." On its home page the PNAC describes itself as dedicated to these propositions: "that American leadership is good both for America and for the world; that such leadership requires military strength, diplomatic energy and commitment to moral principle; and that too few political leaders today are making the case for global leadership."

In many ways the Bush II administration is a Reagan replay. The Reagan administration was a medley of forces and aims.[13] Voodoo economics sank the federal surplus while scrapping the rules of business; less government, more market, and evangelical patriotism—Good morning America, flashback to the American Dream of the 1950s starring America as liberator and beacon of the world; and aggressive foreign policy in Nicaragua, Central America, Grenada, Afghanistan, Angola, and Libya. Forget Vietnam!

The centerpiece of the Reagan program was a tax cut presented as an economic stimulus (the Economic Recovery Tax Act of 1981); the major economic agenda of the Bush II administration—tax cuts for the wealthy—is likewise presented as a jobs program. As David Stockman, the head of Reagan's office of management and budget conceded afterwards, the administration's agenda was to jack up the deficit so high that cutbacks in social spending would be inevitable; a strategy that ultimately failed for electoral reasons ("the GOP politicians of the Congress will not take on the 36 million who get the social insurance checks").[14] The Bush II tax cuts are probably best understood as a political agenda to redesign government and complete the Reagan counterrevolution by eventually eliminating social government altogether.[15] Rather than tax cuts, they are a tax shift from federal to state taxes, which as an economic stimulus is not just ineffective but counterproductive. The affluent don't need the extra dollars; the intent is to redirect it away from government and from welfare recipients who are to fend for themselves. Making tax cuts permanent may permanently attract the (wannabe) wealthy to the Republicans, structurally undermine the Democrats, and achieve a realignment of American politics. As states and cities are in financial crisis they cut social spending and raise taxes, resulting in a double negative outcome for ordinary taxpayers who both lose services and face higher taxes.[16] This hard conservative turn institutionalizes a regressive tax system and further concentrates wealth and power.

The Bush II government came to power courtesy of Reagan-era Supreme Court appointees. It builds on the Reagan administration's judicial appointments and its conservative turn in politics and civil life. With an unprecedented concentration of Washington insiders of the Reagan and first Bush administrations, it builds on accumulated political capital. The Reagan period was an era of the "shadow government" and episodes such as Iran-Contra.[17] Tucked within the Bush II administration is a shadow government centered in the Pentagon with its own intelligence capability independent of the CIA.[18] In the buildup to the Iraq war it provided intelligence that later turned out to be false.

As with Reagan, the support base of the Bush II administration is the Christian right, the white South plus a portion of Jewish votes, wedded through Christian Zionism and the fundamentalist Christian rendezvous with Israel.[19] As in the Reagan years, this administration combines reliance on military strength with moralist language—the cartoon language of Evil Empire and Axis of Evil; narcissistic and Manichean provincialism elevated to globalism.

The National Security Strategy of 2002 parallels the PNAC agenda.[20] Recourse to military force recalls the Reagan policy of rollback (rather than just containment) and its foreign policy of war on terrorism, and continues the Clinton policy of liberal interventionism. The neoconservatives seek to provide a new narrative of America's role in the world that can serve as the successor to the cold war narrative. American global leadership is to create an "empire of liberty." This restates Clinton's liberal interventionism, but now conducted unilaterally. Unilateralism's two components—confidence in one's own strength and lack of confidence in allies—involves two moves. First, power is redefined as military strength rather than as legitimacy or multilateral leadership; second, allies are disparaged. Thus in Robert Kagan's view of power and weakness, "Americans are from Mars, Europeans from Venus";[21] never mind that this celestial classification doesn't suggest historical finesse. Europeans are sissies and multilateralism is a sign of weakness. Power is force and diplomacy is but a tool of deception; a philosophy that is appropriate to the German military staff under Kaiser Wilhelm and the Nazis. These views reckon that success brings might and might makes right: a utopian *Machtspolitik*.

In the process, the neoconservatives perform as intellectual spokesmen who legitimate the role expansion of the military class, which dates back to the 1980s, and as armchair strategists who legitimate the interests of the arms industry (Richard Perle's business connections are instructive).

A neoconservative reaction to 9/11 was that "We are all Israelis now" and the subsequent change in U.S. policy has been described as the "Israelization of American foreign policy." There are close parallels between current U.S. policies and those of Israel in style, methods and objectives. In both countries the "war party" leads, military and intelligence are the leading state agencies, and economics takes a backseat; offense counts as the best defense; diplomacy and multilateralism take a backseat to the garrison state; politics of fear is institutionalized and stark stereotypes guide domestic and international policy. In 1996 Richard Perle and other neoconservatives wrote a policy review for Israel's Likud government that advocated abandoning the Oslo peace process for a neorealist balance of power politics in the region.[22]

The Reagan era drew on nostalgia for America's unchallenged power of the 1950s and the PNAC draws on the Reagan legacy. This produces a double nostalgia that evokes a new American century while looking back to a 1980s era that looked back to the 1950s.

Scenarios and Analyses

The domestic policies of the Bush II administration are consistent with the seventy-year conservative campaign to end New Deal economics, but what about its international policies? How do the various foreign policy designs fit together—political-military strategies, designs such as "redrawing the map of the Middle East," and policies with regard to trade and the world economy?

Foreign policy reflects long-term designs and develops in response to reactions overseas. The two extremes of interpretation are a jam session and a master plan. The most consistent public voices, the neoconservatives, focus mainly on the Middle East and make only sketchy reference to economics (end welfare, privatization, and free market). Long-term planning on the part of the Pentagon and the commanders-in-chief of the regional commands is typically classified.

The Bush II administration seems more preoccupied with the domestic economy than the world economy. Unlike the Clinton years, the Treasury and Commerce are no longer the center of gravity, and the IMF, World Bank, and WTO play second fiddle. Policy toward the WTO is opportunistic and inconsistent, and zigzagging toward the IMF and World Bank.[23] On the other hand, the state-corporate, weapon-petrodollar nexus is stronger than before.

Are the policies of the Bush II administration an ideologically driven project of conservatives and neoconservatives; a resumption of cold war geopolitics; a mutation of neoliberalism; or a combination of all of these? These scenarios are not mutually exclusive; they overlap while appealing to different political factions and audiences. Scenarios that may fit current U.S. policies imply theories that might explain them (table 2.1).

In *Made in Texas*, Michael Lind's account of the Southern takeover of American politics, an extreme right-wing cabal has taken over the government of the world's most powerful country and 9/11 has given it carte blanche. *Made in Texas* is a Karl Rove scenario. In a coalition of parochialisms Southern Republicans outflank Democrats and the Christian right tackles secular cosmopolitanism. As a meticulously calibrated agenda of domestic hegemony building, biased policies are methodically staged as serving the common interest (tax giveaways for the wealthy as a jobs program; curtail civil liberties for security).

Arguably a poststructuralist interpretation would be appropriate for

Table 2.1 Scenarios of Power

Scenarios	Priority	Theories
Made in Texas	Domestic politics	Poststructuralist
Cold War II	Geopolitics	Neo-realism
Neoconservative ideology	Domestic and international	Gramscian
Offensive neoliberalism	Economics and geopolitics	Marxist, Leninist

unpacking this scenario: the Southern takeover of politics is happenstance, does not follow a compelling logic or yield a causally predictable outcome. Dialectics of disaster: without 9/11 this government would be lost.[24] But limitations of this line of interpretation are that by focusing on contingency (and there is contingency, for instance in the way the administration came to power) this ignores the long-term rise of Southern political power. While capturing contingency, this interpretation misses structure, offers presentist description rather than explanation, and does not account for the lack of political opposition.

In the cold war plus scenario, the war party leads and the military and intelligence are back in prime time. During the cold war, the character of power was geopolitical-military-ideological-economic; during neoliberal globalization it was ideological-economic with a strong military; and now by this reckoning, it is again geopolitical-military. From this point of view the neoliberal episode has been an interruption and the real game is power on a global battlefield. This scenario seems to match neo-realist thinking and might be close to practice since this is the theory taught at military academies. Rather than a theory, should it be considered a self-fulfilling prophecy?

This account overlooks, however, that neo-realists had developed alliances with authoritarian regimes in the Middle East, such as that of Saddam Hussein, for the sake of stability and the flow of oil, and because democracy would bring radical Islamic groups to power.[25] To avoid imperial overstretch, neo-realists and many in the Pentagon prefer a rule-based international order and restraint in the use of military force. (Hence the criticisms of Brent Snowcroft, Lawrence Eagleburger, James Baker, and others of war on Iraq without UN sanction.) The neoconservatives break with neo-realism, disparage the international order, advocate taking the offensive, and have greater confidence in the use of military force and, presumably, greater hopes for democracy in the Middle East, inspired by the likes of Bernard Lewis. By capitalizing on 9/11 and targeting the Middle East, they seek to mobilize patriotism, Jewish votes and liberal hawks (mesmerized by "clash of civilizations" talk). They follow a Gramscian strategy of building domestic hegemony and rely on the support of the white and Christian South and the ideological appeal of the target of war. According to Michael Lind, "The strategic brains for George W. Bush's foreign policy were provided by neoconservatives like Paul Wolfowitz, but the Deep South provided the political muscle."[26] However, the alliance of conservatives and neoconservatives is not seamless. Many conservatives and certainly East coast Republicans prefer a neo-realist policy of multilateral cooperation.[27]

Gramscian international relations theory does not apply either for this is a case of hegemony-in-reverse. Never has so much soft power been squandered in so short a time. An administration that in its first year in office scraps five international treaties does not seek international legitimacy. Its recourse to war has prompted the largest demonstration in human history on February 15, 2003 and, for the sake of the "most unwanted war in history," unleashed world public opinion as a "second superpower." This is a crash course in how to lose friends and squander influence. Immanuel Wallerstein notes: "Over the last 200 years, the United States acquired a considerable amount of ideological credit. But these days, the United States is running through its credit even faster than it ran through its gold surplus in the 1960s."[28]

The neoconservative approach is a provincializing globalism that reads global trends in line with American prejudices. Accordingly, its military and intelligence estimates tend to be wrong (as in Afghanistan and Iraq). American economic supremacy is taken for granted rather than examined. The specialty of the armchair strategists is threat inflation. The American military class inflated the threat of the USSR and now inflates the threat of rogue states and terrorism.

In the scenario of offensive neoliberalism, corporations are center stage, in particular energy, military industry, and Sunbelt corporations (including software). In this account, neoliberalism phase 4—following the phases of proto-neoliberalism, rollback and roll-out neoliberalism, discussed in Chapter 1—recombines with the military-industrial complex. According to neoliberalism, "the market rules OK"; and in this dispensation, the market rules OK by force. David Harvey, for instance, interprets the new wars as wars of conquest for the sake of "primitive accumulation."[29]

What pleads against this scenario is that the Bush II administration's economic base is narrow and comprises mainly energy and military sectors. Its economic policies are biased and contradictory, and tax cuts and deficit spending are opposed by CEOs, blue-ribbon business councils, and to some extent even the Federal Reserve, so it is not a typical policy of the "capitalist class." Politics trumps economics in that the fundamental calculus appears to be political (in the sense of party and state-driven) and ideological rather than economic. Unlike neoliberal globalization, policy is not driven by the

Treasury, Wall Street, and international institutions.[30] Corporate partners seem to be co-pilots and economic agendas, which are sketchy in the first place, seem to play a supporting rather than a leading role. The military's overwhelming role outflanks other sectors. The risks entailed in a strategy of offensive war are so momentous that they outstrip corporate capabilities and horizons. Corporations cannot afford to be risk-takers on this scale. If we would further try to read this as a "military adjustment of structural adjustment," the obvious hurdles are that structural adjustment has not been faring well and its logic does not lend itself to military adjustment.

Leaf through a courtside report such as Bob Woodward's *Bush at War* and economic decision makers do not even figure among the cast of characters. The problem with viewing war as accumulation is that it takes propaganda at face value (such as the neoconservative claim that the occupation of Iraq could be paid for by Iraqi oil) and that the cost of conquest and reconstruction is far ahead of and outstrips conceivable material gains. Conventional materialist accounts may overrate the determining role of capital interests—beneficiaries are not necessarily decision makers; ignore the specificity of political processes—the Southern takeover of American politics; and loose sight of cultural overdetermination—9/11 patriotism and the Middle East as target of war. There is no particular "capitalist necessity" to preventive war.

The Leninist theory according to which "imperialism is the highest stage of capitalism" fails to explain when imperialism does *not* occur and therefore fails to explain when it *does*. It declares imperialism a general disposition of advanced capitalism, which doesn't match general experience or the experience of neoliberal globalization. There are no compelling reasons why in the era of deterritorialized hi-tech capitalism and remote control by means of financial discipline (and in the case of Iraq a regime of containment and sanctions), offensive territorial war would suddenly be a bright idea.

If none of these interpretations are adequate by themselves, then what? The most plausible option to understand the new wars is to combine the scenarios of geopolitical, state-corporate, regional, and domestic designs.

Bichler and Nitzan distinguish between the tech/merger and weapon/petrol constellations in the American economy. The years 2000 and 2001 brought several shocks: the collapse of the new economy, Enron, and September 11. In their argument, the first two signaled that the tech-merger wave of expansion had run its course. The main worry of the Federal Reserve and Wall Street now became deflation, not inflation. The administration's shift to expanding the military budget and war (fueling replacement demand for military equipment) served as avenues of reflation. Iraq as the target, in their reasoning, would serve reflation through the implicit agenda of gaining leverage in controlling oil prices, and keeping prices high if necessary. 9/11 provided a political opportunity to merge these agendas. Bichler and Nitzan recognize that no single motive explains the new wars. But their reasoning offers some ground for a convergence of interests between geopolitics and Wall Street; if it doesn't explain the cause for war, it might explain why Wall Street didn't complain more loudly about the turn of affairs.[31]

This theater of mixed signals has something to go on for different actors and audiences. All that is required is sufficient coherence for concerted action, while the meanings of action differ for different players. Different actors perform in different dramas, which audiences take to be a single performance. The scenarios converge provisionally. As in Luigi Pirandello's play Six Characters in Search of an Author, the characters may take over the script in the course of the performance. The scenarios play in multiple theaters—for insider, domestic, regional, and global audiences. Because of the sound-bite nature of American political discourse, the domestic audience is conditioned to expect instant results; geared to short-term outcomes, it is unaccustomed to dealing with long-term projects. Creating a long-term narrative, like the cold war, takes more than British intelligence reports culled from magazines and student essays. Regional and global audiences tick according to different clocks than American audiences.

Capabilities are related to weaknesses. Over time, the United States has created increasingly Pentagon-heavy governments; military assessments lead foreign policy—and do so in the language of control and dominance—and diplomacy trails behind. In the buildup to war in Iraq, the United States addressed the international community in afterthoughts that were zigzagging, sounded insincere and were continually interrupted by muscular Pentagon statements. The United States disparages UN authority and then claims it must attack Iraq to uphold UN resolutions; it must attack Iraq because of WMD, or because of its nuclear threat; or to remove tyranny, effect regime change, and democratize the Middle East. "Disastrous diplomacy" is no incident but a function of the creeping militarization of American government.[32] In the Bush II administration, former war leaders are in charge of diplomacy and warmongers in charge of the Pentagon.

In interpreting the new wars, a matter of balance is neither to attribute too much rationality and coherence nor to dismiss them as right-wing absurdity; there is a limit to "making sense." Rationality of method can go together with irrationality of values and objectives, and the madness is likely to lie in the project itself, in the values and vision driving it. The core problem is the project: who on earth needs another American century? In a speech in Beijing in 1995, Prime Minister Mahathir of Malaysia declared that in his view the coming century would not be an Asian century but a global century. This kind of recognition of interconnectedness is in keeping with the twenty-first century and this wide spirit of diplomacy and magnanimity is glaringly absent from the American cult of power.

Who is the author of these scenarios of power? The usual reading is that 9/11 has been taken as an opportunity by the American war party. But what if 9/11 was a trap and going to war is taking the bait? In the 1960s, the Brazilian guerilla leader Carlos Marighella formulated the aims of revolutionary armed struggle as follows: "It is necessary to turn political crisis into armed conflict by performing violent actions that will force those in power to transform the political situation of the country into a military situation. That will alienate the masses, who, from then on, will revolt against the army and the police and blame them for the state of things." Chalmers Johnson quotes this and draws a parallel with the second intifada of 2000 and 2001, which militarized Israeli policy, and the American reactions to 9/11.[33] In this reasoning, 9/11 has succeeded in unleashing American militarism and leading the United States on the war path, producing the effect that Marighella anticipated domestically on a world scale. The United States has taken the bait. In the words of Jürgen Habermas: "the normative authority of the United States lies in ruins."[34] In this reading, the United States has gained itself another Vietnam and walked into a West Bank all of its own. Whose scenario of power are we in?

Parochial hegemony and transnational hegemony are difficult to reconcile. Domestic selling points may be international nonstarters; domestic strengths, international hurdles. The insular, inward looking and provincial character of American political debate, culture and education make it difficult to resonate with transnational trends. Most American politics takes place in a "cultural cocoon"[35] and Southern conservatism is a cocoon within a cocoon. The Bush II administration builds on learning curves that are mostly of a domestic nature. Unlike the New Democrats, this administration speaks to domestic rather than international audiences. It presents war as liberation and occupation as democracy in a way that might satisfy compliant media and domestic audiences but troubles the rest of the world. Since the American idea of going it alone is a fantasy, international cooperation is needed, but American diplomacy has alienated public opinion and international forums. The policy crafted to produce domestic hegemony is internationally polarizing, destabilizes the Middle East, and is unacceptable in the Muslim world, Europe, and beyond.

CHAPTER 3

Empire as Metaphor

"Globalization" was economic, came along information highways, with the IMF and WTO, government was supposed to be small and corporations large. Occasionally newspapers cautioned that "grown men don't moan over globalization." Now in the midst of the war on terrorism pundits meditate on empire. What is the difference, or is there a difference? Is empire the flavour of the month? Is it the same play performed a different way, or a different play?

In the wake of 9/11 the language and conduct of American politics changed markedly. A steam of articles and books now recommended imperialism: "the logic of neoimperialism is too compelling for the Bush administration to resist . . . a new imperial moment has arrived."[1] Robert Kaplan called for *Warrior Politics* and militant foreign policy. Michael Ignatieff deemed American imperialism necessary. Robert Cooper, a senior British diplomat, argued that in addition to "voluntary imperialism" through the IMF and World Bank, "What is needed is a new kind of imperialism, one compatible with human rights and cosmopolitan values," which he generously referred to as the "export of stability."[2] Until recently imperialism was a left-wing term, but now empire has become a mainstream theme and makes a comeback in everyday language.[3] In this climate, past empires are revisited and whitewashed.[4]

What is the difference between contemporary globalization and empire? This question could be waved away on the assumption that it is academic hairsplitting or on the argument that contemporary globalization, no matter how it is packaged or phrased, is a form of domination. Yet how it is phrased *does* matter in how and to what ends unequal power is exercised and in the agenda of social movements. If globalization equals empire all along, then what is different about the recent imperial turn?

The basic question is simple. Contemporary globalization, though multidimensional, has been primarily economically driven. From the 1980s the dominant project has been neoliberal globalization and empire would mean a profound break, a U-turn that places state and strategic interests rather than corporate interests in the forefront. Neoliberal ideology preaches lean and cheap government (though the U.S. government was always a strong security and law and order state) and empire means big government. Neoliberal globalization hinges on economics and finance, while empire prioritizes geopolitics and military and political power. Neoliberal globalization and hegemony are intrusive, but empire is intrusive to a much greater degree.

Note an ordinary newspaper report of August 2003: "As one of the 24 senior advisors with the Coalition Provisional Authority, the United States-led civilian administration of postwar Iraq, Dr. Erdmann is charged with getting the higher education system back on its feet. While American policy puts the future of Iraqi academia in its own hands, the 20 universities and 43 technical schools must turn to Dr Erdmann for everything from rebuilding looted lecture halls to releasing their budgets. . . . Dr. Erdmann, 36, has little experience in university administration . . .'[5] And so forth. This is empire in action; a bridge further than globalization or hegemony. With the stark innocence of the report's title, "Righting Iraq's Universities," this illustrates the nitty-gritty of empire.

To provide historic context and explain my use of terms, below is a brief periodization (table 3.1). In addition, definitions of basic terms, deliberately conventional definitions, set the stage analytically (table 3.2).

Capitalism = Imperialism?

From some points of view, the difference between globalization and empire is a non-question to begin with.

Imperial corporations. This refers to transnational corporations that "run the world."[6] The argument is that the turnover of large transnational corporations exceeds the GNP of most states and their operations range widely and across state borders. Joint operations of states and corporations, on the model of the East India Company, were part of the capitalist infrastructure of imperialism. The energy and mineral sectors in particular show long-standing patterns of joint state and corporate crossborder intervention, as in the case of the interwar oil majors and the postwar cooperation between

Table 3.1 Phases of Unequal Power Relations

1400>	European reconnaissance and expansion
1600–mid 1900s	Colonialism, imperialism, neocolonialism
1960s>	Contemporary accelerated globalization
1980–2000	Neoliberal globalization
2001>	War on terrorism, preventive war

Table 3.2 International Unequal Relations of Power

Empire	The political control by one polity over the internal and external policy of another[1]
Imperialism	The pursuit of empire
Hegemony	The control of one polity over the foreign policy of another political entity In a Gramscian sense: international leadership based on legitimacy (agreed upon rules, fair procedures)
Dependency	Reliance of a dependent state on economic and political support of a more powerful state, without formal control over internal or foreign policy

[1] Doyle, *Empires.*

metropolitan states, mineral conglomerates, and arms industries (Aramco, Alcoa, Bechtel, Rio Tinto, etc.). Agribusiness, telecommunications, and banks have all been involved in strategic tie-ups of corporate and metropolitan designs.[7] International finance trails international development like a shadow.

The triad of governments, intergovernmental organizations, and corporations takes new shape in the UN's Global Compact, but in fact goes back to colonial regimes and the postwar development era.[8] Agribusiness has long been involved in international food policies, from American food aid to the Green Revolution. New technologies such as bioengineering give corporations a stake in WTO patenting regulations and intellectual property rights. The "revolving door" between U.S. government officials and major corporations and consultancy firms suggests a commonality of interests. The relative retreat of state regulation has been made up for by a role expansion of corporations—in the form of corporate self-regulation (an interesting model is Enron) and in the polite form of corporate citizenship and responsibility.

Yet, for all these interlocking interests, the idea of "corporate imperialism" is a step too far and a contradiction in terms, for it implies nonstate actors undertaking political (not just economic) projects. Political control of the kind implied by empire is of little economic significance and counterproductive in view of the responsibility and accountability it entails. Most transnational corporations can achieve their objectives without control over sovereignty; economic influence of the type provided by the IMF, World Bank, and WTO regulations suffices, along with lobbying and sponsoring political actors. The interests of most corporations (such as financial services, advertising, pharmaceuticals, software, telecommunications) are of a nonterritorial nature and those with territorial stakes (energy, mining, construction, weapons) are relatively few. Most foreign direct investment is concentrated in North America, Europe, and Japan, and a major preoccupation of developing countries is to attract foreign investment. Countries that are in high demand by investors can exact their conditions on investor entry and exit.[9] While corporations come and go, witness the Fortune 500, geopolitics requires a different type of actor and project. The "imperial CEO" is a figure of speech that refers to executives who expand rather than manage their firms. To ascribe imperialism to corporations is to trivialize the term, while disregarding the role of corporations and viewing it solely in economic, apolitical terms is naive.

Economic imperialism. A common view, almost a collective cliché in the global South during past decades is that contemporary globalization is imperialism, recolonization or dependency by another name.[10] Debt, conditionalities of the international financial institutions, and in the cultural sphere McDonaldization all point in this direction. Domination is now exercised through financial and economic regimes. Sanctions on Cuba and Iraq, the Plan Colombia, and the occasional invasion and bombing are outliers in this pattern.

Over time the shadow of empire has been gradually lengthening. Some of the literature on neoliberal globalization since the 1990s reinvokes empire and this usually involves redefining empire in a looser sense. Thus, for Chalmers Johnson imperialism refers not to "the extension of one state's legal dominion over another" but to "imposing one's own social system" by various means. According to Michael Parenti, "By 'imperialism' I mean the process whereby the dominant politico-economic interests of one nation expropriate for their own enrichment the land, labor, raw materials, and markets of another people." In this casual treatment, the actor is "politico-economic interests of one nation" (not even transnational corporations) and the target is a people (not a state).[11]

This builds on a body of literature that dates back to the Vietnam War and analyzes U.S. hegemony and the cold war as imperialism. It typically takes us back to Manifest Destiny and draws a picture of a more or less continuous aggressive and warlike role of the United States, as in the work of William Appleman Williams and Noam Chomsky.[12] Thus, according to Howard Zinn, "aggressive expansion was a constant of national ideology and politics."[13] This homogenizes national ideology, ignores isolationist currents, and refers to dispositions rather than outcomes. These accounts are welcome antidotes to chauvinism, but they are not analytically precise; they are valid but not throughout the whole period. Cultural and post-colonial studies of a historical and interpretive nature have also renewed the interest in imperialism.[14]

The problem is that these views don't usually distinguish between economic regimes and formal political control; in Nye's words, "they mistake the politics of primacy for those of empire."[15] Control exercised by the Wall Street-Treasury-IMF complex means control of *part* of domestic policy and not foreign policy, and falls short of empire. It's true of course that the line between economic and political control is fine. In shaping developing countries' economic policy, structural reforms wield incisive political influence; IMF conditionalities involve political components. Yet this is short of empire and quite different in terms of the *scope* of political influence, its legal *status* and ideological *justification*. These accounts overlook the multilateral framework and rules in which the United States operated; neoliberal globalization is a rules-based order. By overusing imperialism, these accounts are short of words and reasons if empire *does* occur.

Economics imperialism. This refers first, in the words of the economist Ben Fine, to "the colonization of the other social sciences by economics."[16] I think this claim is counterfactual because the influence of economics in social science has been quite limited (with rational choice in the United States as a major exception). Economics does dominate policy, but the blanket metaphor imperialism is more hindrance than help. The charge of *economism* is more appropriate and effective. Hazel Henderson has long argued against economism and notes that "The economism paradigm sees economics as the primary focus of public policy as well as individual and public choices." In her view, "economics, far from a science, is simply politics in disguise."[17]

Empire. According to Michael Hardt and Antonio Negri, imperialism ended in the 1970s and was followed by a new constellation they call Empire:

> The concept of Empire is characterized by lack of boundaries: Empire's rule has no limits. . . . Second, the concept of Empire presents itself not as a historical regime originating in conquest, but rather as an order that effectively suspends history and thereby fixes the existing state of affairs for eternity. . . . Third, the rule of

> Empire operates on all registers of the social order extending down
> to the depth of the social world. . . . The object of its rule is social
> life in its entirety.[18]

Conceptualizing globalization as Empire stretches the meaning of empire to
the point of defining it in contrast to imperialism, which is a little confusing.
This exercise combines features of Foucault (power is everywhere),
Fukuyama (end of history), and Marcuse (hope lies with the multitude).
Encompassing all space and existing outside history, Empire becomes a
metaphysic of power, which is countered by a metaphysic of transcendence
(by the multitude). Hardt and Negri's account of the Empire of globalization as a "smooth space" is thoroughly misleading.[19] Besides, if Empire is
everywhere it is nowhere. That this exercise in poetic license has attracted
so much attention testifies to the trendiness of imperialism. Thus, we can
identify several uses of empire as a metaphor (table 3.3).

In these instances, "empire" is used metaphorically, just as Habermas's
"colonization of the life-world" by capitalist commodification. As a
metaphor "imperial" means domineering, aggressive, and expansive. "Imperialism" is a fighting word that serves mobilizational purposes, but the
question remains what fight, against what and how? Analytical and political
clarity go together. These perspectives reflect two main strands: using empire
as a metaphor and equating capitalism and imperialism.

In the latter view, differences between imperialism and contemporary
globalization fade essentially because of reasoning by similes (capitalism =
imperialism + capitalism = globalization, therefore globalization = imperialism). The equation capitalism = imperialism tells us little because circa
five hundred years of capitalism have not coincided with five hundred years
of imperialism—or, they have but only according to the crudest reading of
history that skips over the nonimperial episodes. Lenin's definition of imperialism casts a long shadow. Lenin's classic definition, according to which
the highest stage of capitalism (= monopoly capitalism) = imperialism,
involves fundamental problems.[20] The assumption that empire is undertaken for the sake of and yields economic gain is simplistic and
counterfactual.[21] While economic gain has been a propaganda point in

Table 3.3 Empire as Metaphor

Corporate imperialism	Transnational corporations
Economic imperialism	International financial institutions
Economics imperialism	Economism dominates policy
Empire (Hardt and Negri)	Metaphysics of power

defense of imperialism, it has often been disputed by business interests and political forces. Equating capitalism = imperialism = globalization = neoliberal globalization creates a transhistorical soup in which nothing essentially changes over, well, two to five hundred years.[22] If nothing really changes, then why bother to analyze at all?

Dispositional definitions of empire, as Michael Doyle points out, fail to explain if the outcome (empire) does not come about.[23] The bouillabaisse approach, viewing history as a stew with everything mixed in, and the failure to use precise terms, makes it impossible to identify different periods, designs, and configurations. If the new imperialism of the late nineteenth century, the cold war, neoliberal globalization and present times are all empire, in what then resides the difference between these periods? At minimum we would have to define different *types* of empire, at which point we are back to square one.

If there were concertation among diverse actors, contemporary globalization might yield a new imperialism, but given the diversity of actors this is unlikely. This is the point of conventional arguments against new empire; as Richard Haass, the former director of policy planning at the State Department points out, the contemporary diffusion of power and resistance, covert and overt is too great.[24] Moreover, a Washington cliché during the Clinton years was that the cost of major war exceeds its benefits: "war may have become a luxury that only the poor peoples of the world can afford."[25] Apparently this view has now changed.

Social movements of the 1990s, local and transnational, target neoliberal globalization, not empire; though they occasionally use the imperialism metaphor, their aims and methods are fundamentally different from the decolonization movements. Examples are the Zapatistas and the World Social Forum. Contemporary globalization, according to the Jamaican economist Clive Thomas, represents a paradigm shift. Analyzing neoliberal globalization *without* invoking imperialism is more effective analytically and politically.[26] This targets unequal relations of power exercised through economic regimes and ideologies—coinciding with shifts in technology, production, and politics, implemented through international institutions and short of political control over sovereignty.

I think the blanket equation contemporary globalization = imperialism is confusing, but not because imperialism is "directional," while globalization is not.[27] Rather globalization too is directional; it is multidirectional since it involves many actors each with diverse projects. I reject it not because, as Anthony Giddens argues, imperialism refers to an intentional and systematic endeavor, while globalization is more complex: "a dialectical process because . . . local happenings may move in obverse direction."[28] Imperialism too was dialectical and local processes moved in multiple directions; thus in the *pericentric* theory of imperialism, the turbulent periphery plays a central role[29] and real imperialism has a weblike and multicentric character. Both imperialism and contemporary globalization are intentional and involve multiple actors. Yet contemporary globalization is marked by a greater diffusion of power, including international institutions and NGOs.

A further argument for rejecting globalization = imperialism is that globalization is plural: *globalizations*; that is to say, there are multiple globalization projects and designs—from corporate globalism to feminist and human rights globalization, and so forth—so that generalizations based on just one mode of globalization are not tenable. In addition, from taking a historical angle on globalization it follows that empire is a *phase* of globalization (as is decolonization). Contemporary globalization means not just Westernization but also Easternization, as in the influence of Japanese and East Asian forms of capitalism. Besides, "the West" is not unified.[30]

In sum, empire is primarily of a political nature, state-centered and territorial and involves central authority, while late-twentieth-century accelerated globalization is intrinsically multidimensional, involves multiple actors, and is in significant respects decentered and deterritorial, involving multiple and diverse jurisdictions (a précis is in table 3.4). Imperialism often sought (unsuccessfully) to impose a clear division between colonizer and colonized; in contemporary globalization, the lines of inclusion and exclusion are blurred.

Can we view contemporary globalization in the light of new combinations of state and corporate designs? In viewing contemporary globalization as a *project* (and not merely an open-ended process), Philip McMichael implies just this. By portraying contemporary globalization as a system that combines "Golden Arches" (global consumerism driven by American firms) and U.S. hegemony, the hidden hand of the market and the hidden fist of

Table 3.4   Differences between Imperialism and Contemporary Globalization

Imperialism	Contemporary globalization
State-centric	Multiple and diverse actors (corporations, government organizations, international institutions, NGOs)
Primarily political	Intrinsically multidimensional
Central authority (metropolis)	Diffusion of power
Balance of power (statist)	Multipolarity and economic interests
Territorial	Nonterritorial

hegemony, Thomas Friedman makes a similar case. So does Immanuel Wallerstein in viewing contemporary globalization as the modern world system in another phase.[31]

Yet neoliberalism and empire make strange bed partners. Both are designs and dynamics of *hierarchical integration*. The difference lies in how and to what ends asymmetric inclusion is exercised. An in-between argument is to view the current shape of globalization as a hybrid that combines features of neoliberal globalization and empire, or imperial neoliberalism. In the next chapter, I argue that this applies to the American imperial turn, which generates the novel formation of neoliberal empire.

CHAPTER **4**

Neoliberal Empire

The United States will use this moment of opportunity to extend the benefits of freedom across the globe. . . . We will actively work to bring the hope of democracy, development, free markets, and free trade to every corner of the world.

—The National Security Strategy
of the United States of America, September 2002.

It is difficult to deal with a great power that is
both schoolmaster and truant.

—Joseph Stiglitz, 2002.

The war on terrorism is accompanied by a vast expansion of military and intelligence budgets and the threat of preventive strikes. It involves the worldwide projection of American military power and a new phase in fossil fuel geopolitics. A 2003 headline sums up the drift in U.S. media: "American Empire, Not "If" But "What Kind.' "[1]

If there is an imperial trend in American policy, what are the characteristics of this empire? If neoliberal globalization was a regime of American economic unilateralism, has this been succeeded by or combined with political and military unilateralism? This chapter probes the emerging features of a hybrid formation of neoliberal empire; a mélange of political-military and economic unilateralism, an attempt to merge geopolitics with the aims and techniques of neoliberalism. This is examined in relation to government, privatization, trade, aid, marketing, and the occupation of Iraq as a case in point. A further, more difficult question is what kind of wider strategy is taking shape amid the turmoil of the new wars.

The Empire of Liberty

Eventually neoliberal globalization began to unravel and faced mounting failures and opposition. Moreover, neoliberal designs may be too multilateral, unpredictable, and cumbersome to ensure American primacy. After all the WTO is a "tariff-trading bourse" with a founding document of twenty-seven thousand pages.[2]

The opening sentence of the 2002 National Security Strategy declared: "The great struggles of the twentieth century between liberty and totalitarianism ended with a decisive victory for the forces of freedom—and a single sustainable model for national success: freedom, democracy, and free enterprise."

Fukuyama's end of history is probably the quintessential statement of American cold war victory. Its fundamental premise echoes endlessly, for instance in President Bush's statement in a speech at West Point in 2002, "The twentieth century ended with a single surviving model of human progress."[3] Thus cold war victory translates into American ideology. That the United States has achieved a status of historical infallibility has become an ordinary, almost unremarkable part of American discourse. In a campaign essay written in 2000, Condoleezza Rice argues that "multilateral agreements and institutions should not be ends in themselves" and American foreign policy should refocus on the national interest. She welcomes relations with "allies who share American values" and notes in passing that "American values are universal."[4] The only problem is that some countries still have difficulty catching up with this reality.

The code word for this project is "Freedom." Freedom is short for "American values," short for "free enterprise," and the cue to the empire of liberty. The Bush II administration took up empire in the name of liberal internationalism, echoing Wilson's pledge to use American power to create a "universal dominion of right" and practicing "Wilsonianism with a vengeance."[5] As Immanuel Kant observed, "It is the desire of every state, or of its ruler, to arrive at a condition of perpetual peace by conquering the whole world, if that were possible."[6]

If the end of history is the definition of *self*, its supplement is Huntington's clash of civilizations, which defines *others*—for instance in the outlandish conspiracy theory that claims an Islamic-Confucian alliance is threatening the West. Next, western allies were cut to size, as in Robert Kagan's analysis of power and weakness. In the process the United States paints itself into a corner of arrogance of power and increasingly views the world through a gun sight.

Nothing defines this period as much as the preoccupation with power in Washington. In Orwellian speak, power too is "freedom." Robert Kagan views multilateralism as the power of the weak—a one-dimensional interpretation that by totally ignoring soft power is revealing in its own right. For the conservative journalist Robert Kaplan, only power counts because ours are not modern but neomedieval times.[7] In relation to Iraq, Pentagon voices declared that "we are now ten times stronger" than in Operation Desert Storm; but not ten times stronger in soft power, not ten times more legitimate. But in mainstream American policy discourse multilateralism and international law figure as no more than "hot air."[8]

The scope of this project, like some classic empires and unlike the cold war, is *universalistic*. "Universalistic empires, in their dominant political culture and/or political practice, do not recognize other polities as legitimate equals." This is in other words "empire without end" (as Virgil described the Roman Empire).[9] Neoliberal globalization was universalistic as an economic regime (free markets are the sole effective system); the war on terrorism is universalistic in giving the United States the exclusive and combined roles of prosecutor, judge, and executioner.

Major previous empires claimed legal status. That the Roman and British Empires brought the rule of law was the basis of their claim to constitute a "Pax." Neoliberal globalization was rules-based, but the new empire is founded on the rule of power, not the rule of law. The United States does not endorse the International Criminal Court, claims preemption from its mandate for American nationals, and uses this in negotiating trade and aid. The United States exists in a state of "international legal nihilism" and its record of breaches of international law has been steadily growing.[10]

These features are encoded in the Bush Doctrine: "Either you are with us, or you are with the terrorists"; and the threat of preventive strike, including nuclear strike. The former sets the terms for universalism and the latter places the United States outside international law.

This project is *kaleidoscopic* and deploys the full register of power— military, political, economic, financial, and ideological. But combining economic and political-military unilateralism does not make for a stronger compound. It yields the suspicion that political-military operations are to make up for failures of the neoliberal project and that war is a diversion from Wall Street blues. Applying the entire arsenal of instruments of power opens up multiple fronts and as many points of contradiction. How for instance do freedom and democracy rhyme with the use of military force? How does the liberal use of depleted uranium ammunitions square with bringing liberty?

There are striking contrasts between neoliberal globalization and the imperial turn. Although the United States avoided international treaties, the cold war and neoliberal globalization were framed by the collective security systems of NATO and other alliances. But the war on terrorism is avowedly unilateral and conducted outside Security Council mandates; while formally pursuing "common security," the Bush II administration disdained not just foes but allies as well.[11] The Bush II administration scrapped international treaties outright and accepts security cooperation only if it can dictate the terms. Rumsfeld's "the mission defines the coalition" means that American military objectives drive international cooperation.[12]

The post-Powell doctrine of hardliners rejects restraints on the use of military force and takes the Pentagon back to before the lessons of Vietnam, back to the cold war; the new willingness to take on "small wars" resumes the pattern of cold war low-intensity conflict.[13] But this administration's reluctance to engage in nation building and making scant resources available for it contrasts with its overseas interventionism, for intervention is messy and small wars yield large ramifications. The "turbulent frontier" gave rise to the *pericentric* understanding of imperialism (i.e. the periphery plays a central role) and applies also now.[14] Sepember 11 as blowback of Afghanistan and the Middle East, developments in Palestine, Pakistan, Kashmir, Indonesia, the Philippines, Central Asia, Georgia, Kurdistan, Liberia, and so on, and Lebanonization in Afghanistan and Iraq, echo this dynamic.

Past empires such as the British Empire transferred a share of their surplus to invest in infrastructure overseas, such as railroads and ports. But the new American empire is not run by a nation on the crest of economic achievement but by a country undergoing structural economic decline, a hyperdebtor nation with a massive current account deficit that needs an annual inflow of $500 billion in foreign funds to keep going, even without empire (discussed in Chapter 9). This is a deficit empire that, rather than investing overseas, drains the world of resources on a gigantic scale; it is a cost-cutting empire that is designed to be cheap, even in such basics as supplies to its troops on the front.[15]

Neoliberal globalization was a regime of market conformity (as defined by the U.S. Treasury) and pressure on developing countries and international institutions to conform to market ideology; the Bush II administration, in contrast, flaunts free-market rules. The new dispensation is regime change (Pentagon-democracy). Regime change in Iraq diverts attention from a war on terrorism that is going nowhere, or is unwinnable, and converts asymmetric conflict to the familiar terrain of symmetric (inter-state) conflict—except that the war reverted to an asymmetric guerilla conflict.

No wonder the United States finds itself in a quandary in Afghanistan and Iraq. General Sanchez, the U.S. commander in Iraq, offered a new rationale for war: "Every American needs to believe this: that if we fail here in this environment, the next battlefield will be the streets of America." Paul Bremer, head of the American civilian command in Iraq, concurred: "I would rather be fighting them here than fighting them in New York.'[16] American power has been greater, of longer duration and greater cultural affinity in the Caribbean and Central America, yet "with how much certainty and confidence is the term "liberal" even today applied to states and societies such as Guatemala, Honduras and Haiti? . . . What reason is there to suspect that America will do better in Afghanistan than it has in Haiti?'[17] The empire of liberty is on display in Afghanistan and Iraq.

Osmosis of Neoliberalism and Empire

While neoliberalism and empire are wide apart, what matters is not merely the contrast but also the osmosis of neoliberal globalization and imperialism, or how they fold into one another. The new policies unfold within a structured setting. The rapid succession from a neoliberal to an imperial project yields a combine of American economic and political-military unilateralism and a novel formation of neoliberal empire. *Neoliberal empire* twins practices of empire with those of neoliberalism. The core of empire is the national security state and the military-industrial complex; neoliberalism is about business, financial operations, and marketing (including marketing neoliberalism itself). The IMF and World Bank continue business as usual, though with less salience and legitimacy than during the Clinton years; so imperial policies come in addition to and not instead of the framework of neoliberal globalization. Neoliberal empire is a marriage of convenience with neoliberalism, indicated by inconsistent use of neoliberal policies, and an attempt to merge the America whose business is business with the America whose business is war, at a time when business is not doing so great.

The combination of business and coercion is not new; the cold war also combined military power and free enterprise. But the habitus of neoliberalism that has taken shape during past decades is more pronounced than cold war free market rhetoric. The neoliberal regime and the imperial turn have in common that they are doctrinaire and involve vast military spending and spin and marketing. Viewed from the United States, continuities between neoliberal globalization and neoliberal empire include:

- State-corporate relations and state intervention in favor of corporate interests (fiscal policy, deregulation of finance, environment, labor, zoning)

- Free market ideology conceals redistribution towards major corporations
- Conservative ideology of authoritarian moralism
- Defunding social government (welfare reform, workfare)
- Funding punitive government ('three strikes and out," Patriot Act)
- Privatizing government functions (prison industry, security tasks)
- Threat inflation, massive defense contracts, militarism
- Marketing and spin
- Internationally: structural adjustment and aggressive trade policies.

Government. Merging neoliberalism and empire yields peculiar outcomes. One of the fundamental contradictions of neoliberal empire concerns the role of government. Neoliberal ideology pleads for small government—though the U.S. government is strong in law and order and regulates by deregulating, which is difficult enough to balance. The neoliberal mindset may be summed up in House Majority speaker Dick Armey's favorite saying, "The market is rational; the government's dumb." But empire requires big government; does this mean that the imperial turn brings dumb government in charge?

The accomplishments of neoliberalism—lean, cheap government—turned out to be liabilities in the war on terror. It was the frailty of its public infrastructures that made the United States vulnerable in the 9/11 attacks, the anthrax scare, and air traffic security. Big government returned in the form of a huge Homeland Security Department, military and intelligence expansion, new surveillance and security systems, propaganda policies, and government support for industries at risk. Establishing the Homeland Security Department, the largest reorganization of the federal bureaucracy in half a century, was initially supposed to be "budget neutral." In line with neoliberal expectations, it was to be cheap, efficient, and flexible (redeploying labor across departments without union restrictions), while matching imperial standards it was to be monumental. Cost-cutting exercises in homeland security were kept from the media. The Pentagon also sought expansion while reorganizing its workforce along flexible lines.[18]

The tension between small-government ideology and big-government reality manifests in economic policy. The Concord Coalition, a budget watchdog group, warns against "a schizophrenic pursuit of small-government tax policies and big government spending initiatives."[19] Neoliberal tax cuts and imperial expansion of military budgets are contradictory moves from an economic point of view (tax cuts and war don't mix)—but not necessarily from a political standpoint.

Privatization. The politics of privatization is that dismantling government means dismantling accountability; the politics of neoliberalism is to treat politics as a business proposition, or money politics, making it as unaccountable as business itself. The Bush II administration took privatization to new heights. G.W. Bush, the only MBA to occupy the Oval Office, is described as "the GOP's CEO" with the "mentality of a successful CEO."[20] The CEO approach to governance involves reorganizing government itself, as in Berlusconi's CEO government in Italy. Bypassing government bureaucracies—in education, the environment, judicial process, fiscal policy, government contracts, intelligence gathering, warfare, and so forth—comes naturally to this kind of administration; the campaign to rollback government is conducted by government. The No Child Left Behind education policy set standards that schools must meet to receive accreditation and funding so high that failure rates may be as high as 70 percent; which means that students are no longer obligated to attend the schools in their district and can opt for private schools, which will then receive government funding. In effect this introduces the controversial system of "school vouchers" through the backdoor and erodes the public education system. Logging and drilling for oil in nature reserves such as the Arctic National Wildlife Reserve also occur by bypassing existing regulations and institutions.

The nation's shift to combat mode in the wake of 9/11 facilitated the authoritarian concentration of power, silenced criticism, and widened the umbrella of "security." Neoliberal practices of outsourcing (to focus on core business) now extend to security and war. Business conglomerates built up during the neoliberal regime cashed in on empire. Examples are the Carlyle Group in defense contracts and Halliburton and Bechtel's contracts for building U.S. bases and the reconstruction of Iraq.[21] Under the security umbrella, government contracts for rebuilding Iraq were allocated without public accountability, or accountability was outsourced—to the companies themselves.[22] Bypassing the CIA, FBI and Defense Intelligence Agency, circles within the administration set up their own intelligence units such as the Office of Special Plans in the Pentagon.[23] Passing the blame for intelligence failures regarding 9/11 and Iraq to the agencies—which had just been bypassed—weakens the agencies and maximizes executive privilege. The habitus of cooking the books Enron-style now extends to policy in intelligence, security, the economy, and the environment. Fudging data and deception become standard operating procedure. The judicial process in relation to suspected terrorists is politicized by reference to security. Terrorism Information Awareness means unlimited surveillance with limited accountability. Security voids the Freedom of Information Act.

Security operations are increasingly outsourced to private military contractors such as DynCorp and MPRI, some of which are subsidiaries of Fortune 500 firms. The annual global market in private military contracts is estimated at $100 billion. These services include training foreign troops, low-intensity conflict overseas, security for president Karzai in Afghanistan, airport security, and military recruitment. While these mercenary forces are paid for by the American taxpayer, they don't operate under military rules, are unaccountable and "allow the administration to carry out foreign policy goals in low-level skirmishes around the globe" without attracting media attention.[24] This turns overseas conflict into another business proposition—just as prisons in the United States have been privatized and turned into a "prison-industrial complex."[25] Thus neoliberal empire extends profitable domestic practices overseas.

The accounts of terrorism for the public and for insiders differ markedly. In the media, terrorism is duly presented as the archenemy of "freedom," routinely viewed through the lens of Jihad and clash of civilizations. But the Rand Corporation, a Pentagon subcontractor, in testimony to congressional intelligence committees presents an entirely different view. Here Bin Laden is "a "terrorist CEO,"

> essentially having applied business administration and modern management techniques learned both at university and in the family's construction business to the running of a transnational terrorist organization. . . . Just as large multinational business conglomerates moved during the 1990s to flatter, more linear, and network structures, bin Laden did the same with al-Qa'ida. . . . Bin Laden has functioned like the president or CEO of a large multi-national corporation: defining specific goals and aims, issuing orders and ensuring their implementation. . . . And as a venture capitalist: soliciting ideas from below, encouraging creative approaches and "out of the box" thinking. . . .[26]

One view is a Jihad stereotype while the other assimilates al Qaida into the neoliberal mindset as a decentralized transnational enterprise. The account of terrorism for insiders is businesslike: in this view, essentially two business empires compete, using similar techniques. Meanwhile both perspectives ignore the opponent's politics.

A vivid example of neoliberal empire was the plan for a futures market in political instability in the Middle East. It was set up at a Pentagon website on the principle of using market signals as a source of information on political trends; it was a mutually advantageous combination of online betting and intelligence gathering, for isn't the market the best source of information? Revoked within days under pressure of Congress, it illustrated the novel possibilities of neoliberal empire and war as business.

Neoliberal empire is a tricky project. Neoliberal globalization sought to establish accountability transnationally via political-economic principles (transparency, accountability, good governance); the Bush II administration shows decreasing transparency (empire requires secrecy), accountability (empire requires broad executive privilege), and good governance (civil liberties and due process impede the concentration of power).

Remote control via remote sensing satellites, unmanned drones, and airborne surveillance is sufficient for containment (such as maintaining no-fly zones), but empire requires on-the-ground control involving ground troops and special forces. Universal empire yields imperial overstretch, including military overstretch and the overcommitment of American troops. Forsaking UN authorization in Iraq means that the "coalition forces" consist mainly of GI boots; preparing for war and not for peace means that policing falls to coalition boots rather than UN peacekeepers; and relying on hi-tech rapid deployment means that boots on the ground are thin. This has stretched American forces so much that deployment in Iraq outlasts military morale and National Guards and Reserves are deployed overseas contrary to their expectations. In summer 2003, twenty-one of the Army's thirty-three combat brigades were overseas, though normal doctrine calls for the deployment abroad of one brigade in three while the other two retrain. While the Pentagon contemplates expanding its troop size (a very costly proposition), it outsources security tasks to private military contractors. Law enforcement in Iraq was outsourced to DynCorp International in a $50 million contract.[27] But if privatization has trouble keeping electricity flowing in the United States, would it be more reliable in providing security and services in a war zone?

By another account, the United States suffers from "imperial understretch" because it does not have the capabilities that empire requires. "Neither the public nor Congress has proved willing to invest seriously in the instruments of nation building and governance, as opposed to military force. The entire allotment for the State Department and the U.S. Agency for International Development is only 1 percent of the federal budget."[28] Neither does the United States have the cultural mentality and outlook that empire requires. Unlike the British during their imperial career, Americans have no desire to stay overseas; "when Americans do live abroad they generally don't stay long and don't integrate much, preferring to inhabit Mini Me versions of America, ranging from military bases to five-star 'international' (read: American) hotels."[29]

During the Vietnam War, the budget squeeze of Johnson's Great Society and the war effort led to a major slump; now a scarlet deficit economy faces a budget squeeze between monumental tax cuts, expansion of military spending, and the cost of war and occupation. The expansion of military spending marks a shift from a gigantic to a colossal military force. In a globally wired economy with a large service sector and a failing new economy, a transition to a war economy is not as easily achieved nor as rewarding as during the cold war. It breaks with the long-built American strategy of achieving primacy by promoting free market policies, which are less rewarding since the United States has turned into a consumer and service economy.

Trade. The opportunism of the Bush II administration in macroeconomic policy does not help bring about a new international coalition. Proclaiming free trade while imposing steel tariffs and adopting a farm bill with hefty subsidies to American farms demonstrates that the United States favors free trade only if it does not damage its interests, which is nothing new, but the signal is louder than before and clashes with WTO rules.

Increasingly free trade, a core tenet of U.S. hegemony for decades, is politically driven. U.S. trade representative Robert Zoellick is a signatory of the PNAC; in his view, "Trade is more than economic efficiency. It's about America's role in the world."[30] Although the rules were biased, neoliberal globalization was nevertheless a rule-based international system of "institutional envelopment." The global trade regime "institutionalizes closed markets in rich countries, coupled with rapid liberalization in developing countries."[31] Agricultural subsidies in Europe and America run at $1 billion a day, six times annual aid flows to developing countries. Europe imposed higher tariffs than the United States, but this changed with the Bush II administration. "In the past several months the United States has compiled a long record of violating trade rules and has single-handedly blocked an agreement to provide medicines for the world's poorest nations."[32] The WTO awarded Europe the right to impose $4 billion worth of trade sanctions against the United States for giving tax breaks to American exporters. The American steel tariffs and the farm bill (increasing agricultural subsidies by 10 percent to $20 billion per year) were calculated to secure a Republican victory in the 2002 Congressional elections. An analyst commented: "The most important trade negotiator is Karl Rove. . . . He really made the call on steel and on farm. He counts the votes."[33] Thus, domestic votes took priority over multilateral trade; politics trumps international economics. Progress on agriculture, textiles, and garments—the promise of the WTO Doha round—stalled. According to William Finnegan, free trade as pursued by the Bush II administration is a "complex and sophisticated agenda" and "a system of control." "We practice free trade selectively, which is to say not at all, and, when it suits our commercial purposes, we actively prevent poor countries from exploiting their few advantages on the world market."[34]

With WTO negotiations stalled, the U.S. government opts for what Robert Zoellick calls "competitive liberalization" via bilateral or regional trade talks. The Free Trade Area of the Americas (FTAA) faces opposition from social organizations and Brazil and other countries. Bilateral free trade agreements have been completed with Singapore—a strategic bridgehead in Southeast

Asia,[35] and Chile—a bridgehead in Mercosur at a time when the FTAA faces opposition. Free trade talks are underway with Morocco, an unlikely American trade partner but a bridgehead in North Africa and the Arab world. The wider plan is to create a U.S.-Middle East free trade zone by 2013, stretching across a region of twenty-three nations in North Africa and Asia. Free trade talks are also ongoing with Thailand, India, and South Africa. But conducting trade negotiations simultaneously at WTO, regional and bilateral levels weakens the influence of the WTO.[36]

Marketing. Regime change in Iraq came on the administration's agenda soon after 9/11. Andrew Card, Jr., the White House chief of staff, explained why the rhetorical campaign on Iraq started suddenly in September 2002: "From a marketing point of view, you don't introduce new products in August."[37] Thus neoliberal marketing principles carry over into government operations.

Neoliberal empire comes with marketing campaigns worthy of corporate causes. In 2001 the White House hired Charlotte Beers, a Madison Avenue top brand manager who was formerly with J. Walter Thompson and Ogilvy & Mather advertising agencies, to rebrand the United States: "to sell the U.S. and its war on terrorism to an increasingly hostile world" (she has since resigned). In the Arab world the reaction was disinterest; as the editor of the Egyptian newspaper *Al Ahram* remarked after a meeting with Beers, "she seemed more interested in talking about vague American values than about specific U.S. policies."[38] The crux is that the United States treats "anti-Americanism" as a communications problem and not as a reaction to its policies. Rather than change policies, the idea is to repackage and market them.

Long before the Iraq war started it was carefully marketed as a "blow for freedom." Operation Iraqi Freedom followed Operation Enduring Freedom in Afghanistan. Keywords sustained the campaign narrative such as regime, coalition forces, war of liberation, thugs, death squads, terrorists.[39] A by-product of marketing policy, rather than just consumer products, is that authoritarian ideological drill is hammered down daily by all communication channels.

The Rendon Group was responsible for public relations in the Gulf War and produced the horror fantasy of Iraqi soldiers ripping babies from incubators in Kuwait. They worked for the CIA to boost the image of the Iraqi National Congress, the U.S.-backed Iraqi opposition group; John Rendon, the head of the group, came up with the name.[40] The Rendon Group was probably responsible for the choreography of tearing down Saddam's monument in Baghdad. "Saving Private Lynch" was another Rendon product, delivered just when a feel-good news story was welcome; afterwards the whole story turned out to be fake.

In the wake of 9/11, the Pentagon strengthened its ties with Hollywood.[41] The American military has increasingly become a marketing operation replete with slogans and fluff: full spectrum dominance, dimensional hi-tech operations. The military's main new asset, ICT, is a commercial Silicon Valley product, so the Pentagon carries the flag of new economy marketing. Major new weapons systems are untested. The Pentagon may turn into another Enron. Military victories in Afghanistan and Iraq are elaborately staged media operations. Even a supporter such as Thomas Friedman observed that the real situation in Iraq "underscores how much the Pentagon's ideological reach exceeds its military grasp."[42] Neoliberal business is characterized by an inverse relationship between marketing and product, with more effort and quality going into marketing than the product. Customers are supposed to buy the marketing rather than the product; and salespersons often begin to believe their own story.

Table 4.2 compares neoliberal globalization (1980–2000) and neoliberal empire (2001>).

Occupational Hazards in Iraq

> The Bush team has now created the very monster that it conjured up to alarm Americans into backing a war on Iraq.
>
> —Maureen Dowd, 2003

The American and British occupation of Iraq is a highly unusual episode in the annals of conquest. I know of no other occasion in history where a conquering force did not merely purge the top leadership but shut down the entire country. Iraq's entire government and civil service, armed forces, police, firefighters, hospital staff, teachers, and faculty were sent home and all production facilities stopped. Governance at all levels was shut down on the assumption that the Baath party penetrated everywhere; which might be true but doesn't carry the demonic meaning that U.S. officials attribute to it. The invaders came with a minutely detailed war plan but without a peace plan other than protecting oil and other critical facilities. For the people of Iraq the outcome was unprecedented chaos, total breakdown of governance, security, services, production, employment, and wages. What forestalled total disaster is that before the onset of war the UN Oil for Food program had distributed basic food supplies to the population to last for several months.

The conduct of the war itself was unusual. First the country was brought to its knees by twelve years of sanctions. It was later disclosed that the reason why bombardment at the onset of war, the phase of Shock and Awe, was so brief was that in reality the war had begun months earlier; under the pretext of reacting to Iraqi violations of the no-fly zone, U.S. and British forces had

Table 4.1   Continuities/Discontinuities between Cold War and Neoliberal Globalization

	Neoliberal globalization	Neoliberal empire
Central arena	Economics and finance	Geopolitics
Key actors	Wall Street-Treasury-IMF, World Bank, WTO	U.S. government, Pentagon, military industries
State	Lean government (except military)	Big government
Key state agency	Treasury, Commerce	White House, Pentagon, intelligence
Interests	Nonterritorial Market share	Territorial as well Political-military control
Project	Shareholder capitalism	Empire of liberty
U.S. foreign policy	Uni-multipolarity Market conformity Financial and market discipline	Unipolarity Regime change Military discipline and economic incentives
Trade	WTO, regional and bilateral	Tariffs, bilateral free trade, WTO
Ideology	Universalistic (free market for others, at home if convenient)	Universalistic (U.S. primacy)
Media	Advertise global brands; propagate free market	Propagate fear and boost U.S. military
Style	Corporate marketing, spin	Government marketing policy, the Pentagon marketing war
Conflict management	Humanitarian intervention Collective security	Preventive war Permanent war

been bombarding Iraqi strategic sites and communication facilities for months. The guerilla war that has ensued suggests that Iraqi forces have opted for tactical retreat.[43]

In Afghanistan, the CIA bought the Northern Alliance with millions of dollars to act as their proxy in an inhospitable land (just as the United States had funded the Mujahideen to act as a proxy against the Soviets, and produced the Taliban regime). The United States bought victory at a price that divides Afghanistan for a long time to come, turns it into "warlordistan" and cedes influence to the Northern Alliance previous supporters, Russia,

Iran, and India. Since the warlords have been appointed governors, all that victory in Afghanistan produces is a mayor of Kabul and an upsurge of crime, opium production, human rights abuses, and instability in the south. Afghan warlords have a lasting stake in controlling the pipeline territories, which ensures the enduring segmentation of the country. Over the years the United States has merely shifted its support from southern to northern Afghanistan. Meanwhile American media present swift victory in Afghanistan and Iraq as major triumphs.

In May 2003 the Security Council authorized the creation of the Development Fund for Iraq, controlled by the United States with advice from the World Bank and IMF. A presidential executive order issued in May exempts, on the grounds of national emergency, all companies, contracts, and proceeds relating to Iraqi petroleum products from suits of practically any kind. The U.S. Export-Import Bank has come forward to act as guarantor for companies doing business in Iraq and explained in a release that "The primary source of repayment is the Development Fund for Iraq, or another entity established under the auspices of the Coalition Provisional Authority."[44] Thus, the threat-profit, war-business nexus works on both ends. At the front end, no-bid contracts are awarded under the shelter of security; at the rear end, risks or losses are written off to the Development Fund for Iraq and any wrongdoing or environmental damage is granted sweeping immunity beforehand. Thus for companies doing business in Iraq a no-risk situation has been created; the game is rigged and unaccountability institutionalized such that corporations can only win. Thus regardless of the outcome of the war for the United States—it has been called "a monetary Vietnam that already accounts for around 15 percent of the U.S. annual budget deficit"[45]—the corporations come out as major winners. In neoliberal empire, conflict is a business proposition. When financial engineering runs into roadblocks at home, with growing scrutiny in the wake of Enron, war becomes an alternative source of "serious money."

The matrix for the new Iraq that the U.S. government envisages is essentially the neoliberal model of a minimal-state country. U.S. options in Iraq "revolve around the privatization of all state enterprises within 18 months and the creation of an independent central bank—an institution that exists in no other country in the region. It seems that the U.S. vision is of a "state-free" Iraq."[46] A former U.S. energy secretary proposed to "make Iraq our new strategic oil reserve": "In one blow, the U.S. can free itself from OPEC, be repaid for the war and create jobs for Iraqis."[47] Another proposal is to distribute Iraq's oil revenues in a way that bypasses state institutions.

> U.S. officials are weighing the merits of a provocative proposal to
> distribute a portion of Iraq's petroleum wealth to its 24 million citi-

zens by sending periodic oil revenue checks to every Iraqi household. Similar in concept to Alaska's Permanent Fund, which last year paid $1,540 to every man, woman and child who met residency requirements, the proposed Iraqi fund would represent a radical departure from traditional state control of oil revenue.

Cheerleading comments suggest,

> "It's an economist's dream," said Robert Storer, executive director of Alaska's Permanent Fund. "You distribute money to each individual in Iraq, and they use it in whatever way best suits their purposes. It's a great way to deal with the rebuilding of the Iraqi economy." . . . "The worst thing for the United States as the steward of Iraq is to be seen as keeping all the debt-holders whole and pumping a lot of money into oil refining, while the public gets nothing," said Stephen Clemons, vice president of the New American Foundation, a centrist think tank that is promoting the concept. "That kills us on the hearts-and-minds side."

When critics argue that this deprives the state of funds to finance public health, education, and transportation needs, the rejoinder is: "That's one of the reasons you set it up. . . . You don't want politicians using all those funds. That's democracy, and I love it."[48]

Thus dismantling the Iraqi state is cast as an American hearts-and-minds triumph. These proposals suggest an Iraq without a state other than for law-and-order and security purposes. This would stunt the Iraqi government regardless of which political forces would emerge from the occupation. It is an Iraq without a collective purpose or identity and with minimal infrastructure, a caricature of the economies that the IMF and World Bank have sought to implement in developing countries and the transition economies of Eastern Europe. The experience of postcommunist Europe suggests that if a one-party controlled economy is instantly opened up to unregulated capitalism, patronage networks rapidly turn into organized crime. The attempt to keep senior Baath party members from holding office recalls a cautionary lesson from the experience of developing countries: it doesn't work to first eliminate a country's social, political, and cultural capital (by imposing modernization as westernization) and then to count on people's "entrepreneurial spirit" to take over from scratch and create a middle-class society. The reason this has failed everywhere is that it is based on an ideological misreading of the experience of the West and the United States itself.

Guerilla war in Iraq places the U.S. for a dilemma. One option is to internationalize the occupation, but other nations would join only under UN authority and mandate. For the United States, this would mean sharing power and a steep climb down from hyperpower altitude. International accountability would mean opening the books of war as business and wider United States strategies in the region. An alternative is to indigenize policing and security, but Iraq's managerial capacity is implicated with the Baath party or its exiled opponents; training juniors to police the country builds cadres that can later challenge U.S. authority and are difficult to give security clearance. For a host of reasons, the American capacity to manage this process is short. At the time of the Gulf war, President Bush I said, "We have more will than wallet." The Bush II administration had still more will and less wallet.

Strategy Matters

> The strategic mind is readily identified and, on the whole, rather
> simple as well as straightforward. It is drawn uncontrollably to
> any map of the world, and this it immediately divides into
> spheres of present or potential influence.
>
> — J. K. Galbraith, 1979

How to characterize this configuration? *Aggressive unilateralism* brings us back to the unipolar moment of the 1980s. The National Security Strategy of 2002 introduced the doctrine of *preemptive strike*; but since this only applies to imminent and ongoing threats, the appropriate terminology in international law is *preventive war*. Since, in addition, the assessment of future threats depends on unverified intelligence that may turn out to be false or exaggerated—as in the case of Iraq's weapons of mass destruction and nuclear preparations—the actual terminology is *offensive war* (or "war of choice"). Another heading is the *war on terrorism*. But the Iraq war was not motivated by combating terrorism (claims linking al Qaida and the Saddam government were unfounded). The occupation of Iraq is imperial, but Iraq is a country of geostrategic, geo-economic and regional importance, so this may be an exception rather than a pattern. Afghanistan, left to its own devices with pipelines and warlords, and Liberia demonstrate that the United States, not surprisingly, is not interested in empire per se. Empire then is part of the configuration but not a necessary part; so imperialism is not a foregone conclusion and the term should be used provisionally. Given the available instruments of neoliberal globalization, recourse to territorial incorporation and formal empire is likely to be exceptional.

An element that is constantly hammered on in all administration statements is that war—against terrorism, rogue states, for the sake of regime change or freedom—will be open-ended. Days after 9/11, secretary of defense Donald Rumsfeld interpreted the war on terrorism thus: "Forget about "exit strategies"; we're looking at a sustained engagement that carries no deadlines."[49] According to Rumsfeld, "the nation must be prepared to defend itself 'against the unknown, the uncertain, the unseen, and the unexpected' and must prepare its forces 'to deter and defeat adversaries that have not yet emerged to challenge us.' " This requires "spending billions building a military that will be capable of meeting any threat, anywhere, at any time."[50] The Pentagon has adopted the doctrine of permanent war and is developing a new generation of weapons systems that bear no relation to the war on terror.

Ralph Peters, a former army intelligence officer assigned to future war, formulates the philosophy of "constant conflict" in these terms: "We are entering a new American century, in which we will become still wealthier, culturally more lethal, and increasingly powerful. We will excite hatreds without precedent. . . . The de facto role of the U.S. armed forces will be to keep the world safe for our economy and open to our cultural assault. To those ends, we will do a fair amount of killing."[51] The assumptions of permanent war include superior information management and software, cultural self-confidence, and, apparently, the anticipation of worldwide hatred.

The Pentagon is now planning "a new generation of weapons, including huge supersonic drones and bombs dropped from space that will allow the U.S. to strike its enemies at lightning speed from its own territory. Over the next 25 years the technology would free the U.S. from dependence on forward bases and the cooperation of regional allies, part of the drive towards self-sufficiency spurred by the difficulties of gaining international cooperation for the invasion of Iraq. The weapons are being developed under a program codenamed Falcon (Force Application and Launch from the Continental U.S.)." Global-reach missiles are planned in two stages, a small version that is to be ready by 2006 and a larger program that will be ready in 2025.[52]

Several elements are striking in these developments. One is the reliance on technology—which is taken up in Chapter 6. Second is the shift back to a war economy; defense spending in 2003 again stimulates the U.S. economy. Third, what underlies and sustains the prospect of "permanent war" is a rigid posture of cultural alienation from the rest of the world—a theme that is taken up in Chapter 7. The reliance on technology and nimble expeditionary forces counts without the real ramifications of conquest. The Iraq war shows that U.S. forces need to be on the ground much longer than expected. While force transformation is supposed to mean less is more (i.e. less troops, more technology), the U.S. army now requires more troops. Being strangers in a strange land involves unanticipated pitfalls of its own.

The axis of evil doctrine has been widely ridiculed; there is no axis and "evil" is Sunday sermon talk. There is a tendency to make light of current

U.S. policies. They may be viewed as "inarticulate imperialism"[53] or light-weight improvization politics, narcissistic and impervious to contradictions because the American leadership is confident it can afford the price. But long-term planning underlies at least some current policies. Being "misunderestimated" and in some respects made light of allowed the administration to proceed with less scrutiny than if it ponderously set forth its plans. But a state does not station a million soldiers in 350 bases and 800 military facilities in 130 countries across the world to have a jam session. Spending on armed forces for many years in excess of all conceivable rivals combined at 40 percent of world total defense spending would suggest strategic planning. It is in the nature of strategic planning that it should not be fully disclosed to either domestic or foreign audiences. Have $400 billion military, will travel.

According to Leo Strauss, the maître of the neoconservatives, some are fit to lead and others to be led, as in Plato's Republic. Deception of the ruled is a basic policy tool of rulers, as in Plato's "noble lie."[54] According to Robert Kaplan, deception is part of imperial policy and the U.S. government should operate "in the shadows and behind closed doors," outflanking Congress and the media.[55] The neoconservatives were casual about the public reasons given for war in Iraq and inferred wider strategic objectives (as Wolfowitz conceded, the threat of weapons of mass destruction was presented as the cause for war only for "bureaucratic reasons" because this was what all parties could settle on). The intelligence scandals that erupted in Britain, the United States, and Australia reflect casualness on the part of the rulers and reluctance of the ruled to play their part.

The Iraq war was supposed to be an opening move toward "redrawing the map of the Middle East," which at times was presented as a Wilsonian project for reshaping the region. Never mind that the means contradict the end. Another objective may be Central Asia. In the oil industry, Caspian basin oil and gas reserves are regarded as so vast that they dwarf those of the Middle East. In this setting of energy geopolitics, Afghanistan and Pakistan figure not just in their traditional role of military buffer states but as "Pipelines-tans." Iran, China, and Russia are contenders for influence in the region; this is where new U.S. bases in Uzbekistan, Kyrgyzstan, Kazakhstan, and Tajikistan fit in.[56] If these reserves need up to ten years to come on stream, leverage in Iraq and the Middle East gives the United States advantage in the intervening time. Control of Iraqi oil means leverage in controlling oil prices; avoiding the shift in oil trading from the dollar to the euro may be a further consideration.

United States bases in Egypt, Djibouti, and Yemen secure the Red Sea. Relocating U.S. bases from west Europe to the "new Europe"—Poland, Bulgaria, Rumania—creates a chain of United States bases and military alliances that runs from Poland to Turkey and from Central to South Asia, slicing through the Eurasian landmass and through any potential or emerging geopolitical rapport between the European Union and Russia and possibly China. This may serve as the infrastructure of another American Century. Gradually the contours of a plan emerge that combines coercion of unruly states with economic incentives; the components include:

- Experiments with neoliberal empire in Iraq and Afghanistan.
- Fossil fuel imperialism, i.e. resource-based international leverage.
- A global grid of U.S. bases, to be supplemented or substituted by global-reach missiles and space-based weapons.
- Security assistance in regional instability and terrorism.
- Bilateral and regional free trade agreements.
- Protection of U.S. patents through the WTO.
- Aid on condition of accepting U.S. conditions.

Economic incentives involve the IMF and World Bank as gatekeepers of the international financial system, aid, and trade access. The fine print of U.S. aid (for instance $15 billion for HIV victims in Africa) is that receiving countries exempt American nationals from the International Criminal Court, accept Genetically Modified Food (GMF), and cooperate in the war on terror. The GMF condition alone makes it practically unacceptable for African countries because it would exclude them from European markets. This agenda ranges from the "imperialism of free trade" to formal empire. The international financial institutions and banks are part of the infrastructure of hegemony, as before; the new icons of neoliberal empire are airbases and pipelines.

By the turn of the nineteenth century at the height of the "new imperialism," western colonial powers occupied 97 percent of the world's landmass. Now if we collate the areas that are targets of American coercion or under different types and degrees of American control, we almost arrive at a similar total. It includes those classified as rogue states (Iraq, Iran, North Korea) or accused of harboring terrorism (Sudan, Syria, Somalia), American protectorates and satellite states, failing states, and developing countries under the regime of the international financial institutions. But twenty-first century empire differs from past empires precisely because of contemporary accelerated globalization. This is a blowback world and "All around the world today, it is possible to see the groundwork being laid for future forms of blowback."[57]

Neoliberal globalization involved international institution building and "institutional envelopment" that claimed legitimacy—even if it rested on the ideological grounds of market fundamentalism. It could boast appeal in view of the alleged success of Anglo-American capitalism (never mind that social inequality was rising steeply) and its pull in international financial markets, thus giving countries a stake in the project while leaving them little choice. The project of endless war is short on all these counts—legitimacy, appeal, and closure. With the United States placing itself outside international law and international institutions and surrendering even the pretense of legitimacy, what remains is rule by force. This is not just empire but naked empire and global authoritarianism, in the process dismantling the international institutional framework that the United States has helped build over decades. American capitalism now commands as much appeal as Enron does. There is no charm to American hard-line policies and unwillingness to revise policies, particularly in the Middle East. By disregarding allies and international institutions, the United States gives countries an exit option. They cannot opt out of international financial markets and credit ratings, but they can opt not to take part in an exercise of power that does not include them.

Control Risks, a U.K.-based international security consultancy in its Risk Map 2004 report describes American foreign policy as "the most important single factor driving the development of global risk." It notes that many in the private sector "believe that US unilateralism is creating a security paradox: by using US power unilaterally and aggressively in pursuit of global stability, the Bush administration is in fact precisely creating the opposite effect."[58]

One of the implications of neoliberal empire is that distinctions between public and private domains have eroded; the public domain has been privatized. What matters is not merely the link between threat and profit and war and business, but what kind of business: privileging military contractors means that the U.S. economy has become uncompetitive. The military industrial complex has been a major source of distortion (as in the economic shift from the Frost Belt to the Sunbelt and the consequent rise of the conservative South) and structural inequality in the American economy and politics. The growing role of private military contractors who operate outside national and international law implies that private actors can unleash global instability or global crisis.

CHAPTER 5

Global Inequality
Bringing Politics Back In

The data on contemporary human inequality are dramatic and widely known. Now about a third of the world population—1.3 billion people—live on incomes of less than one dollar a day. Taking two dollars per day as the poverty line, 2.8 billion out of 6 billion people lived in poverty in the early 1990s.[1] The UN Development Program (UNDP) reports:

> Consider the relative income shares of the richest and poorest 20% of the world's people. Between 1960 and 1991 the share of the richest 20% rose from 70% of global income to 85%—while that of the poorest declined from 2.3% to 1.4%. So, the ratio of the shares of the richest and the poorest increased from 30:1 to 61:1 ... by 1991 more than 85% of the world's population received only 15% of its income.[2]

Overall discrepancies in income and wealth are now vast to the point of being grotesque. The discrepancies in livelihoods across the world are so large that they are without historical precedent and without conceivable justification, economic, moral, or otherwise. Several circumstances with regard to global inequality stand out. While global economic integration has grown over the past decades, global inequality has increased. In a clear rupture with the pattern over previous decades, global inequality has increased sharply since the 1980s. The growth of extreme poverty coincides with an explosion of wealth over the same period. Conventional arguments to explain global inequality have been losing their validity over time, rapidly so in light of the recent widening of global inequality. Economists lead the way in global poverty research and operational research and technical analyses predominate. Research and policy focus on *global poverty* rather than *global inequality*. While international institutions set the agenda in world development their institutional maneuvering room is restricted. Does this explain why current approaches to reducing global poverty are fundamentally incoherent?

The main concern in this chapter is to look beyond measurements of global poverty to global inequality. This prompts the question of what light growing global inequality sheds on the conventional arguments that explain inequity and inform policy. The closing section examines contemporary perplexities from the viewpoint of political considerations.

Global Inequality

The emergence of global inequality as a theme implies a horizon that is global and adopts human equality as a norm. Equality as a general sensibility has come with liberalism and socialism,[3] though it has deeper religious roots. As a theme global inequality goes back by and large to the mid-twentieth century. As a global sensibility, it is part of the postwar era shaped by the United Nations and the adoption of the Universal Declaration of Human Rights. UN agencies such as the UN Development Programme, UNRISD, UNICEF, and UNESCO have done much to monitor world-scale inequality. As part of the creation of global order and representing a worldwide momentum that places all nations on a common platform, UN agencies embody and have educated the world to a global sensibility, while being part of the international power structure.

Global inequality evokes what has been termed the "second great transformation," the transformation from national capitalism to global capitalism. Themes that ring familiar from the time of the first great transformation—the "social question," the "victims of progress," the divide between rich and poor—are now amplified on a world scale. Domestic differences endure and now come back as global differences, too. Yet, the global setting is quite unlike the national settings in which these questions were first faced.

One hurdle is that while in domestic society the good life can be discussed, the international domain has long been viewed as an anarchic, Hobbesian domain. Within societies there is a social contract, but on a world scale? There are crossborder rights, such as the right to development, but is there a crossborder social contract? Solidarity has deep cultural and national roots but so far, according to many, thin transnational roots. The question "can egalitarianism survive internationalization?" elicits profoundly different answers. Some perspectives take the viewpoint of moral obligation and others that of risk; there are egalitarian and nonegalitarian perspectives on global inequality.[4] With regard to social justice, the spectrum of views ranges from *distributive statism* to *distributive cosmopolitanism*, with *moral federalism* as an in-between position.[5] These wide disparities match the uneven character of international relations. Andrew Hurrell signals a "combination of density and deformity" in international society:

> There is now a denser and more integrated network of shared institutions and practices within which social expectations of global justice and injustice have become more securely established. But, at the same time, our major international social institutions continue to constitute a deformed political order, above all because of the extreme disparities of power that exist within both international and world society.[6]

Measuring Global Poverty

Humans measure what they treasure.

—Hazel Henderson, 1996

When the first major overall gap in human inequality emerged in the wake of the industrial revolution the differences were not yet large. They have been widening ever since, though not in a steady fashion. Estimates of the income gap between the fifth of the world's people living in the richest country and the fifth in the poorest are as follows:[7]

1820	3 to 1
1870	7 to 1
1913	11 to 1
1960	30 to 1
1990	60 to 1
1997	74 to 1

The earliest measure of world-scale inequality, Gross National Product, was followed by GNP per capita. The Gini coefficient that measures inequality within societies (0 means that all share equally and 1 means that one individual receives all income and wealth) applies on a global scale as well. A conceptualization that was prominent in the 1980s, basic human needs, has been virtually abandoned in poverty research.[8] While the consensus is that poverty refers to lack of resources, the most common measure remains *income poverty*. The UNDP uses the notion of *human poverty*, measured in terms of education, health, housing, and income.[9] A further yardstick is *capability poverty*, which "reflects the percentage of people who lack basic, or minimally essential, human capabilities," and gives rise to a capability poverty measure.[10]

Initially the unit of analysis was typically the nation (matching the UN frame of the world) and what was taken as global inequality was an aggregation of national statistics. Subsequently, differences *within* societies—rural and urban, gender, regional, ethnic, ecological—have been taken into account. Reports now also often recognize the difficulties of adequately measuring poverty.

Major sources of data such as the World Bank's World Development Reports and the Human Development Reports of the UNDP set forth global poverty data in language as plain as the business pages with easily assimilated graphs and diagrams and occasional striking comparisons. This finding found its way into many newspapers: "Today, the net worth of the world's 358 richest people is equal to the combined income of the poorest 45 percent of the world's population—2.3 billion people."[11] Another recent study finds that the richest 1 percent of the world have income equivalent to the poorest 57 percent.[12]

Statistics on global poverty are now abundantly available; it would not be difficult to fill this chapter entirely with data, along with laments on difficulties of measurement and hand-wringing policy perspectives. The measures and data are problematic indeed. A handbook of poverty research identifies the following underresearched areas in national poverty research: the power structure and its implications for poverty, the control and manipulation of statistics, and the structural framework of primary research.[13] These gaps also apply to global poverty research. Power relations are entirely absent from the leading accounts; the manipulation of statistics makes for an interesting subtext of global poverty research;[14] and macroeconomic research tends to be concentrated in the international institutions.

Global poverty, a late-modern notion, implies an economic turn and brings us into a world of economic statistics. With this comes an air of matter-of-factness that is quite unlike older ideas and measures of difference (along the lines of religion, race, civilization, or nation). The terrain of poverty and inequality is dominated by economists and empirical sociologists and defined and communicated by means of numbers. That with regard to poverty we inhabit a statistical universe is not unusual; numbers lead the way in studies of development, population, and environment. From the way global inequality is conceived it follows that economists do the primary research. The salience of economics is appropriate in that without economic data we could not map or conceive of world-scale poverty; yet it implies that the parameters of debate in economics frame the perceptions of global inequality.[15] Much debate concerns econometrics and technical questions of measurement—which are appropriate measures, purchasing-power parity, by actual exchange rates, according to which US dollar value, weighted by population, whether and how to draw the poverty line, and so forth?[16] With regard to poverty research in the United States, Mishra observes, "The near-obsessive concern with the definition and the count of the poor is clearly driven by the ideology and politics of social welfare" and by disputes between conservatives and liberals,[17] and to some extent this holds true for the global situation.

What is missing is a problematization of poverty itself. Economists tend to use culturally flat definitions of poverty, as if monetary income measures hold universal validity. Wolfgang Sachs distinguishes a wide register of *frugality*, as in subsistence economies; *destitution*, which arises when subsistence economies are weakened through the interference of growth strategies; and *scarcity*, which arises when the logic of growth and accumulation takes over and commodity-based need becomes the overriding logic.[18] Of course it is possible to capture this under "poverty," but is it insightful?

Data on global poverty have become part of a new conventional backdrop. In the course of the 1990s and in the wake of the 1995 World Social Summit in Copenhagen, poverty alleviation became an international policy focus. Declarations on the part of intergovernmental institutions and governments to reduce poverty by half by 2015 are common fare of fin de millennium international politics. This policy objective exists alongside the neoliberal policy framework in an awkward cohabitation—*bien étonnés de se trouver ensemble*.

The emphasis in research and policy is on *poverty* rather than inequality. In most societies, poverty is a politically sensitive theme while inequality is not. Inequality is a relatively safe theme for after all there are many positions, philosophical and political, in relation to inequality. It may be viewed as necessary, inevitable, or even beneficial in relation to a particular mode of progress. A classic liberal view holds that inequality of outcomes may be acceptable as long as there is equality of opportunity. Poverty, on the other hand, is politically sensitive and challenging for it undermines social cohesion; hence how to conceptualize and measure poverty are matters of political dispute.[19]

On a world scale, arguably, it is the other way round. Here poverty is a safe theme: the numbers are worrying, but isn't poverty mostly concentrated in distant lands? Has unequal development not been the rule of history particularly since the industrial revolution? Doesn't technological change make poverty inevitable? Of course developing countries are lagging behind, particularly in Africa and South and Southeast Asia, but the rising tide of free trade and global economic integration will eventually lift all boats.

Global inequality is a different kind of theme for it measures not just the condition of the world's majority but the gap, and the growing gap, between them and the prospering minority. In that global inequality maps relative deprivation it challenges the legitimacy of world order in a way that mere poverty statistics, accompanied by benevolent policy declarations, do not. According to Robert Wade, "New evidence suggests that global inequality is worsening rapidly. There are good reasons to worry about that trend, quite apart from what it implies about the extent of world poverty."[20] Phrased in a different way, "The non-poor and their role in creating and sustaining poverty are as interesting an object for research on poverty as are the poor."[21] Economists and the international institutions that employ them routinely ignore differences of power; by prioritizing poverty over inequality power relations, and the responsibilities they entail, are eliminated from the picture.

Examining Global Inequality

On the assumption that knowledge and power interact it would stand to reason that the *findings* on global inequality cannot be neatly separated from the world order that *produces* global inequality. One way to enter into the core of global inequality is to ask where the data depart from the conventional policy wisdom.

First, a general assumption is that inequality within countries is largest in the poor countries. The figures however bear out that the steepest inequality is within the United States and United Kingdom. Considering the comparative degree of income inequality within countries, Bob Sutcliffe observes, "It is common to read disparaging references in the Western press to the inequality in a country such as India, so it is salutary to note that . . . inequality in the UK and in the USA is much greater than in India . . . in the richest country of all, the USA, the poorest part of the population are poorer than in almost any other developed country."[22] "The per capita income of the poorest 20 percent in the United States is less than one fourth of the country's average per capita income—in Japan it is nearly half."[23]

The second steepest social inequality is documented for the United Kingdom where inequality has been increasing since the mid-70s. In the United States the Gini coefficient began to rise in the 1970s. "In the period 1977 to 1990, the Gini coefficient for distribution by individuals of disposable household income in the United Kingdom rose by some 10 percentage points, from around 23 per cent to around 33 per cent . . . this increase is 21/2 times the increase in the United States over that period." Since the 1980s, the trend of growing inequality is being observed throughout Europe, also in staunchly egalitarian societies such as Scandinavia and the Netherlands.[24]

Second, the conventional assumption is that neoliberal globalization and free trade lift the tide so all boats rise. However, those countries and time periods where this policy has been most consistently implemented show the steepest *increase* in inequality: the United States, United Kingdom, and New Zealand in the 1980s to 1993.[25]

This effect is being replicated the world over. An overall growth rate of 5 percent during the postwar "golden age" of capitalism (1950–73) was accompanied by decreasing inequality between and within societies. There has been a sharp break in this pattern—except in East and Southeast Asia. "For the majority of the developing and transitional economies, the North-South and East-West income gap in the late 1990s is higher than it was in the 1980s or 1960s." Since the early 1980s income concentration has risen virtually everywhere: "this trend towards an increase in inequality is perplexing and marks a clear departure from the move towards greater egalitarianism observed during the 1950s and 1960s."[26]

All reports and analyses document the same pattern. "Between 1987 and 1993 the number of people with incomes of less than $1 a day increased by almost 100 million to 1.3 billion."[27] Taking the 1985 U.S. dollar standard, the number of persons who live on less than one dollar per day "rose from 1.2 billion in 1987 to 1.5 billion today and, if recent trends persist, will reach 1.9 billion by 2015."[28] Robert Wade concludes that

> the bulk of the evidence on trends in world income distribution runs against the claim that world income inequality has fallen sharply in the past half-century and still faster in the past quarter-century ... world income distribution has become much more unequal over the past several decades and ... inequality accelerated during the 1980s, whether countries are treated equally or weighted by population.... [W]orld income distribution became markedly more unequal between 1988 and 1993.... World inequality increased from a Gini coefficient of 62.5 in 1988 to 66.0 in 1993 ... the share of world income going to the poorest 10% of the world's population fell by over a quarter, whereas the share of the richest 10% rose by 8%.[29]

Thus thirty postwar years of growth with improving equality have been succeeded by twenty years of growth with increasing inequality.

Third, the "East Asian Miracle" is often presented as a major turnaround in international development. While East and Southeast Asian countries as a whole deviate from the pattern of increasing global inequality, inequality *within* these societies has increased: "In some economies, including China, Hong Kong, Malaysia and Thailand there have been significant increases in inequality, especially in the past ten or fifteen years," associated with differences between high and low-skill groups, between rich and poor regions and rural-urban differences.[30]

Fourth, to growing global inequality there are two sides at least. The least developed countries lag more and more behind and within countries the number of the poor is growing; on the other side of the split screen is the explosive growth of wealth of the hyper-rich. The world's 7.3 million millionaires (2003) include 512 billionaires and 58,000 "ultra-high net worth individuals" (with assets of more than $30 million).[31] The wealth of the world's three richest men is now greater than the combined gross national product of all the least developed countries, with a total population of 600 million.[32] It makes sense to contemplate extreme poverty and extreme riches side by side, for this alone explains world economic growth occurring simultaneously with growing poverty; this is brought out by focusing on global inequality, not just global poverty.[33]

Fifth, the nexus between global inequality and domestic inequality is insufficiently examined. The general tendency is for global and domestic inequality to move in tandem, so that increasing global inequality is grosso modo accompanied by growing domestic inequality.[34] Specifically, a common view is that "increased wage dispersion in the OECD countries is due to increased competition from low-wage economies,"[35] while "globalization of capital gives business a great deal of leverage in vetoing national policies."[36] Pressures on wages, productivity, labor conditions, and trade unions in advanced countries have been rationalized by referring to labor discipline in low-wage countries, particularly in East and Southeast Asia.

But there are more subtle interconnections as well. Inequality in advanced countries (even growing inequality as in the United States and United Kingdom) may seem acceptable in light of glaring and growing global inequality. Perceptions of poverty in Britain used to be shaped by the images of the Depression but are now more shaped by images of Third World poverty.[37] Televised images of extreme poverty in Africa and Asia may work not merely as a compassion wake-up call but also as a domestic pacifier. Global inequality, then, tends to sustain power structures and inequality within countries, overtly as well as covertly, and helps privileged strata to maintain their status.

Sixth, the risks that global inequality poses are discussed with increasing frequency, also in the wake of the 9/11 attacks. Economic failure according to Jeffrey Sachs raises the risk of state failure. "Failed states are seedbeds of violence, terrorism, international criminality, mass migration and refugee movements, drug trafficking, and disease," and this "significantly affects US interests in military, economic, health-related, and environmental areas."[38] Robert Wade mentions another angle: "The result is a lot of unemployed and angry young people, to whom new information technologies have given the means to threaten the stability of the societies they live in and even to threaten social stability in countries of the wealthy zone."[39] A conventional assumption is that it is possible to contain these risks within the global margins and that a combination of "aid governmentality," tactical sorties and enhanced border security can control their spillover effects.[40] Yet, environmental degradation doesn't recognize borders and neither do migration, transnational crime, and terrorism.

Seventh, conventional wisdom holds that free markets and democracy advance together. But how does democracy function in the face of growing inequality? One consideration is that "democracy has made income gaps in regions such as Latin America more visible and looks more and more like an accomplice in a vicious circle of inequality and injustice."[41] John Gray observes that in societies that follow neoliberal policies middle classes are falling and working classes are being "reproletarianized." "Meanwhile, the overclass increasingly plants itself behind the high walls of suburban developments, Latin-American plantation style, where private funding, not taxation, covers all services. The whole picture of democracy and free markets advancing together, of free-market capitalism sprouting bourgeoisies all over the world, is generally false in today's world."[42] The Washington consensus assumption that civil society acts as a countervailing power and democracy keeps government in check cannot apply if official corruption is sustained by transnational corporations and forces beyond the reach of the domestic public.

Eighth, conventional wisdom focuses on poverty, but inequality is different in that it brings political dynamics to the foreground. For instance, comparing data across countries, "It is interesting to observe that some middle-income countries with relatively similar GNP per capita (Poland, Malaysia, Venezuela, Brazil and South Africa), are characterized by very different degrees of inequality ... the Gini coefficients of Brazil and South Africa are much higher than those of Poland and Malaysia."[43] By focusing on poverty such findings escape economists.

Conventional Wisdom for Beginners

Global inequality trails the career of modern development policy as its dark shadow. During this career that stretches well over fifty years standard arguments that have conventionally served to neutralize findings on global inequality have been losing their validity and recent increases in global inequality don't help.

According to Simon Kuznets's classic argument, income inequality in developing countries would first rise as workers left agriculture for industry and then fall as industrialization would take hold, so inequality would follow an inverted U pattern, the Kuznets curve. This has been applied on a world-scale as a global Kuznets curve. "The global economy would be viewed as having weak stratification if there is significant 'mobility' of nations between groups of nations changing rank or catching up."[44] In other words, the prediction is that of long-run economic convergence. Subsequent World Bank research qualifies this as *conditional convergence*, conditional upon investments in human capital, and research and development.[45] But the sharp increase in global inequality from the late 1980s belies this expectation.[46]

Another conventional argument goes back to classical political economy and the early catch-up strategies in Central Europe and the Soviet Union: through modernization and industrialization, late-comers to development will be able to catch up. Modern development theory adapted these expectations and dependency theory challenged them: the timing and geopolitical setting of catching-up matter and entrenched patterns of dependence and structures of power intervene. With hi-tech and the information revolution, arguments centered on technological change go through another cycle of high expectations and dim outcomes. The scope for "associated dependent development" through technology transfer by means of foreign direct investment is limited by the assembly and *maquiladora* type of low-wage industrialization and by patenting arrangements through which transnational corporations control technological innovation and dissemination.[47] Do the newly industrializing countries break out of this pattern? In spite of their efforts at industrial upgrading, East Asian tiger economies such as Korea continue to be technologically dependent on advanced countries and transnational corporations.[48] Information technology does not essentially change this equation and the scope for technological leapfrogging is limited; witness the global digital divide.[49]

An argument that has been stubbornly repeated throughout the career of international development is that the best anti-poverty strategy is *economic growth*, with some variations on how best to achieve this; in a word, the blessings of trickle-down. On this ground, "economists who espouse the cause of the poor" are routinely accused of "becoming unwitting accomplices in the perpetuation of poverty."[50] The real friends of the poor are market forces and market friendly policies (a "pull-up approach," according to Bhagwati).[51] However, growth may be a necessary but is certainly not a sufficient condition for improving inequality. What matters is not simply growth but *how* growth is achieved. Second, what matters is the *quality* of growth; a major contribution of human development economics has been to build the case for pro-poor growth as the most *efficient* growth. Third, the trend of widening global inequality in tandem with world economic growth refutes this expectation at a general level, while ample country experiences discount it as well. Fourth, more significant still is the widening inequality in advanced countries, occurring again in conjunction with economic growth. If trickle-down does not occur in these robust democracies and in the world's richest country middle classes live in "fear of falling" and the minimum wage is not a living wage,[52] then on what grounds is this supposed to deliver in the weaker polities of developing countries and on a world scale?

Economic growth, industrialization, and conditional convergence are far too generalizing to be useful and on the whole falsified by several decades of accumulated experience. If these conventional views seek to explain economic convergence, how then do we explain the actual experience of divergence?

Current discussions signal various causes of growing inequality, some that were in effect before the 1980s (faster population growth in developing than in developed countries and deteriorating unequal terms of trade) and others that are specific to the recent period, in particular technical change and financial liberalization.[53] Cornia attributes the increase in income inequality to a rise in earnings inequality and emphasizes as the main explanations skills-based technical progress (reducing demand for unskilled labor), the impact of trade liberalization, IMF policies generating recessions (which adversely affect income distribution), financial deregulation, and enlargement of the financial sector (resulting in a shift to non-labor incomes) and the erosion of labor institutions (greater wage flexibility, reduced regulation, erosion of the minimum wage, dilution of trade union power, and higher labor mobility).[54] Apart from technical change, most of these factors are the outcomes of neoliberal policies. The effects of technical change can be channeled by means of industrial policy interventions, as in most newly industrializing countries, but neoclassical policy prescriptions delimit this option. Liberalization and deregulation bet on the strong, privilege the privileged, help the winners, expose the losers and prompt a "race to the bottom." Although this is a broad stroke representation, it is plausible to view neoliberal policies as the central dynamic in widening domestic and global inequality since the 1980s.

The perception that global inequality is more threatening a theme than poverty holds widely, yet it may be less pertinent in the case of the United States. The United States has greater tolerance for inequality than any advanced society: materially and socially, as the most unequal among developed societies, and in terms of political culture and development philosophy. In the United States, "the Reagan administration replaced the war on poverty with a war on the poor. . . . Not poverty as such but pauperization, i.e. dysfunctional and deviant behaviour on the part of the poor was now identified as the main problem of the 1980s, and the early 1990s reflected this shift in agenda from a concern with poverty to a concern with the poor."

"From this viewpoint, then, poverty is no longer an issue. The social problems confronting Americans are now those of welfare dependency, out of wedlock births, criminality and other dysfunctional behaviour on the part of the lower strata of the population."[55] This discourse blames the victims, defines welfare dependency as the problem, and views welfare cutbacks as the remedy. Inequality of outcomes is taken as matter of course and poverty is seen as an enemy in that it shows up the cracks in the culture of success. This deeply embedded strain has been reinforced in recent years.[56]

Transposed on a world scale this entails a policy of slashing foreign aid, upheld by Congressional majority, in a nation that ranks already as the world's stingiest foreign assistance donor (the United States transfers circa 0.1% of GNP to developing countries annually while the internationally agreed UN target is 0.7% of GNP). As part of a relentless campaign for corporate deregulation, conservative think tanks rail against "foreign welfare" on the same grounds as welfare is blamed in the United States: "economic assistance impedes economic growth." International welfare does not work, Congress should eliminate aid, adopt a long-term policy for eliminating development assistance and instead adopt policies to promote "economic freedom" (read: free market) in developing countries.[57]

Thus, while international institutions declare reducing world poverty a global priority, in the host country of the headquarters of most of these institutions poverty does not rank as a viable political issue. The international institutions are part of an institutional power grid whose global impact and dynamics they measure and report on and as such are subject to ample political pressure. They are intermeshed with and politically and financially dependent on the international political and economic balance of forces. The international institutions based in the United States depend on congressional budget allocations, Treasury backing, directors and trustees appointed by the U.S. government, and commercial financial infrastructures and credit ratings (the World Bank is a bank with triple A rating). Subject to multiple pressures from the Treasury, Wall Street, and American neoconservatives—as well as from critical NGOs and social forces in the South—the international institutions have little room to maneuver. A way out of the crossfire is to *depoliticize* the global situation and agenda as much as possible. By this logic, the object of concern is not global inequality but global poverty, the instrument of analysis is economic data processing, and the bottom-line remedy is freeing up market forces, now with a human face.

Consequently, a general trend in policy and discourse is towards hegemonic compromise and papering over significant differences in approach on the part of powerful stakeholders, in particular by using the same terms with different meanings.[58] Bemoan outcomes and confine discussion of causes to technical analyses. For international institutions this translates to intricate balancing acts between signaling concern without rocking the boat. UNDP typically follows a two-track approach, addressing "aid fatigue" on the one hand (so it's necessary to demonstrate success) and urgency on the other, for instance: "human development over the past 30 years is a mixed picture of unprecedented human progress and unspeakable human misery—of human advances on several fronts and retreats on several others."[59]

In poverty research in North America, Mishra distinguishes between social engineering and social structural approaches, which matches differences between economic and sociological approaches. The former "tends to concern itself with research problems closely related to issues of policy and administration. It could also be described as 'operational' research. . . . [It] tends to abstract the problem of poverty from the larger social structure and sees it largely as an administrative problem that can be solved by policy makers by applying 'rational' methods." The social structural approach, in contrast, is not policy oriented; the focus is "on broader structural issues and their relationship to poverty."[60]

In relation to global inequality the social engineering approach prevails, as it does in development thinking generally. "Operational research" is the overriding tendency in development studies that are dominated by the same international institutions that produce and supply the economic data, embedded and enframed in their institutional discourses. The development industry is to a significant degree a subcontracting industry of the international institutions and their intergovernmental infrastructures. Their apolitical disposition is passed on to development studies in various ways. The international institutions exercise their influence not merely directly (by subcontracting research, funding NGOs, etc.) but through their agenda-setting influence, much like the haute couture houses set the tone in another fashion conscious industry. Development studies focus on questions of regional, national, or local development; when it comes to the global level, "world development" is hardly on the map beyond the macroeconomic data of the IMF, World Bank, UN, OECD, and WTO. The research capacity to address world development tends to be concentrated in the international institutions.

The human development approach, which is currently the most influential synthesis in development thinking, centers on capacitation, enablement, and empowerment. This is part of a wider "capabilities turn" from development economics to business management, and one of the responses to the massive increase in global inequality.[61] Empowerment is now upheld across the world as a magic wand to dispel growing inequalities. Capacities however do little to alter unequal relations of power. The old saying is give a man a fish and he will eat for a day, teach a man how to fish and he will eat always.

But nowadays in many places by the time people have learned how to fish, they will likely find their shores emptied by large hi-tech fishing vessels from Japan or the West, under contract with their own governments. Governments North and South hammer on education and training as today's magic charm. But training, in poor neighborhoods, doesn't solve the problem of employment growth.[62] In business management, empowerment means skill upgrading for lower cadres so that with the downsizing of middle management they will supervise themselves and junior staff. Capabilities, skills, and education are resources and forms of power themselves, but there is more to poverty than a deficit of skills.

It helps to put this in historical perspective. Paul Bairoch notes that around 1750 the share of the Third World, China included, in world industrial production stood at about 73–78 percent, dropped to 17–19 percent in 1860, and to a minimum of 5 percent in 1913. Technological change alone does not explain this precipitous decline, which is not intelligible without political intervention of the kind usually summed up under the heading imperialism.[63] In view of this historical backdrop, to account for contemporary unequal development chiefly in terms of unequal capabilities is shallow; or more precisely, if capacities matter, so do unequal relations of wealth and power, which are capabilities magnified.

The poverty reduction strategies proposed by international institutions—such as economic growth, good governance, "building democracy by strengthening civil society," empowerment—are welcome in themselves; yet in the absence of scrutiny of macroeconomic policies and international power dynamics, they exonerate the powers that be and, at the end of the day, abide by the conservative cliché that the poor are to blame for their fate. These approaches now come in standardized packages such as the World Bank's *Sourcebook on Participation* and UNDP's *Overcoming Human Poverty*.[64] These treatments seem to address a parallel universe in which there are no major powers—transnational corporations, banks, Western governments, international trade barriers and institutions—that *produce* and reinforce poverty and inequality. Detailing microeconomics while ignoring macroeconomics, probing micro-politics while skipping macro-politics, they are profoundly apolitical texts. Good governance, democracy, participation? How about good governance, democracy, and participation in the IMF and World Bank? How about transparency and accountability of Wall Street, the U.S. Treasury, the IMF, and World Bank?[65] Does combating poverty in retail while leaving it alone wholesale make sense? If these policy recommendations were matched by inquiries into the role of corporations and governments in the North, by advocating changes in international standards and law, they might be credible; without it they come across as fig leaf exercises in hegemonic compromise.

Thomas Pogge draws attention to the international borrowing privilege—regardless of how a government has come into power it can put a country into debt; and the international resource privilege—regardless of how a government has come into power it can confer globally valid ownership rights in a country's resources to foreign companies.[66] In view of these practices, corporations and governments in the North are accomplices in official corruption; thus, placing the burden of reform solely on poor countries only reinforces the existing imbalance.

To gain deeper insight we must turn to social structural approaches. Attempts to conceptualize global inequality in terms of conventional frameworks in sociology face several difficulties. *Global stratification*[67] has fractured into analysis of gender, race, and ethnicity; class analysis transposed on a transnational scale presents problems of its own. The contemporary dispersal of capital, the complex interweaving of capital, finance, and governance and the intermediary role of international institutions defy the conventional instruments of class analysis. The idea of a transnational capitalist class[68] usually refers to a trans-Atlantic, Fortune 500 class and excludes East and South Asian capital, faces methodological problems and falls short of an overall global stratification analysis.[69]

Several frameworks that sociologists have typically brought to bear on global inequality have gradually been relegated to the margins or overshadowed by other themes. World system theory posited world inequality as a major theme.[70] But this approach itself is tied to macroeconomic data, particularly the long wave (the Kondratieff cycle) and in the end follows economistic lines of analysis, verging to a capitulation of sociology to evolutionary economics, or rather bookkeeping on a world scale. Analyzing global stratification by core, semi-periphery, and periphery countries[71] does not yield data that differ much from the stratified data sets used by the international institutions (such as high-, middle-, and low-income developing countries). Dependency theory has been sidelined by the development of newly industrializing countries and emerging markets, and has been overtaken by the debate on globalization that dominates in sociology as elsewhere. Sociology, anthropology, and geography make distinctive contributions to migration, labor markets, ecological and cultural changes, and gender, race, and class dimensions of global inequality. Several of these concern the downstream consequences of macroeconomic policies; they reflect that the main strength of sociological methodology and theory remains the "society," while transnational sociology is not as well developed. Similarly, while the nexus between poverty and migration, poverty and violence and political instability examined in political science[72] and geography is relevant, it fails to penetrate the core issue of global inequality.

We can consider several studies that straddle transnational political economy, sociology and political science and probe dimensions that depart fundamentally from the dominant economic approaches to inequality. Next, by combining them a plausible perspective emerges. Moving from the general to the specific, this suggests the following lines and levels of inquiry:

1. At a structural level, examine inequality of power between and within states.
2. At a general procedural level, examine how inequalities of power affect decision-making processes.
3. Examine the institutional location and workings of major international institutions.
4. Examine policy frameworks and policies.
5. Examine decision-making processes on a case-study basis.
6. And examine policy outcomes.[73]

The upshot of these analyses is to bring politics back in and to zero in on unequal power relations as a major factor in growing global inequality.

Politics of Perplexity

What kind of world economy grows and yet sees poverty and global inequality rising steeply? The foregoing analysis suggests several observations. (1) Neoliberal policies are largely responsible for rapidly growing global inequality in the past decades. (2) Most research and policy accounts are of an operational nature. They tend to be ahistorical and apolitical; in view of overreliance on neoclassical economics they are atheoretical as well. Their matter-of-factness is impression management only; under the surface are many conflicts about measurements and their implications. (3) The growing density of international networks (such as the "associational revolution" and intercultural connections) generates growing pressures for global reform. International power structures and institutions however are tied in with neoliberal policy frameworks, either because of profound commitments (in the United States and to some extent Britain, home of the nineteenth-century Manchester school), or through hegemonic compromise (European Union, Japan, OECD). What ensues is fundamental policy incoherence between neoliberal policies that widen global inequality on the one hand, and attempts to reduce global poverty on the other.

According to John Ruggie, what is needed is "a new embedded liberalism compromise."[74] Proposals for global reform such as a "global third way," a global new deal and global social policy are increasingly widely discussed.[75] But the contemporary international conditions of density and deformity, referred to above, both account for (density) and delimit (deformity) these contributions.

In 1979, Thomas Rowe distinguished four different approaches to poverty domestically and internationally: *socialization, integration, isolation,* and *revolution.* It is interesting to reflect on how these come across when juxtaposed to current approaches to global inequality.

- *Socialization:* "Deprived must acquire the values and behavior that bring rewards to the more privileged in the dominant system. With self-help and aid from the privileged the shortcomings of the deprived must be eliminated."[76] Here the basic source of the problem is viewed as internal to the deprived. This describes the thrust of current mainstream development policy; it is a disciplinary approach in that aid is conditional.
- *Integration:* "Deprived must be allowed to participate as equals in the system. Exclusive attitudes and behavior on the part of the privileged and dependent and exploitative relationships between deprived and privileged must be broken." Here the basic source of the problem is viewed as external to the deprived. This describes the critical approaches of dependency theory, the New International Economic Order, and contemporary global justice.
- *Isolation:* "Deprived must reclaim or develop the values and behavior necessary for the good life. . . . [T]he values and behavior derived from the dominant system are inherently destructive and must be rejected." Rowe focuses on isolation "from within," by radical social movements of a traditionalist or "fundamentalist" kind. This also describes voluntary delinking or dissociation from the dominant system, or localism, as in post-development approaches. In addition, isolating the deprived is also a policy imposed from without—as politics of containment and concentrating the poor in ghettoes and, internationally, in the "global margins."
- *Revolution:* "Escape from inequalities requires fundamental change in the dominant system." Revolutionary approaches have been waning after the end of the Soviet and Chinese alternatives. Growing differentiation in the global South has further undermined joint collective action. Most armed struggle movements in the South have shifted from the bullet to the ballot[77] with the exception of separatist struggles, armed Islamic groups from Algeria to the Philippines, and insurgency in Nepal and Peru.

Presently, more than two decades hence, three of these approaches are being implemented side by side by the same and by different actors; a précis, updating and expanding on Rowe's categories and with brief notes on contemporary outcomes, is in table 5.1.

Policies of isolating the deprived, or "others," go back a long way. "Beyond the pale" is an old expression. In the 1960s, Maurice Duverger spoke of the metropolitan world "slipping into a comfortable and mediocre civilization of consumption, a sort of air-conditioned Late Roman Empire . . . in which the essential is to hold the barbarian beyond the *lines*." About the same time, J. M. Albertini saw the industrialized world, both capitalist and socialist, becoming "islands of prosperity which can maintain their position only by atomic power."[78] The zones of prosperity and deprivation are now also identified as zones of peace and of turmoil, which is taken up in the next chapter.

Between the zone of peace and the zone of war, there is no peace. The borders are ever turbulent. They are the site of enhanced border security,

Table 5.1 Four Approaches to Global Inequality

Approach	Prescriptions	Policies	Outcomes
Socialization	Deprived must conform to standards set by the privileged	Modernization, human capital, empowerment, good governance, civil society	Capacitation does little to alter the overall structure of power and privilege
Integration	Deprived must be treated on equal terms	Foreign aid, foreign direct investment, democracy, participation	Aid is decreasing, FDI is concentrated in the North, international institutions are not democratic
Isolation	Deprived must stay apart, or be kept apart; contain the effects of poverty	From without, contain: • migration • conflict • disease	Strong borders, migration restrictions, "humanitarian intervention," war on terror
		From within: • Delinking, localism • Separatism • 'Fundamentalism'	Neonationalism remains attractive, yet delinking is a dead end
Revolution	Achieve break in global system	Armed struggle in favor of delinking or radical change	Waning after end of Soviet alternative; shift from bullet to ballot

rising visa restrictions, human trafficking. Instability and conflict in the zones of poverty—and dreams of greener shores[79]—create refugee streams, asylum seekers, and human smuggling. At the same time, declining fortunes and "fear of falling" amid the depressed middle and working class in the advanced countries fosters the rise of right-wing political forces, as in several European Union countries, and an association between immigration and crime. The human rights of those who cross the border between zones don't rank high on their profile. Australia's policy of detaining refugees, in effect for ten years, is a case in point. Their remote location, deep in the interior in Woomera, confined and kept from inspection is telling in itself.[80] On one side of the border, in the global margins, there is discipline—the financial and developmental regimes of the international institutions and conditional aid, or coercive intervention in case of turbulence (as in Sierra Leone, Somalia, Bosnia). In the ghettoes, banlieux and favelas, another discipline and surveillance is in operation—the punitive discipline of "zero tolerance" policing, racial profiling and incarceration. Those who cross the border zone do so at their peril, facing humiliation, disenfranchisement, punishment, and risking death.

Three of the four approaches outlined by Rowe are now simultaneously in effect. In addition they interact in several ways, so they could be viewed as three modalities of the same approach. *Socialization* has increasingly become the imposition of disciplinary regimes, as in IMF conditionalities, World Bank structural reform, and WTO stipulations. *Integration* into the world order takes the shape of the "safety net" that comes with structural reform on a conditional basis. *Isolation*, or social exclusion, then, comes in only as part of a wider picture: the same areas and people that are being marginalized (cordoned off by low credit ratings, trade barriers, security measures, immigration rules) have first been incorporated into disciplinary regimes of debt repayment, stabilization lending, and aid governmentality. Together, these policies could all be viewed as different modalities of a single process of *conditional, asymmetric integration.* Thus, global apartheid and global integration, scenarios that are usually viewed as being wide apart, are being practiced simultaneously, with the note that integration refers to *hierarchical integration.* It goes without saying that these processes of asymmetric inclusion are internally contradictory. Cultural and political globalization promoted by transnational enterprises, media, and intergovernmental arrangements, militates against isolation policies. Disciplining, democratization, and containment are out of step with one another. Thus global hierarchical integration has turbulence built-in. It is against this dramatic and turbulent backdrop that we consider the main perspectives that now underlie policies in relation to global inequality: global risk management and global justice.

During the golden age of the postwar capitalism, a guiding principle in international policies was mutual interest. In the 1960s and 1970s this was the leitmotiv of international cooperation for social democratic, socialist, and developing countries: helping developing countries achieve development and equal status is in the interest of advanced countries, which stand to benefit from a growing and balanced world economy economically and in terms of political stability. This inspired proposals for a new international economic order, the Brandt Commission, and the North South Commission. This outlook has gradually faded for several reasons. The new international division of labor and investment in low-wage economies turned with wages rising in newly industrializing countries, the share of labor cost in production decreasing due to technical change, and concentration of investments in the advanced economies and selected emerging markets; transnational corporations can achieve growth without investing in the least developed countries. The end of the cold war and developments in military technology lower the security risk from poor countries. Yet, some risks have increased. Accordingly risk assessment and management have moved up on the international policy agenda.

After spelling out the risks global poverty poses to the interests of the United States, Jeffrey Sachs pleads for "a strategy of foreign assistance that is commensurate with U.S. strategic interests." This involves income transfers to poor countries, which don't have to be large: "small amounts of help at crucial moments can tip the balance toward successful outcomes."[81] In other words, this is a plea for the status quo, now no longer as muddling through but with the novel dignity of a "strategic approach."

Risk management raises many questions. Who defines risk? Risk to whom? In this example, risk is defined solely by reference to national interest and so is in effect a realist balance of power approach. This ignores global risk. Alongside global inequality, environmental risk, international financial and economic instability, conflict, transnational crime and terrorism, and migration are the most salient global problems. These cannot be properly understood from a "national interest" point of view. This awareness underlies current discussions about a new architecture of international finance and the provision of global public goods. Yet, multilateral cooperation is but one way to manage global risk; unilateral policies are another. In promoting the interests of American corporations worldwide, the United States actively promotes globalization, yet it views the risks this entails only from the standpoint of national interest. For security, a missile defense shield; to contain "rogue states," preventive strikes; to contain local conflict, humanitarian intervention. In relation to wider risks, the United States pulls out, as it did with environmental risk when it pulled out of the Kyoto protocol.

As part of contemporary flux, considerable mentality changes are underway. The justice claims of developing countries are widely perceived as legitimate. Yet they are being neutralized by international institutions that translate development needs into disciplinary regimes, or are kept from acting on more critical assessments by the existing international *rapports de force*. Media personnel in the advanced countries who have seen their personal fortunes improve keep a considerable moral investment in the overall system.

Global justice, the normative approach of social movements, global ethics, and human rights, is a profound dimension of contemporary dynamics. It recognizes that the global rendezvous is not just a large numbers game but a matter of human engagement and solidarity; the world is more interconnected also emotionally and morally. Economic and empiricist views in being morally flat deny the fundamental interconnections that exist between the poor and privileged, and in doing so commit the fallacy of misplaced realism. They overlook, for instance, that global environmental problems require cooperation between rich and poor nations, which is unlikely to come about in the face global injustice.[82]

Engaging global inequality and global poverty is morally right. "The new global economic order we impose aggravates global inequality and reproduces severe poverty on a massive scale. On any plausible understanding of our moral values, the prevention of such poverty is our foremost responsibility."[83] It is economically beneficial, as human development economics and growth and equity analyses demonstrate. Global poverty reduction meets the mutual interest of stakeholders. It confers strategic benefits by contributing to political legitimacy and stability and reduces the risk of conflict. Besides it is doable: "For the first time in human history it is quite feasible, economically, to wipe out hunger and preventable diseases worldwide without real inconvenience to anyone—all the more so because the high-income countries no longer face any serious military threat."[84] Why, then, in the face of moral, economic and strategic considerations—each weighty and together overwhelming—is there no significant action to address global poverty? If we discount the conventional argument according to which economic growth is *the* antipoverty strategy as falsified generally and a fortiori by recent trends, the sole plausible remaining reason is of a political nature (using "politics" in a wide sense).

In the twentieth century many more people have died from poverty than from violent conflict. "The few years since the end of the Cold War have seen over 200 million deaths due to poverty-related causes," far more than the deaths due to violence.[85] Yet conflict management ranks much higher on the agenda than combating poverty. Why are western governments "doing so very little toward the eradication of severe poverty abroad even while they are prepared to spend billions on other humanitarian initiatives, such as the NATO bombing of Yugoslavia?" A cynical answer, according to Thomas Pogge, is that "helping the world's poorest populations emerge from poverty tends to strengthen their states and thus to weaken our own, while bombing Yugoslavia tends to reinforce the existing power hierarchy."[86] Addressing global poverty will affect global inequality, which in turn will affect domestic inequality and thus reduce the manoeuvring room of dominant political and economic elites. This suggests that we must consider global inequality *as part of the balance of power*, and global poverty as part of the price being paid for maintaining global inequality.

Balance of power is not meant here in a realist sense as interstate balance of power, but as *rapports de force*, a loose constellation of interwoven political and economic interests and cultural habitus that is not unified or homogeneous but has yet, so far, sufficient momentum to deflect alternatives. Nor is the assumption that this is a conscious strategy or design, at any rate in its overall outcomes, but rather the outcome of many diverse acts of self-interest and risk avoidance on the part of privileged actors. If many among the privileged abhor poverty, they blame the poor and rely on economic growth as the remedy, and if these beliefs fail, they may still desire privilege, or fear losing it, more than they abhor poverty. The self-serving orthodoxy of neoclassical economics, the trappings of privilege, the charms of power, and the cult of celebrity, all concur to maintain the overall balance of power. And so the world's hyper-rich and the poor majority are intertwined in a joint rendezvous, mirrors to one another—but at quite a remove, which is about the size of the planetary field.

The combination of density and deformity in international conditions makes for fundamental instability, witness global justice movements from Seattle onwards. The global justice approach has hurdles to spare. If social justice and ethical standards don't apply domestically, the likelihood of their prevailing transnationally is even less. Isn't it a strange expectation that poverty elimination worldwide could conceivably succeed at a time when the middle class and working class in developed countries see their incomes stagnating or falling and are increasingly exposed to risk in their job security, social benefits and pensions? If socioeconomic inequality is on the increase in developed countries, what would be the prospect of its diminishing on a world scale? Yet this may be one of the most sensitive pressure points in the global situation. If global injustice is being neutralized by clichés and passé economics, this is not the case with domestic injustice. Growing inequality in advanced countries cheek by jowl with stupendous wealth from financial transactions and rising remuneration of CEOs, even as their companies collapse, leads to growing disaffection.

The policies that are now in place are fundamentally incoherent. Neoliberal policies widen the global inequality that poverty reduction strategies seek to mitigate. International financial institutions count on "conditional convergence" while inhibiting the required conditions from materializing. International institutions urge state action while trapping states in structural reform. Human capital investment is deemed essential but structural reform requires government spending cutbacks. Hence, not surprisingly, the expectation is that the objective of reducing global poverty by half in 2015 will not nearly be met. "There is no strong evidence supporting any trend towards greater income equality across countries."[87] According to the 2003 Human Development Report, many regions will not meet the goals set for 2015 for several decades or in some cases not until the next century.

Perhaps revolution does come in, but in quite a different fashion than the old state-centric notions of revolution. A contributor to a discussion on the implications of technological change notes: "Poverty is a choice the world has made. It is a political choice. The information revolution will be another instrument to implement that choice. Only a governance revolution would represent a real change. And to link the information revolution with democratization is naive in the extreme, parallel to the current leap of faith linking democratization and open markets."[88] John Gray strikes a different note: "I fear that, given the strength of the project of a global free market, it will take some significant economic upsets and some significant political turmoil for social thought to be sufficiently reworked so that the operation of the world will be more compatible with vital human needs."[89] This is a reasonable agenda for the next chapters.

CHAPTER **6**

Conflict
Technologies of Work, War, and Politics

Since the fall of the Berlin Wall in 1989, over 4 million people have been killed in violent conflicts. An estimated 90 per cent of those killed are civilians, primarily women and children.

—Mass Violence Is Not Inevitable, 1998

The truth is that many conflict areas today are closer than our vacation destinations.

—Adolf Ogi, federal defense minister
and president of Switzerland

Glossy advertising for travel and consumerism is one way in which the brave new world of globalization is taking shape. Technology gives instantaneous access across the world. Credit cards open any doors and platinum cards open doors even wider. International brand name goods are available everywhere, frontiers are fading, borders are for crossing, mobility is unlimited, consumer choice growing, and communication instant.

On the other side of the split screen, poverty and inequality are subsumed under "development" and delegated to international agencies such as the World Bank, which translate development into disciplinary regimes. As to violence, opinion articles offer "the Golden Arches theory of conflict prevention" according to which "No two countries that both had McDonald's had fought a war against each other since each got its McDonald's."[1]

With regard to the means of violence as with production, the state no longer has the preeminent position. Economies no longer necessarily hinge on the national market and states no longer hold a monopoly on the means of coercion. Criminal organizations and paramilitaries also organize flexibly, embrace the free market and source internationally for contraband, weapons, and profit. They too represent the "magic of the market place." Urban gangs, rural militias, and warlords replay the game of states. The creeping privatization of security arrangements shows how unfettered market practices erode the public sphere also in crime and conflict. Flexible technology enables minor states to afford weapons of mass destruction. As the nuke race between the superpowers draws to a close, other chains of conflict unfold involving biochemical weapons, environmental warfare, and niche conflicts.[2] The nation state has become one institutional domain among several and state authority is making place for a multiscalar network of governance structures from the local to the global, which operates on uneven premises and leaves glaring gaps. The nexus between profit and taxation as it used to exist is no more, hence the fiscal crises of states and the privatization of services. This institutional interregnum is often described under the shorthand "globalization."

What is the relationship between globalization and conflict? How does the leading script of contemporary globalization, neoliberalism, affect the politics of violence and conflict? Let's signal some paradoxes or anomalies of contemporary globalization and conflict. Globalization brings increasing bordercrossing and borderlessness, but there is no let up in border conflicts. Borderlessness for capital, communication, travel, and consumption, but borders for labor and border policing to contain migration and conflict. While new technologies carry the gloss of the borderless world in the making, they do double duty in border control, containment, and surveillance. Neoliberal globalization weakens state capacities and in weak states conflict and crime proliferate. Globalization shrinks the world, but leading political accounts ("Jihad vs. McWorld," "clash of civilizations," etc.) portray a deeply divided world. The need for supranational governance is growing in order to manage conflicts, but multilateral institutions are being weakened. Under no-nonsense capitalism, unprofitable sectors have been shrinking throughout the world—typically health care, education, social services—while conflict and security are growth industries. "Transparency" in international finance and development suggests a world of visibility, legibility, and accountability, but transparency is mostly one-way.

So globalization is a unified field for some and thoroughly partitioned for many. What else is new? The sunny side of globalization is rapidly expanding mobility and the ideology of borderlessness; and the dark side is an all-too familiar world of poverty and growing cleavages and conflict. How do the two sides interact? Refurbished politics of containment and preventive war seek to keep the two sides apart.

Globalization and conflict involve multiple dimensions. Technologies enable accelerated globalization. In security and politics as in economics, globalization is a package deal; transnationalization both requires and prompts informatization and flexibilization. Conflict and security are also economic sectors, as in the arms industry, crime networks and paramilitaries in developing countries.[3] Conflict and security have become growth industries—the erstwhile war economy reborn as part of the post–cold war economy. Trend-spotters recognize the opportunities for profitable investment in privatized security; the "Criminal-Industrial Complex" is anticipated to be a "major growth industry." "The $70 billion hypersafety industry (1995) will continue to grow at 9 per cent per year through the turn of the century."[4]

In local arenas, new interests interplay with vested security interests. Cold war blowback feeds local and regional conflicts while new dynamics emerge. Thus, the need for interoperability between NATO and former Warsaw Pact countries prompts East European countries to release outdated weapons (and explosives such as Semtex) on the global arms market, which feeds into local conflicts and terrorist networks.

While a distinction is often made between the cold war era and contemporary globalization, common to both is modernity, which raises the wider question of the relationship between conflict and modernity, between military technologies and progress. After all, modernity through most of its career has been modernity at war.[5]

How globalization and politics of conflict and security interact is too wide a field to be adequately surveyed in a single chapter, so this discussion concentrates on three themes: technology, geopolitics, and asymmetric conflict. Focusing on technology serves to shift the attention from globalization events (its *histoire événementielle*) to the infrastructure of globalization. Focusing on violence is to zero in on the dark side of globalization; conflict and security reveal the Janus faces of globalization. A point where these dimensions—technologies, the political economy of violence, geopolitics—intersect is asymmetric conflict, or conflict across technology gaps. This includes humanitarian intervention, which is also termed humanitarian militarism.[6] The central riddle is how is it that the era of accelerated globalization is so deeply mired in politics of containment?

The first section of this chapter argues that economic and military technologies change in tandem and correlate with political changes. Contemporary globalization exhibits institutionalized schizophrenia—relative borderlessness within the world of Ronald McDonald and borders without. It follows that the key problem is conflict that takes place at or beyond this dividing line, as in Thomas Friedman's Golden Arches theory.

The two faces and two worlds of globalization meet in the new politics of containment. The closing query is if the worlds of accelerated globalization are managed and policed by politics of containment and remote-control technologies, are there counterpoints that signal different forms of engagement?

Technologies of Work and War

The principle that technologies of work and war move in tandem is well established. Historically, economic progress and arms races often went together. Thus the emergence of modern capitalism in Northern Italy was accompanied by rival military improvements.[7] Economic and military leadership often go together and are intertwined in notions of international hegemony. The stage for the military-industrial complex was set in the nineteenth century when military production was the industrial locomotive in France, Germany, Russia, and Japan. The twentieth-century military-industrial complex extends to high tech, witness the affinities between IBM and the Holocaust and between the Pentagon and the Internet and Silicon Valley. "The connection between war and technoscience has long been intimate; now it is integral."[8] Military, intelligence, and space technologies are intimately interwoven in the development of information and communication technologies.

Speed differentials have always been essential to military strategy. With flexible technology this has moved into overdrive. The Iraq war set the latest standard of "smart warfare." Flex tech has become the basis of contemporary strategy. Rapid deployment forces have become a general strategic formula. Military equipment has literally become lighter.[9] Lean multitask mobile forces and smart military outfits follow the same principle as the automation of production: "using knowledge so that less capital and labor may have to be expended."[10] The soldier in electronic warfare, like the multitask worker in flexible production, becomes a multi-skilled operator, a software soldier. Parallel trends in the organization of production are flexible system production, just-in-time manufacturing or Toyotism.

Like production and business, warfare has become knowledge intensive, to the point of "knowledge warfare" in which "each side will try to shape enemy actions by manipulating the flow of intelligence and information."[11] Information management, "info doctrine," "knowledge strategy" along with policies of "knowledge procurement," simulation and cyberwar are part of this reorientation. Command and Control, C2, has become Command, Control, and Communication, C3 (C3I with Intelligence) and next, Command, Control, Communications, Computers, Intelligence,

Surveillance and Reconnaissance, or C4ISR.[12] As military endeavour becomes a network effort, connectivity is crucial and includes shielding software and communication lines from hackers and enemy infiltration. C4ISR is multiscalar and involves the decentralization of coordination tasks. Like flexible production, war involves a network of global and local coordination efforts: globally via satellites, locally via on the spot decision-making, and just-in-time assembly and delivery of custom-made threats.

Force modernization or the Revolution in Military Affairs (RMA) is to bring the armed forces in line with information technology, build a knowledge-intensive smart military force, and scale back cold-war type heavy equipment.[13] This is a long-term project that also applies to NATO forces.[14] It means a greater role for technology in combat—such as unmanned drones, satellite-guided missiles, precision-guided munitions, and advanced ICT. In addition, Rumsfeld wants the entire military to be "speedier and deadlier, the hallmark of the Special Operations forces."[15] Special forces played a major part in Afghanistan and Iraq.

Surveillance technologies in civilian and military spheres follow parallel tracks. Closed-circuit television monitoring in security-sensitive public areas and production sites, satellite remote sensing (Geographical Information Systems), automatic vehicle location systems, and cell phone monitoring add up to "total tracking" capabilities. Employee productivity and work habits can be monitored through computer use. Remote sensing can be automated with in-built trigger alerts in response to anomalies; financial and currency markets also partly operate via computer-set trigger thresholds. The Terrorism Information Awareness project of the U.S. department for homeland security seeks to merge extant databases.

To inform C4ISR it takes flexible intelligence. Conventional intelligence followed standardized techniques such as the indiscriminate "electronic vacuum cleaners" of electronic intelligence gathering, the equivalent of mass production. What is needed now is precision-targeted information. According to a CIA analyst: "To tailor routine intelligence to particular consumers' interests, we need the ability to produce different presentations for each key customer. We envision final assembly and routine finished intelligence at the 'point of sale.'"[16] In other words, just in time (rather than just-in-case) intelligence.

According to the Pentagon's Joint Vision 2020, U.S. forces must have "access to and freedom to operate in all domains—space, sea, land, air and information" and achieve "Full Spectrum Dominance"—"to defeat any adversary and control the situation across the full range of military operations."[17] In information war, communication, media and education policies become part of overall military strategy. A country's information structure is essential in national competitiveness and is relevant from a military point of view. According to an intelligence analyst, "The essence of Information Warfare and Information Operations is that the aim of conflict should be to manage the perceptions of an enemy leadership.... An integrated IO strategy would therefore incorporate covert action, public affairs and propaganda, diplomacy and economic warfare."[18]

Collective security operations, as in the Gulf War and the Balkans, are being succeeded by "modular coalitions as crises arise" or "temporary plug-in/plug-out alliances," which "parallels the efforts of the world's largest corporations to form 'strategic alliances' and 'consortia' to compete effectively."[19] Thus similar transnational combinations of cooperation and competition emerge in business and war: network capitalism and network war. Just as production technologies influence war, war shapes business. Management and the organization of labor in industry have long been profoundly influenced by military examples.[20] Business and competition are now often likened to warfare, boardrooms make increasing use of war games, and studies of war strategy are summer reading for CEOs.[21]

RMA entails several points of tension. The economic spin-offs of this type of military expansion are likely to be much less than the military Keynesianism of the cold war economy. The cost is higher and the spin-off lower because it relies on commercial sources of information technology that depend on international markets.[22] Technology is often viewed as a silver bullet or a general-purpose snake oil; but applying new technologies gives rise to anomalies. For instance, throughout history a key military concern has been to augment combat force and lethal capability, but now in several arenas the problem is *excess* military capability.[23] An American private comments from Iraq:

> A lot is made of our military's might. Our Abrams tanks, our Apache helicopters, computers, satellites, this and that. All that stuff is great, but it's essentially useless in peacekeeping ops. It is up to the soldiers on the ground armed with M-16s and a precious few words of Arabic.[24]

Applying high tech requires the reorganization of force structure lest there is a mismatch between cutting-edge technology and cumbersome command and control lines. The paradox of RMA is that to implement it requires a centralization of command, which force modernization seeks to overcome. A problem in joint operations is that collective security operations require a coordination of C4ISR that may not be attainable politically.

Technologies of Politics

> The interdependent world looks more and more like the weather
> system described by chaos theory; influenced by millions of vari-
> ables, its causality does not follow a linear model, and
> consequences are not proportionate to causes.
>
> —Jean-Marie Guéhenno, 1998

Since war is the continuation of politics by other means we must also consider the technologies of politics. Technologies cannot be divorced from politics; they embody a politics and their application is thoroughly political. Parallels between power and technology are an old theme. As every analysis of power confirms, different forms of power (political, economic, ideological, and military) are interdependent and change in parallel ways.[25]

In sociology, connectivity has given rise to the notion of the network society.[26] A related notion is "network capitalism" and to characterize the public-private partnerships in the politics of aid and intervention Mark Duffield speaks of network war.[27] Geoff Mulgan makes a further argument on the relationship between technology and politics. In his view, the heavy technologies of industrialism in the mass production phase were paralleled by heavy command-and-control politics; standardized production was matched by standardized administration and regulation, standardized politics, and coalitions. These involved top-down hierarchical relations between government and the governed, and within bureaucracies, parties, and trade unions. Light touch-button technology, on the other hand, correlates with lateral relations and information flows within organizations and light network politics. Thus technologies of social cooperation in production, governance and collective action tend to move in parallel ways.[28]

One need not look at technology to arrive at similar observations. Laclau and Mouffe describe contemporary politics as "hegemonic" and characterized by unfixed identities and fragmented space in which nodal points nonetheless matter. In hegemonic politics, political coalitions are not stable as in old-time politics because the subjectivities are not as stable.[29]

It has been argued that the technologies of domination and emancipation are structurally similar in that both concern capabilities, while the difference lies in the values, objectives, and methods that guide action.[30] Since the Enlightenment and the model of the bourgeois revolution, progressive politics has been sprinkled with pleas for unity. The desire to forge a grand coalition of opposition forces leads to a search for a central counterpoint that would unite all dissident social forces. This may reflect nostalgia for "old politics" characterized by clearly divided camps and neat ideological boundaries. But increasingly the case for a "convergence of radicalisms" fails to persuade because in such pleas the interests and subjectivities involved tend to be taken as given and static, rather than as being constructed and reworked in the process of political articulation. Analyses of collective action and social movements, then, confirm the observation that politics, from above and below, has become more "flexible."

Alvin Toffler argues that in military technology "the new communications networks favor democratic nations."[31] They depend on "the ability to exchange information, to swap data, and to promote a free flow of information around the network, so that people can assemble the tactical pictures, they can relate their stuff together.... Societies that freeze the flow of communications, the free flow of ideas and data, will not, by definition, be able to make much use of such systems." In fact, the "soldier and the civilian are informationally intertwined."[32] According to Rand Corporation analysts, the best way of fighting terrorism is "netwar";[33] but netwar requires decentralization of command and control.

This would give a different twist to the conventional Washington consensus that links the free market and democracy—with some ifs and buts. "Democratization is inimical to imperial mobilization."[34] War and democracy don't go well together and media manipulation and information war are not all that helpful to democracy either.[35] Besides, the new technologies obviously favor information-intensive societies.

Technologies of work, war, and politics are intertwined but their interrelations are uneven within and across countries. Just as not every industrial production system is up to flexible system production, so "not every army in the world is culturally or politically (let alone technologically) capable of using" the information-intensive C4 systems.[36]

ICT leapfrogs across the conventional boundaries between modes of production. Masai herdsmen in Kenya now use mobile phones and wireless radio to manage their herds. Such technological crossings are not new—as in plantations organized on industrial basis and trends such as agro-industry, "miracle seeds," and biogenetic engineering. ICT enables long-distance nationalism such as Tamils in Toronto and London sponsoring the Tamil Elam struggle in Sri Lanka, or Kurds in Germany rallying against the Turkish government. Alternative or rival globalization projects, such as Islamic globalisms,[37] are likewise made possible by ICT. ICT also enables criminal organizations and terrorist networks to operate flexibly over larger terrains and to cooperate transnationally more effectively than previously.[38] In police methods, crossborder policing and transnational information exchange are viewed as achievements of the knowledge society.[39]

The situation is contradictory in several respects. That we are heading towards a borderless world is one of the familiar ideologies of globalization. At the forefront of economic change this is supposed to be a time of deterritorialization, or even dematerialization.[40] In politics, sovereignty has become increasingly decentered. Yet, in the view of strategy analysts, "Most wars are still about territory. . . . The key requirement for military force remains the ability to take and hold strategically important territory, or at least to control those that live there. Air and sea strategies must therefore always be assessed in terms of their impact on land strategy. This is as close a constant as we are likely to have in the study of war."[41] It is as if Napoleon's saying that "the policy of a state lies in its geography" still holds.

This applies even more if we consider regional politics than if we take a big-picture approach to geopolitics. In most regions we find that the reports of the death or retreat of the state are exaggerated and territorial politics driven by "national interest" is quite alive. For instance, Israel's politics in the Middle East is thoroughly "Westphalian." Egypt's relations with Sudan are a regional eco-politics shaped by its interest in the Nile waters. Similar considerations apply to the relations between Turkey and Greece, Russia and China, China and Japan, India and Pakistan, the Balkans, and so on. In most regions countries continue to behave according to national interests that include territorial considerations.[42]

While territory matters and we cannot understand conflict and security otherwise, territorial considerations themselves are embedded in and criss-crossed by economic, ecological, and cultural politics. Obviously the United States' commitment to the Washington consensus cannot be understood within a territorial or Westphalian framework. The French politics of fran-cophonie, in Africa and on issues of international trade in services and the WTO transcends Westphalian interests. Indeed, territorial considerations themselves are profoundly structured by national narratives and imaginaries. They are shaped by cultural fictions that can become "fighting fictions."[43] Milosevic's take on Kosovo is a case in point. Israel's Westphalian strategies are meaningless outside the framework of Zionism and the "Jewish state," or what Avishai Margalit calls "the kitsch of Israel."[44] The same applies to relations between India and Pakistan, and the Kashmir question. It gener-ally holds for conflicts of the type referred to as "ethnic," as in the Balkans, Sudan, or Tamil Elam in Sri Lanka: they are culturally overdetermined.[45]

In strategy analysis, perspectives that combine *culture* and *strategy* have a considerable lineage.[46] According to a recent account, "Strategic behav-iour cannot be beyond culture"; "Adversity cannot cancel culture"; "Strategic culture is a guide to action"; "Strategic culture can be dysfunctional"; and the conclusion is that "all dimensions of strategy are cultural."[47] If "culture rules" in strategy, then what about international affairs? According to the constructivist turn in international relations theory "ideas and discourse matter."[48] This brings us from realism to "cultural realism" and the post-structuralist turn in international relations theory takes this further.[49]

These considerations come back with a twist in Jean-Marie Guéhenno's observations on contemporary political leaders. "Their political agenda is vague and while they may define their objectives in very broad terms, their identity and goals may be more accurately described as a style than as a program.... [S]trategy then is no more than a pattern of action, linking together situations that are otherwise disjointed.... Just as corporations compete to create 'brands,' political actors try to establish a 'style.'"[50] This understates political economy and interest: what underlie brands are market positions, and presumably what underlie leadership styles are interests. It's just that interests cannot be separated from cultural narratives just like products can no longer be separated from their brand images. "In diplomacy, style is often substance."[51] What then would be the element of coherence in such strategic "styles"? Interest, ideology, image, style, or all of these?

The old saying that "language is a dialect with a navy and an army" confirms the significance of linguistic and discourse analysis. "Hate speech" from Rwanda to Serbia, and in slick packaging by NATO and the Pentagon, is a case in point. Divergent perspectives on the role of discourse and images in conflict[52] do not necessarily contradict one another but can function at different levels of awareness, all feeding into the role of media in conflict.[53] Media, then, are an integral part of network and conflict politics. In Lebanon, Hezbollah aimed television broadcasts in Hebrew at Israeli soldiers. Information war changes the politics of protest: "information wars tend to be public-relations battles for Western attention, hence the adoption of English as the universal language of protest. It is assumed that the way to Western decision-making is through the media and public opinion."[54]

The question of style suggests furthers parallel between the technologies of work, war, and politics. All along the military has also been an aesthetic and sign-intensive domain actively concerned with impression management and the "politics of appearance."[55] The American missile defense program or "Star Wars" has found its way under fluffy headings such as "future imagery architecture." With the increasing importance of marketing and media, economics has become sign and design-intensive[56] and so has politics.[57] Thus, work, war and politics are all also semiotic and aesthetic projects, tied up with libidinal economies. A précis of interrelations between technologies of work, war, and politics is in table 6.1.

Technology Matters, But

The upshot so far is that modes of production and modes of destruction interact. Accordingly, technology may serve as a crosscutting angle from

Table 6.1 Technologies in Diverse Domains

Technologies	Work	War	Politics
High tech	Flexible production	Smart war	Governance
ICT	Connectivity	C4ISR	Connexity
Flexibilization	Just-in-time	Rapid deployment	Interactive decision making
Informatization	Knowledge intensity	Information war	Deliberative democracy
	Multi-task worker	Software soldier	Empowered citizen
Information circulation	"Learning organization"	C4ISR vs. command structures	Lateral politics, e-government, referendum
Information management	Marketing, branding, logo	Information Operations	Spin, style
Aesthetics	Sign & design intensity	"Spectacular war"	Media politics
Organizational structures	Concentration & decentralization	Concentration & decentralization	Decentralize, regionalize, internationalize
	Network capitalism	Network war	Network society
	Mergers & acquisitions, joint ventures	Modular coalitions	Coalition politics Plug-in/plug-out alliances
Space	Deterritorializing	Territorial	Neo-medievalism, "electronic feudalism"
	Bordercrossing	Border control	Border negotiation

which to view the patterning of human affairs—not merely looking from production to social relations and from production relations to politics (as in Marxist accounts), but all the way across, from technology to production, politics, and war. Technology then may be viewed as a deep structure of the rhythm of history made visible.

So no doubt technology matters, but is this a matter of technological determinism? An alternative view is that it is not technology as such that determines but the capabilities of which technologies are an expression. What underlies technology is human capability: technology is encapsulated human skill, or crystallized labor, in the Marxian frame. Technology is social relations made durable, packaged and routinized, a form of "social mapping."[58] Thus, production, politics, and war all reflect growing human capabilities in diverse domains, socialized in forms of cooperation and social practices, and exteriorized in the form of technology. Technology, then, is an enabler and a necessary but not a sufficient condition for action. If anything, what would be at issue is capabilities determinism. But that's not quite true either.

The other major component, besides ability, is will; technology is only half the story, the other half is political will or motivation. According to Henry Kissinger, defeat in Vietnam was due to a failure of American will power, a "failure of nerve." In the war on terror it is said again, "Our vulnerability is in our political will."[59] At times this is referred to as morale. Adolf Hitler put it boldly:

> Any resurrection of the German people can take place only by way of regaining external power. But the prerequisites for this are not arms, as our bourgeois "statesmen" always babble, but the forces of will power. . . . The best arms are dead and useless material as long as the spirit is missing which is ready, willing, and determined to use them. . . . [T]he question of regaining Germany's power is not, perhaps, How can we manufacture arms, but, How can we produce that spirit which enables the people to bear arms.[60]

Indeed, not just technology but also political will is changing in the brave new world. One wonders, for instance, where the spirit of sacrifice is to come from in conditions of high affluence. And what of the kind of national cohesion that is required to "produce the spirit of war" in an era of multiculturalism and transnationalism? This suggests that propaganda and politics of representation acquire crucial importance at every step of the way. That warfare itself has become a multilevel spin operation we see in the Gulf War, the Allied Force Operation in Kosovo, Afghanistan, and the Iraq war, where media manipulation is a crucial component of strategy.[61] These information operations are embedded in narratives and representations that explain how the brave new globe is divided, which is taken up in the next chapter.

Asymmetric Conflict

The politics of violence draws on competitive advantages of weapons, organization and information. Business is a play of margins—drawing rents from temporary advantages in technology, production, marketing, and distribution. Likewise violence involves playing margins of protection.[62] The world circumstance ranges from agricultural and industrial to knowledge societies. Include indigenous peoples and the spectrum runs from the Paleolithic to the post-industrial. The politics of violence involves a play of technology or capability differentials across terrains and social contexts. In the nineteenth century colonial armies could control large populations by means of simple technological leverage— "We have got the Maxim gun/And they have not."[63] By virtue of the same principle, warlords with access to modern weapons can now destabilize states. Even small arms, which are in plentiful supply, make a lot of difference. "In Uganda, an AK-47 can be obtained for the price of a chicken. In Swaziland, the same weapon has sold for $6."[64]

The Westphalian state system assumes a level of technology that enables states to effectively monopolize the means of coercion within their borders. In many countries this kind of control is no longer available; state sovereignty can no longer be guaranteed by force of arms internally. In weaponry as in economics, flex tech alters the relation between regions and nations, between the local and the global. Complexity and uncertainty characterize the environment of foreign military intervention.[65] Part of this equation is asymmetric conflict, which ranges from the classic repertoire of small wars and counterinsurgency to episodes such as the traumatic intervention in Somalia.

In this setting the information advantage of advanced societies may be of limited purchase, as demonstrated in Iraq, Bosnia, and Kosovo: "Modern sensors come into their own when observing a conventional order of battle, but have more trouble monitoring urban militias, rural guerrillas or crude mortars on trucks."[66] ICT is the wave of the future, but to what extent does information really constitute an advantage on the ground?

> In general, high-quality information systems work best when they are linked to a physical capacity to attack enemy assets, or to defend one's own. The focus on information systems as targets misses the point that, today, information is easily stored, reproduced and accessed.... [I]t is therefore important not to exaggerate the West's information advantage.[67]

If this forms part of the security dimension of global risk society, what are the trends in risk and conflict management? Conflict management now refers to the overall spectrum of conflict prevention, conflict transformation, conflict resolution, humanitarian action and intervention, aid, and postconflict rehabilitation. Western countries are keen to be active on either *end* of this spectrum, in conflict prevention or postconflict rehabilitation, rather than in the middle, for that requires real engagement with local affairs.[68] Here the trend is to subcontract to NGOs and regional and Third World security forces.

Another trend is to recycle the national security apparatus that has been underemployed since the end of the cold war, by redeploying conventional organizations and techniques of control and surveillance. This applies to the way intrastate conflicts in third states are managed as well as to policies against terrorism, crime, and drugs.

In relation to drugs, the main trend remains the War on Drugs, even though drugs are part of consumerism, "prohibition" type policies are out of synch with contemporary levels of individualization and social and consumer choice, and with present technologies such a war is not winnable. Legalizing drugs would be more realistic; it would give room to social choice and decriminalize the drugs trade. It would imply accepting a greater degree of individual and collective risk management. Prohibition policies achieve the reverse and are a boon to both crime and police organizations. "Zero tolerance" in urban policing is another instance of command-and-control politics.

Phrased differently, if due to, among other things, technological changes, we are experiencing a miniaturization of conflict—so that armed conflict, more than before, is no longer the prerogative of states but accessible to groups within states—the appropriate response would be a flexibilization of conflict management. Westphalian balance of power politics and the doctrine of preventive war are out of step with techno-logical, political, and cultural processes. While there is a place for state politics (no doubt a larger place than is granted in "retreat of the state" arguments), it needs to be supplemented with more flexible and imagi-native approaches to conflict management.

New Politics of Containment

The key work on strategy lessons learned from the Vietnam War in the United States is Harry Summers's *On Strategy*. It concluded that the Pentagon should only go into war with the backing of congress and should avoid "quagmires," so there should be an exit strategy. The Pentagon can no longer afford fighting wars that are undeclared, have no legitimacy and no public support.[69] In the era of media warfare, body bags erode public support; Operation Restore Hope in Somalia is a case in point.

> The fact that the first requirement of intervention in a conflict is now a credible exit strategy, like a debt-collector venturing into a rough neighborhood, is symptomatic of a lack of confidence.

Another symptom is the search for ways to influence events from a
safe distance, especially through air power. This fits with the notion
that we are dealing with criminal elements who must be punished
if they cannot be coerced.[70]

This involves a historically novel notion of conflict management without
risk to life, without sacrifice, without tears. This may be termed a "postheroic
style of warfare" or fighting and killing without dying.[71] Airborne warfare
and smart technology seem to make the dream of clean risk-free warfare
come true. The 78 day air war against Yugoslavia in 1989 yielded zero
American combat casualties. Conflict management without body bags: isn't
there a parallel between LAPD helicopters circling over risky neighborhoods
of Los Angeles and NATO planes bombing targets in Serbia and Kosovo
from a safe altitude? Yet at some point ground forces have to come in, in
Kosovo as in Los Angeles.[72] A showcase moment in Los Angeles was police
beating Rodney King, a black truck driver. A showcase moment in the clean
war was Srebrenica July 1997.[73] How to provide safe havens for a population under threat if the terms of engagement are no risk to the lives of the
peacekeepers?

Smart war without tears is made possible by global and long-distance
optics and cartography. Jim Scott's *Seeing like a State* refers to a gaze "from
above," an engineering and managerial gaze that shapes nature (as in scientific forestry and huge dams) and society (as in urban and development
planning), which he contrasts with local optics.[74] Macroeconomics exhibits
similar features, and military parallels include what Paul Virilio calls "seeing
from the air"[75] and seeing from space. They all represent the essential technological illusion: the illusion of control.[76]

The circumstance that distinctions between military and civilians often
can't be made from the air and smart weapons aren't all that smart is made
up for by overall lack of involvement in the local stakes, whether it concerns
Iraq, Kurdistan, Bosnia, Kosovo, Rwanda, Somalia or Sudan. Not to mention
Sierra Leone, Liberia, or Burundi. Casualties on the other side don't count
and are not even counted or reported. This matches the view of the world
split into an advanced zone without major conflict and a backward zone of
"Iraqs and Ruritanias" where "small wars" continue. This outlook often
involves the reification of "fundamentalism" or ethnicity, the objectification
of ethnic conflict, and the perception of combatants and their conflict as
somehow irrational, savage. In caricature and cartoon fashion—and isn't
this cartoon politics?—this adds up to a picture of supermen in the air, or
airborne angels, and savages on the ground and we recognize the profile of
the Angel of Progress.

This optics comes with a global panopticon view that sees the world in terms of geopolitical objectives, strategic resources (oil, strategic minerals, diamonds, gold), and military choke points. In this view, relations across zones—nicely bifurcated as advanced and backward—are reduced to strategic and corporate interests, and threats and obstacles to these interests. Global panopticism comes with

- *representations* that proclaim globalization divides (à la Huntington),
- which require *politics of containment,*
- which are enabled by remote-sensing *technologies*
- and operationalized in *policies,* such as
- regime change (Afghanistan, Iraq, Palestine, Liberia, Iran),
- embargoes and sanctions (Cuba, Libya),
- blockade (West Bank and Gaza),
- humanitarian intervention (Somalia, Bosnia, Kosovo),
- aid governmentality
- and immigration control (visa restrictions, border policing).

Downstream consequences are that containment politics inadvertently creates or fosters totalitarian control (as in Iraq, warlord territories in Afghanistan, Sierra Leone, etc.) and authoritarian politics and rent seeking within the contained zone.[77] It increases military vulnerability in border control (witness Israel) and fosters seeking loopholes and crime (as in the upsurge in human trafficking). It mixes up military and police functions (or deterrence and compellence).[78] The objective of containment is not to settle or resolve conflict but to contain security risk, and arguably containment politics sustain conflict. The underlying motif is that there is no interest, no motive, no capacity, and no political tools for engaging local realities. This matches the politics of hopelessness of neoliberalism, a politics of betting on the strong without providing for the losers. A parallel in the United States are the twin phenomena of ghettos and gated communities. Fifty years hence a perspective on neoliberal globalization may be that it produces world-scale American capitalism, fosters a technologically and economically driven growth, as in turbo capitalism, and is fundamentally unable to address inequality.

Let's try to pinpoint the contours of the new politics of containment more accurately. Also during the cold war, containment was but a headline and not a full account of what was going on, which included interventions across the dividing line, such as corporate joint ventures, building political alliances, covert operations, and rollback interventions. Now likewise, containment is only part of the register, part of the security dimension, along with other forms of engagement such as stabilization lending, development cooperation, foreign direct investment, and so forth. A schematic comparison of cold war and accelerated globalization politics of containment is in table 6.2.

The predecessor of current containment politics is the policy of dual containment of the close of the cold war, aimed against communism and "extremism."[79] Yet the globalization divide differs from the cold war in several ways. There is no clear enemy. The terrain of capitalism versus communism has made place for capitalisms with Anglo-American capitalism in the lead. The East bloc policy of confinement ("the wall") is no more. But the globalization divide is no more fluid than the cold war divide. Now walls emerge on the other side, to keep intruders out (as in Israel's fence, U.S. borders and air traffic security, EU visa requirements). And if the overall axis of difference has shifted from East–West to North–South, differences *within* North and South are as large as or larger than those between North and South. So while the security apparatus of the globalization divide builds on existing security structures, the terrain, the stakes and the policies are radically different.

The cold war was won; is the globalization divide winnable? And what would winning mean? Can the new politics of containment work? September 11 suggests that it doesn't. The U.S. defense system distinguishes between A category threats to national survival, B threats to national interest, and a C category of minor conflicts.[80] September 11 promoted a C category threat to A level. Do the politics of divided globalization and containment inspire a politics of subversion and resistance? Cliché spillover factors are transnational terrorism and crime. Do the technologies that enable the new containment also enable its subversion? Graffiti on the Islamic university in Gaza read: "Israel has nuclear bombs, we have human bombs."[81]

Table 6.2 Politics of Containment

Dimensions	Cold War	Contemporary Globalization
Ideology	Free World vs. Communism	Clash of civilizations, etc.
Boundaries	East–West	North–South
	Ideology, political system	Development indicators, poverty
	Alliances	"Culture"
Threat	Communism	Rogue states, terrorism, crime
Risk	Domino theory	Economic crisis: contagion theory
		Politics: "new barbarism"
Infrastructure	National security states	Modular coalitions

Containment or Engagement?

> How to shore up anchor states while satisfying disadvantaged
> minorities is a huge challenge for international diplomacy at a
> time when the US Congress seems determined to cutback aid and
> multilateral institutions.
>
> —B. Slavin, writing in *USA Today*

> A connected world defies the rules of zero sum games, where an
> advantage for someone else means a disadvantage for me.
>
> —Geoff Mulgan, 1994

Scratch the kitsch of globalization and there is glaring inequality, misery, and conflict. In the early 1990s, U.S. national security advisors conceded that "extremism" is born out of "exclusion." According to the 2002 National Security Strategy, the greatest danger lies "at the crossroads of radicalism and technology."[82] Now along with the political economy of "permanent war," novel features are a globalized social Darwinism and a development-security nexus.

Long-distance optics and remote-control technologies create, maintain, or enhance the illusion of separation between conflict managers and combatants, which at the same time is being dispelled by live media reporting that brings long-distance suffering close to home (but suppressing civilian casualties and "collateral damage," as in Afghanistan and Iraq). Thus one set of technologies enables dualistic engagement while another ambiguously suggests solidarity or reflexive engagement. Remote sensing presents the paradox of distant engagement.

Connexity is a two-edged sword that separates (by enabling surveillance and inflicting injury over long distance that separates perpetrators from victims) and unites (by establishing a moral nexus between actions and consequences, reporting and public awareness, engagement and responsibility). Enhanced technological capabilities inevitably involve enlargement of responsibility. This dual track applies to technologies of war as it does to other technologies—such as the capacity to build large dams that can annihilate hundreds of villages or their livelihood, to biogenetic engineering or genetically modified food. The present juncture is part of a historical crossroads.[83] The essential problem of contemporary globalization is that technological capabilities and economic changes are ahead of institutional and political capacities: growing capacities, also for conflict, coupled with inadequate institutions.

Is it too much to expect coherence between politics of containment and politics of engagement? The idea of a world split in advanced and backward regions may look superficially valid in view of the different stakes, weapons, and methods of conflict in diverse theatres, but since it overlooks western complicity in conflicts and the spillover effects of conflicts, it is ultimately Mickey Mouse politics. The role of western powers in conflicts the world over includes colonial legacies and blowback of the cold war, financial and economic regimes, double standards, arms exports,[84] appetite for strategic and valuable resources, and state-corporate alliances that sow the seeds of conflict (as in Angola and the Democratic Republic of Congo).

When considering perspectives on conflict and security what matters also is how they construct reality and the policy framework they imply.[85] Constructivism applies not only in past and present but to the future too; the way realities are constructed may hold a reconstructive potential as well. Both the way in and the way out are matters of perspective and representation. Since in security issues threat-inflation and worst-case scenarios predominate the margins for progressive scenarios seem slim.

One scenario is that neoliberal empire will not have a long career and U.S. policy will revert to unilateralism with a multilateral face. An alternative scenario is two spheres, one under U.S. unilateral control and another governed multilaterally under the International Criminal Court. At any rate it is necessary to think ahead. We need enabling diagnoses and scenarios but could only enable democratic trends if we would recognize them. This is not taking a normative leap but taking stock of trends that are already in motion. Of course, if the new grows within the womb of the old, new trends are intermeshed with current malpractices. If we don't heed the complicity of actors in the configuration we misread the unfolding drama; if we don't consider the innovations that are taking shape we miss the contours of change. While recognizing that to each coin there are at least two sides, let's signal several ongoing trends.

- A counterpart to the business of war is the "Business of Peace," that is partnerships with the private sector in conflict prevention and transformation.[86] An example is efforts to restrict trade in diamonds and other resources from conflict zones. Thus a counterweight to network war is network peace.
- Ongoing changes in understanding sovereignty should not merely be viewed as a loss, as "perforated sovereignty,"[87] but also in a forward sense. Thus the international recognition of sovereignty has become de facto conditional on respect for the human rights of the population.[88]
- This ties in with trends towards postnational citizenship. Borders offer protection, but one of the causes of conflict is "hard sovereignty," along with winner-takes-all nationalism. A forward option is to experiment with forms of shared sovereignty such as

transborder human rights regimes.[89] In the Great Lakes region of Africa, for instance, such arrangements would enable people fleeing warlords in one state to find refuge in another without immediately being categorized as "refugees." Eventually this could evolve in the direction of "regional sovereignty." Related notions are Sakamoto's civic regionalism, Ulrich Beck's "cosmopolitan state" and the idea of cosmopolitan justice.[90]

- "Make law not war" or strengthening the international legal order.[91] Trying human rights violations and war crimes under international legal standards, as in the War Crimes Tribunals of Rwanda and Yugoslavia, is becoming established practice. These tribunals do not make up for the absence of international forces when the conflicts occurred, yet they set precedents for international law. Other reforms are restrictions on the trade in conventional arms[92] (though the elimination of nuclear weapons is more remote than ever).

- The role of NGOs. The range of organizations active in complex emergencies involves relief and development agencies, medical organizations, international institutions, human rights organizations, legal offices, military outfits and police organizations coming together in novel combinations. This is the oft-criticized new governmentality of aid; yet it also means an extension and deepening of the international public sector that acquires an increasingly transnational character. Linking relief and development strengthens a developmental approach to complex emergencies that may involve a more participatory approach and, at least, a chance for local empowerment.[93] The involvement of NGOs (diverse as they are) makes for a different organizational mix and may contribute different ways of relating to actors on the ground. At times the role of NGOs expands in multitrack and people-to-people diplomacy.[94]

- The reform of international institutions is part of the wider agenda of international governance. Reform of the UN, the Security Council, and the international financial institutions to make these more responsive bodies from the point of view of planetary citizenship has long been on the agenda.

This is a time when global networks exist but not global society. Global communications and instant live reporting on violence in far-off places, even if filtered through stereotypes, involve ripple effects and awareness of long-distance suffering as well as political and ultimately legal ramifications. Early warning imposes obligations. According to the Geneva Convention, preventing genocide is a moral and legal obligation that overrides all international norms. Arguably we are experiencing the gradual emergence of a de facto global moral economy in real time, which generates new demands. Early warning necessitates early response; hence the preoccupation with conflict prevention. On a broad canvas these dilemmas form part of human evolution: the networks of social cooperation gradually widen over time while the institutions lag behind. In history when new inventions and opportunities emerge, conflict usually predates cooperation and cooperation arises, in part, in order to regulate conflict.

CHAPTER 7

Globalization North and South

A major feature of the global condition is the glaring hiatus between wealth and poverty. One would like to say it is a feature of global experience, but for how many of us is it a matter of experience? Worlds of experience are segmented and representations across the fence are coded. Global poverty is routinized—"the poor will always be with you." Aid fatigue is periodically interrupted by emergencies that prompt selective media attention and out of the sky relief campaigns. Refugees are objects of charity, asylum seekers objects of scrutiny, illegal immigrants are criminalized along with drug traffickers, crime syndicates, and terrorists. Wealth and poverty are both relative and contextual, and according to the soap stories that make up the comfort zones of capitalism "the rich also suffer." The steady succession of development fixes and failures is papered over by global economic management; poverty alleviation and development are being outmaneuvered by macroeconomic management in the vague expectation that a rising tide will lift all boats.

One of the features of collective reflection today is the profound discrepancy between perspectives North and South. On either side, representations in media and social science are schematic and together make up a stylized encounter of stereotypes and off-the-shelf knowledge. Since global inequality is a major part of the collective condition, it would loom large in collective reflection, but does it? The wide discrepancies between the worlds of experience of the world's poor majority and the world's privileged minority in the North are echoed in media and social science. Social science

107

in the North takes itself to be at the forefront of collective understanding, while it is mostly too self-engrossed to take into account the experiences and perspectives of the world majority. Whether it concerns modernity, globalization, or history, it tends to represent narrow western or northern views.

The North is often better known in the South than the South is in the North. Yet in the South the engagement with northern perspectives is often out of context, out of touch with their historical context and cultural variations. New Age scientists in the North are foraging mystical and shamanic traditions worldwide without much understanding of the actual variations in philosophy and practice. In the South, scholars seeking to negotiate modernity scrutinize the European Enlightenment—Kant, Hegel, Habermas—without adequate understanding that rationalism was a program, not a reality, that to the Enlightenment there was also a dark side, and the romantics were part of the Enlightenment too (Herder, Carlyle, Nietzsche).

Lack of depth and nuance, lack of experience and understanding on either side. Schematic understandings North and South of modernity, capitalism, poverty, development, religion, cultures. The North–South hiatus in experience and reflection has us living in a cardboard world, making gestures to cut-outs rather than real figures. No wonder that émigrés from the South in the North have been so influential in fiction and social science, for they—along with migrants, transnational activists, and NGOs—bridge the different worlds of experience.

North–South inequality runs very deep, *n'en déplaise* globalization and the "deterritorialization of poverty" (the rich in the South and the poor in the North). This involves not only material differences and differences in power, but also different cultures and perceptions. It relates profoundly to world images and perceptions of globalization that are held also among the middle class in the South.[1] Of course, the South is in the North and the North is in the South, and privilege and poverty are no longer neatly geographically divided. Yet the overall distinction between North and South, crude as it is, still makes sense. In demographic terms they are the minority and majority world. They are *worlds* because they make up complete life worlds. The division does not simply run between middle class and underclass—as if globally these share similar consumption patterns, life styles, and values. In some respects they do, but obviously class and status are not the only variables. Thus the middle class in the South shares many of the majority's economic and political frustrations and in varying degrees identifies with the culture, the nation. The poor majority and the middle class in the South suffer domestic political incompetence and corruption, Western double standards, geopolitics, and share national and regional destinies.

Existing analytics—such as dependency, imperialism, exclusion, conspiracy theories, clash of civilizations—are not adequate for dealing with the new relations that come with contemporary globalization. Representations "across the fence"—such as judgments on ethnic politics, Islam and terrorism—interact with changing security designs. Rather than the interplay of modernities and capitalisms, they project a segmented world.

Thus, the economics of dependency overlooks reverse dependency, such as the dependency of deindustrializing regions in the North (Wales, Scotland) on investors from East Asia (Japan, South Korea, Taiwan). The notion of boomerang effects—such as the debt boomerang (indebtedness in the South curtailing demand for products from the North)—is too blunt to monitor and capture the multiple links and their ramifications. Risk analysis and the globalization of risk can be relevant tools, but risk to whom? What about the risk to the global majority of the excess consumption of energy and resources by the privileged minority? Another account of contemporary globalization refers to the *exclusion* of the majority of humanity who are kept from life in the fast lane. But exclusion is too blunt a terminology to grasp the new uneven links that are developing in the framework of accelerated globalization.[2]

Globalization evokes much anger and anxiety in the South and tends to be experienced as yet another round of northern domination and concentration of power and wealth. In the slipstream of hundreds of years of weary experience, the common metaphor for globalization in the South is imperialism or neocolonialism revisited. Analytically this is mistaken, as argued in Chapter 3. But we cannot neatly distinguish between accounts and conditions, perceptions and realities. Perceptions make up realities, subjectivities and conditions are interwoven, and how situations are evaluated is part of their reality. Constructivism as a common premise in social science means taking seriously the politics of representation at every step of the way, including the representation of representation. While the metaphor of imperialism doesn't apply, nevertheless the widespread feeling that this is another round of domination is a political reality. What is common to both imperialism and contemporary globalization is the sense of powerlessness and frustration on the part of the global majority; only now the dynamics of deprivation are different.

So are the geopolitical circumstances. The world of the 1970s is no more. Then the momentum of decolonization was still in motion, the Nonaligned Movement was strong; the East bloc provided a counterbalance and alternative scenarios such as the new international economic order seemed to make sense. But during the last thirty years, in the wake of the recycling of petro-dollars and the ensuing debt crisis, globalization has come with a new hegemony of finance capital, resembling in some respects Hilferding's turn-of-the-century epoch of finance capital. Open space is shrinking. Delinking as an option was overtaken by the new international division of labor in the 1970s and localism in the sense of building alternative enclaves has little future. This is why the "new protectionism" is a loser strategy. Countervailing power is now located in the diffuse realm of global civil society, civic organizations, and NGOs.

In addition there are regional anxieties, such as double standards in the Middle East, India's worries about rivals in the region and Southeast Asian concerns about the fragility of Indonesia; along with border disputes and secessionist struggles.

Frustration fosters paranoia and conspiracy theories are a convenient shortcut. Lashing out against "Jewish financiers" and George Soros, as the Malaysian prime minister Mahathir Mohamed did, is not of much use. A popular conspiracy theory in the Middle East centers on Zionism in league with the United States because of the Jewish American lobby.[3] In parts of Africa, the Caribbean, and among many African Americans, the main conspiracy is white racism and its machinations. If we enter into the minutiae of international development politics the argument makes sense enough.[4]

Part of cultural and symbolic violence is the hegemony of western institutions and politics of representation. In the absence of an alternative coalition that is strong enough, western notions are the ruling notions. On McPlanet, even dissent, as Ashis Nandy notes, has become standardized and western forms of dissent and notions of rights and justice set the tone.[5]

These perspectives in the South are mirrored by conspiracy theories in the West—such as Jihad against McWorld, the clash of civilizations, the Islamic bomb. Conflicts in the South are trivialized as remote skirmishes, as in Fukuyama's end of history, or yield doomsday perspectives, as in Kaplan's end of the world.[6] Illegal immigrants, criminal organizations, terrorists and drug traffickers threaten the citadels of civilization. The issue is not that these phenomena don't exist; the issue is politics of representation.

Representations of Global Divide

> For the foreseeable future, the world will be divided between a post-historical part, and a part that is still stuck in history.... Clearly, the vast bulk of the Third World remains very much mired in history, and will be a terrain of conflict for many years to come.
>
> —Francis Fukuyama, 1992

Collective history is a mirror and prism of existential dilemmas and cultural leanings. Usually the way out is to try and identify trends that seem broad and structural enough to generate a minimum of consensus. Until recently a cliché among strategy analysts was that, in the words of Michael Mandelbaum, major war while not impossible is "obsolete in the sense that it no longer serves the purpose for which it was designed."[7] Mandelbaum views this as part of a wider trend of "debellicization" or "warlessness."

> Warlessness is the product of developments that have their origins in the West over the last 200 years and that have gained strength in recent decades: the decline of orthodox communism ... and the concomitant spread of democracy ... the expansion of commerce, making war between and among trading partners, if not wholly irrational, at least increasingly expensive; the reduction in the average size of Western families ... making each son more valuable and less dispensable; and perhaps even the waning of religious faith and with it the collapse of confidence in the existence of a world to come, placing a higher premium on remaining alive as long as possible in this one.[8]

This is a variation on the classic argument that "well-established republics do not fight their own kind."[9] Since this diagnosis is confined to the western world it recalls Fukuyama's end of history thesis that splits the world in an advanced part where war has gone out of fashion (the cost are too high and the risks too great in relation to the gains) and a backward part where small wars proliferate.

Some time ago Hillel Schwartz predicted that "the 1970s would see the Politics of Despair, the 1980s the Politics of Desperation, the 1990s the Politics of Catastrophe, and that the 21st century would be the Era of Annihilation."[10] At the turn of the millennium, the apocalypse retail trade has been especially active and offers ample choice in apocalyptic scenarios. One that stands out is the *new barbarism* thesis. This argues that these are times of ethnic pandemonium, as in Robert Kaplan's neo-Malthusian accounts of violence and mayhem in Africa and the Balkans. In this view, the deterritorialization of economies is being matched by the reterritorialization of identities. Identity politics and multiculturalism, in the conservative view, are part of a syndrome of intensifying niche conflict, neo-tribalism, and social fragmentation. Scholars skilled in arithmetic inform us that about ten thousand societies are tucked within 180 nation states.[11] In this perspective, ethnic fragmentation is a counter scenario to universalist politics. The new barbarism thesis (or

"Kaplanism") matches a definition of conflict management as risk containment and a "creeping coup" scenario of conflict management.

> "Kaplanism" posits the need for a more authoritarian approach to global governance ... we will start thinking in terms of "humanitarian sorties," rather than participatory distribution systems. If the military take on this role and, in effect, take on partial governance of "failed states," without consent or invitation, one must conclude that a process that could be described as a creeping coup is indeed under way, filling the policy vacuum created as the United Nations developmental agencies are abandoned as an expensive failure.[12]

Other chilling scenarios are Huntington's clash of civilizations and Barber's Jihad versus McWorld. What these views share is that the assumption of progress and the evolutionary trend of gradually widening circles of social cooperation turns into reverse, to ever narrowing modes of cooperation and standards of action—from universalism to particularism, from secularism to communalism, from nationalism to ethnicity, from cosmopolitanism to localism.

Considered more closely, two fundamentally different perspectives on the causes of conflict vie for prominence. One view emphasizes the politics of difference—hence growing conflict; another emphasizes growing homogenization, courtesy of corporate globalism and McDonaldization—hence alienation, inequality and conflict. If these diametrically opposite frames of explanation are both deemed plausible and are both pessimistic, then let's step back and also reflect on pessimism itself as a taken for granted common sense.

Paranoia comes natural and easy, has definite survival value, and is thoroughly familiar to the brain. Evolutionary psychology holds that the roots of paranoia go back to primeval hunting times. In politics and social science, paranoia analytics have a formidable lineage; besides, new technologies also inspire paranoid scenarios.[13] But for all its superb analytics, is paranoia also fertile soil for identifying constructive ways forward? If we need to organize the future because that's where we will spend the rest of our lives, then on what premises do we organize the future?

There is a pessimism of the right as well as of the left and sometimes it's not easy to keep them apart. Pessimistic scenarios on the right offer dim diagnoses of trends past and present. The prediction that "the world staggers toward inevitable war" annuls the "peace dividend" and justifies rearmament.[14] Both the pessimism of the left and the right is based on a bleak view of human nature, a pessimistic anthropology. But while the pessimism of the right fears the forces of insubordination and instability, left-wing pessimism fears the forces of domination and the way the wheels of power turn. New technologies are ever used for narrow ends and domination by capital now comes in the shape of multinational enterprises and the WTO.

The two hypotheses of why globalization creates conflict, growing homogenization and growing particularism, come together in Amy Chua's account of rampant global market forces that set the *World on Fire*.[15] Since market forces are culturally embedded, growing inequality unfolds along ethnic lines and inflames "long suppressed ethnic hatreds." Her central case is the Chinese minorities in the Pacific Basin, from which she generalizes to worldwide cleavages. Chua produces another version of ethnic pandemonium, now caused not by insufficient modernization but by global economic integration. The problems of her thesis are that she reckons mainly with the top stratum of ethnic Chinese and not with the many who are assimilated into Southeast Asian cultures; she generalizes the scenario of ethnic polarization worldwide, and in the process reifies ethnicity and ignores or downplays interethnic relations.

Discourse serves multiple purposes, not necessarily in logical ways, and I don't mean to give a functionalist account; yet we can distinguish several layers of discourse that sustain the empire of liberty. A general framework of discourse shields and sustains the "chauvinism of prosperity." With 5 percent of the world's population, the United States absorbs vastly disproportionate amounts of the world's energy, capital, and commodities. The United States, for instance, has more cars than registered drivers. To naturalize and justify this spectacular imbalance, discourses such as Fukuyama's end of history argue that others are backward and mired in history (and might catch up, without mentioning that global catching up is an ecological impossibility). With 5 percent of the world's population, the United States spends 40 percent of world's total military spending. Threat assessments provide specific rationales; at a broader cultural level, various discourses project assorted global divides, all variations on the classic theme civilization versus barbarism. Within this general setting one set of discourses addresses *internal frontiers*. With 5 percent of the world's population, the United States has 25 percent of the world's prisoners. Blaming the victims as in the neoconservative "war on the poor" provides discursive order. All these accounts suggest a world that is deeply divided, along different lines, while it is globalizing (a brief précis is in table 7.1). In fact most depictions of world politics are characterized by a "two worlds" thesis.[16]

Table 7.1 Representations of Global Divide

Theme	Keywords for "others"	Source
Clash of civilizations	"Islam has bloody borders," "the age of Muslim wars"	Huntington
McWorld	Jihad	Barber
Lexus, Golden Arches	Olive tree	Friedman
"Kaplanism"	New barbarism	Kaplan
	Ethnic pandemonium	Moinyhan
Market-dominant minorities	Ethnic polarization	Amy Chua
End of history	Small wars	Fukuyama
Warlessness		Mandelbaum
Liberalism	Terror	Paul Berman

Ethnic Politics?

Specific accounts that split the world from the viewpoint of the West are "ethnicity" and "fundamentalism." Consider one example. During three months in 1994 in Rwanda close to 1 million people were killed and 2 million displaced in a conflict between Hutus and Tutsis. Another ethnic conflict, another manifestation of ethnic mayhem. Except that this was not an ethnic conflict; it was primarily a *political* conflict between well-organized factions, in particular the *Akazu* or small house around the Habyarimana regime and the Rwanda Patriotic Front whose position in Uganda had become precarious.[17] This is just an example of how *ethnicity* is being banded about as a signifier of mayhem, inspires sweeping generalizations and speculations on primitive human nature and archaic solidarities, and in the process functions as a new imagery and code of racism. Civilized peoples have nationalism while "others" indulge in ethnicity.

Representations of ethnicity—as of "fundamentalism"—are replete with references to irrational crowd behavior, mass pathology, and "evil leaders."[18] They are variations on the theme of the "bestial crowd," a recurrent motif from Plato to Freud: "the crowd as swinish multitude, as many-headed-hydra, as wild beast."[19] In this regard the barbarism thesis of the left mirrors the new barbarism thesis on the right and the right-wing view of ethnic conflict through the lens of moral turpitude, anomie, and decadence. "Socialism or Barbarism" has a long lineage in left-wing thinking, from

Friedrich Engels through Rosa Luxemburg to Samir Amin and others.[20] This thesis combines cultural prejudice with economic determinism and an underlying assumption of popular disorganization and cultural and political entropy.

An alternative perspective is that generalizing about ethnicity is of little use because ethnicity is plural and refers to a wide variety of expressions. We can distinguish different types of ethnicity, and to each type there are strands of domination and emancipation. Are those who are suspicious of ethnicity also suspicious of nationalism? Nationalism is ethnicity writ large and arguably the core problem is the politics of nationalism rather than ethnicity, for the other side of the story is that every form of ethnic conflict without exception arises from nationalism taking the form of monocultural control.[21]

What is termed "ethnic politics," rather than archaic and anarchic expressions of popular emotion, identity politics gone berserk, is often an orchestrated, methodical and opportunistic mobilization of cultural differences. The problem of ethnic conflict, notes Maynes, "is less one of bad leadership than of inadequate structures."[22] A complex and dynamic understanding of "ethnic politics" means engaging the "hidden economies of armed conflicts"[23] and the deep political economy of violence. It means entering the labyrinth of local politics. Conflict situations usually involve a layered crisis that cannot be simply reduced to a single set of problems.

Beyond Blowback

In American media the 9/11 attacks have been routinely interpreted through the lens of the "clash of civilizations";[24] as if Huntington's thesis was the prophecy and 9/11 its fulfillment. "Jihad 101" led the media interpretations, as part of a configuration that Timothy Mitchell refers to as "McJihad."[25] Just as routinely, American media avoid discussion of United States policies in the Middle East and avoid using the dreaded P word for Palestine.[26]

An approach to 9/11 that does take into account American policies is blowback. This reiterates how during the cold war the United States supported conservative religious organizations as a countervailing power in the fight against communism. The United States supported the Mujahideen during the Afghanistan war of 1979–89, the way Israel sponsored Hamas in the Occupied Territories as a counterweight to al Fatah and leftwing Palestinian groups. As part of anti-Soviet operations in Afghanistan, the United States—and allies including Saudi Arabia, Egypt, Pakistan, China, and Israel—inadvertently created networks of violent Islamic groups that have since been active in Algeria, Egypt, Yemen, Bosnia, Kashmir, the Philippines, and elsewhere. In the Middle East the returnees from the Afghan front, trained and armed by the CIA and others, are known as "Arab Afghans." In this view, Bin Laden and al Qaida are part of cold war dialectics and an outgrowth of anti-Soviet policies.[27] Since they are also an extension of Saudi oil wealth, Middle East policy is part of the equation. For decades the United States and others relied on oil supplies from the Middle East while sustaining oligarchies, pouring oil revenues into the region while politically alienating it, particularly through virtually unconditional support of Israel. Thus American policies created the resources, capabilities, and motives for political antagonism in the region. During the cold war the imbalance of economically strengthening and politically alienating a strategic region was compensated for by the struggle against communism; the United States, Israel, Saudi Arabia, and others conducted joint operations from Afghanistan to Zaire. As part of its own balancing act Saudi Arabia supported both anticommunism and conservative Islamic movements. When the cold war unraveled, so did the alliance. The Afghanistan Mujahideen established the Taliban regime. Meanwhile the Gulf War brought American military bases into Saudi Arabia, Kuwait, and the Gulf Emirates.

The implication of blowback, originally a CIA term, is unintended consequences of past security operations. While this implies admission of past involvement, it takes politics out of ongoing events by treating them as the unanticipated consequences of past actions. The same organizations that the United States promoted in the eighties were declared the new enemy in the nineties, renamed fundamentalist, with the clash of civilizations serving as the new enemy doctrine. Yesterday's freedom fighter literally became today's terrorist. The "clash of civilizations" is primordialism warmed over that blames the victim and takes politics out of the equation: yesterday's allies were created and then recast as today's enemies.

The Interplay of Modernities and Capitalisms

The global divide as represented by Huntington, Bernard Lewis, and others suggests that the new threats are a matter of failed modernity or resistance to modernity. An alternative explanatory framework may run as follows. Ours is not a world of simple modernity or simple capitalism that exists in varieties of more or less, further or earlier, differentiated along a single-track path. That was the old panorama of evolutionism, progress, developmentalism, modernization, Westernization. Part of the problem is that the language of social science and politics invites the use of the singular—modernity rather than modernities, capitalism rather than capitalisms, industrialization rather than different types of industrialization. This generalizing language is in use across the political spectrum, right to left, and is inhospitable to nuanced thinking.

It is tempting to conceive of modernity as a single historical sphere, to which there may be different roads but which is ultimately a singular experience. What matters in that case is only a before and after: pre- and postmodernity. Of course, within modernity differences run between early and advanced, high, radical, neo modernity, and at the edges of modernity there are variations as well—peripheral, failed, truncated and hybrid modernities, but these all refer back to more or less of a single modernity. On the other hand, from here it would be a small step to recognizing spatial-temporal variations—such as European, American, Japanese, Asian modernities, and variations within each of these (such as West, Southern, Eastern, and Central European variants). Another argument is to distinguish among different *sequences* in modernization processes, as is common in Asian perspectives. The idea of different modernities is now widely accepted; a similar case can be made with respect to different capitalisms (discussed in Chapter 9).

Multiple modernities and capitalisms are each shaped by historic and geographical circumstances and take on a different character on account of different modes of fusion and articulation. Acknowledging the geographical and historical differentiations of modernity, capitalism, industrialism is one issue; analyzing their interrelations is another. What is the relationship between difference and sameness, between the variations and the theme? These are not different realms that are neatly separated—modern and premodern, North and South, and so on. Besides the different modernities in Asia, the Middle East, Africa, the Americas, and Europe, there is the *interaction* of modernities and capitalisms. Understanding this interplay is a major key to contemporary dynamics. "We live in a world in which competition is not only a feature of inter-firm relations, but of the relations between different capitalist economic systems."[28]

The theme of post-Fordism, for example, brings together discussions on capitalism and industrialization, but is usually discussed as if it concerns dynamics in the advanced economies of the North only. Yet the actual options available and directions taken are likely to be more influenced by the interactions among different modes of capitalism than is indicated by merely examining varieties in the North, as if these represent the front end of capitalism (which is not tenable in view of the rise of Pacific Asia) and as if the front end would not be affected by the rear. For instance, if "national variants of Fordism" include peripheral Fordism (Mexico, Brazil), hybrid Fordism (Japan), and "primitive Taylorization" (Southeast Asia),[29] the question is how are they related?

While post-Fordism and postmodernity are important analytics, for a complete understanding we should consider the relations *between* post-Fordist economies, newly emerging markets, and developing countries. Consider for instance the ramifications of the East Asian economies. East Asian firms have been new investors in deindustrializing regions of the North and in Eastern Europe, thus affecting regional uneven development in the North. Labor standards in newly emerging markets (lower wages, longer working hours, less unionization) affect labor standards in multinational corporations in their operations North and South. The bogus rhetoric of less government intervention in newly emerging markets is being used to reinforce structural reform globally and government rollback in the North. Financial crises in emerging markets—the Tequila crisis, Asian crisis, Latin American crisis—reverberate worldwide and have led to reconsidering the architecture of the international financial system. It has generated the notion of contagion as a successor to the cold war domino theory. Thus, links *between* economies in the North and the newly emerging markets affect developments North and South. This unfolds at the level of material exchanges and economic and financial regulation and at the level of images and discourse. These diverse spaces are not simply stray parts and add-ons in a random arrangement but part of a structured, dynamic, and self-reflexive configuration. The articulation of different capitalisms and modernities is being processed and channeled through the nodes of global capitalism and global hegemony.

Imperial continuities—the British Empire succeeded by U.S. hegemony—have shaped the global career of capitalism. Nesting in the interstices of empire and hegemony and carried on its waves, Anglo-American capitalism—the least regulated of all forms of capitalism—has become the dominant form of global capitalism. Its economics, neoclassical economics, has become the norm of economic thought. As part of global hegemony, differences are erased in the terms in which they are being acknowledged—as more or less of the same, early and late along the same course. Globalization has overtaken development or, more precisely, developmental globalism has become the successor to developmentalism; structural adjustment has become the successor to modernization. Both refer to alignment in the global ranks, the subsumption of differences under a single standard set by the center.

The clash of civilizations was originally a funding proposal that Samuel Huntington wrote as director of the center of strategic studies at Harvard University. It turned out to perfectly serve the purpose of a new postwar enemy doctrine. It echoes the American sense of geographical and historical distance from other continents. In other cultures that have been intimately interacting crossculturally for ages, the exaggerated perceptions of difference with other cultures to the point of a worldwide clash of civilizations, are often viewed as a bizarre premise. This contributed to the rapid dissolution of worldwide solidarity with America in the wake of 9/11. When the United States adopted a binary mode (either with us or with the terrorists) it projected its continental island mentality on the world.

The "two worlds" matrix belies the interplay of modernities. Stereotypes conceal ongoing interactions. Each culture uses reified images of others to sustain its internal status quo. Orientalism in the North and Occidentalism in the South are mirror operations. Conspiracy theories in the North serve the purpose of threat inflation; in the South they shield governments and elites from criticism. In both they conceal the actual interactions that take place—which to maintain the paradigm of difference are treated as exceptions to the rule.

CHAPTER **8**

Hyperpower Exceptionalism

Today's era is dominated by American power, American culture, the American dollar and the American navy.

—Thomas Friedman, 2000

Discussions of globalization often focus on Americanization and many discussions of Americanization focus on popular culture, media and consumerism, as in the familiar litanies of Coca-colonization, McDonaldization, Disneyfication, and Barbie culture. These are all highly visible, within many people's range of experience and easily communicated, so they receive overwhelming attention. But the focus on culture belies the significance of American influence in economics, politics, and security, though it is less visible on the street. Besides, American cultural influence and what Joseph Nye calls "soft power" is rarely adequately linked to the other dimensions of American influence,[1] yielding an approach that is culturalist and ignores the relations between soft and hard power. This chapter combines the themes of American exceptionalism and American international influence and in the process seeks to correct the culturalist approach to "Americanization."

If we take global problems seriously and thus the need for global reforms (such as global environmental regulation and regulation of international finance) and then turn to their political implementation, we naturally arrive at the door of the United States. Progressive social forces and international institutions the world over make proposals for global reform, and their list is considerable and growing, but without American cooperation they stand little chance of being implemented. In this regard the world's sole superpower is also the world's major status quo power. The world leader, then, turns out to be a global bottleneck and in this light American conditions and problems become world problems.

The thesis of American exceptionalism in American social science holds that the United States is a special case. If we take this claim seriously what does it imply for U.S. leadership? What does it mean when a country that by its own account is a historical exception sets rules for the world? This chapter revisits the arguments of American exceptionalism and asks how this spills over into the international arena.

This is not meant as another round of anti-Americanism; that would take us back decades and onto conservative terrain. We may appreciate or admire American society for its many contributions—its cultural mix as an immigrant society, the vitality of its popular culture, its technological and economic achievements—and yet be concerned about the way it relates to the rest of the world. In the words of the British historian Timothy Garton Ash, "I love this country and I worry about its current role in the world."[2] This discussion seeks to take a clinical, matter of fact look at American conditions and their consequences for global conditions. The argument under examination is whether American exceptionalism is important for understanding contemporary globalization and accordingly, whether the margins of political change in the United States hold implications for global change.

Furthermore, the aim of this discussion is not to revisit the globalization as Americanization thesis. That is a variation on the modernization = Westernization = globalization thesis and an extremely narrow take on globalization. I view globalization as a long-term historical process of growing worldwide interconnectedness, far more diverse in nature and far longer in duration than modern American influences. Thus globalization also involves Easternization and South–South flows.

This treatment overlaps with the hegemony literature in international relations but differs by taking into account American domestic politics. It also differs from the conventional cultural imperialism thesis; overall American impact may be largely a matter of what Johan Galtung called "structural imperialism": shaping other societies through structural leverage, rather than just through direct political intervention,[3] which includes but goes beyond the cultural industries. Economic policies, international politics, and security too are "cultural," but covertly rather than overtly so, and less visible in everyday life.

American laissez-faire has promoted a worldwide shift from stakeholder capitalism to shareholder capitalism; world economic management led by

Washington-based institutions and neoliberal globalization have brought increasing global inequality; and in world politics, the United States blocks the formation of global public goods and institutions unless they can serve as instruments of American power.

The literature on the world's largest and foremost developed country is vast and multivocal; this treatment is pointed, focused on American exceptionalism and global ramifications. Difficulties in this inquiry are to avoid taking American ideologies for realities and to both heed American exceptionalism and problematize it. The closing section criticizes American exceptionalism as a self-caricature and considers counterpoints. The first part of this exercise is easy in that there is ample literature on American exceptionalism, mostly from American sources, and the key themes are familiar; this part is a précis organized in brief vignettes. The second part probes the international ramifications of American exceptionalism. This is less widely talked about, more controversial and tucked into specialist literatures (such as on transnational enterprises, international politics, and military affairs).

American Exceptionalism

The profile of American exceptionalism (AE) is fairly familiar. Its origins lay in "the merger of the republican and millennial traditions that formed an ideology of American exceptionalism prominent in American historical writing."[4] Another familiar line of reasoning follows Werner Sombart's question of 1906, "Why is there no socialism in the United States?" AE is a controversial thesis also in the United States. Thus it is argued that "because of American heterogeneity we have not had a singular mode or pattern of exceptionalism."[5] (Chapter 1 discussed exceptionalism within American exceptionalism and the role of the American South and Dixie capitalism.) Nevertheless, AE remains broadly endorsed by influential American thinkers across a wide spectrum, in history, labor studies, and race relations; in political science it has taken on salience through a major work by Seymour Martin Lipset.[6] American exceptionalism of a kind has also been signaled abroad, often with admiration, from de Tocqueville to Gramsci, Ralf Dahrendorf to Jean Baudrillard.

There are wider differences of opinion on accepting or rejecting AE, especially among American historians, than on the components of AE itself. Major strands of AE such as laissez-faire ideology and the power of business have been fairly continuous over time. Lipset notes that "Prolonged postwar prosperity refurbished the classic American anti-statist, market-oriented values,"[7] which have been further reinforced under the Clinton and Bush administrations. The decline in trade union membership has been ongoing and corporate hostility to organized labor and illegal corporate tactics against organized labor have increased over time.⁸

This treatment is not a critique of AE; the focus is not AE per se but its international ramifications. To a certain extent AE is understandable in relation to American fundamentals: a vast, resource rich continent without foreign wars on its territory; a history of settler colonialism and a recent modernity; a nation of immigrants and a huge interior market; the fourth largest population and the first among developed countries. By the same token this is a warning light that the American *Sonderweg* reflects fundamentals in which others cannot follow. As a Bostonian remarked to de Tocqueville, "those who would like to imitate us should remember that there are no precedents for our history."⁹

Yet we cannot avoid problematizing AE. AE serves a double function as a summary account of American historical and geographical particulars *and* as an ideology. In its former role AE is widely referred to, yet contentious; and as an ideology AE is a self-caricature that is as old-fashioned as the weary stereotypes of "national character" in other nations. As such AE itself is a form of "Americanism" and part of what it purports to describe; I detail critical points in the concluding section. It's quite difficult then to draw a line between AE as social fact and as ideology. On the premise of social constructivism (or the idea that societies are constructed on the basis of people's beliefs and common sense) it makes sense to assume that both spill over into the international arena. So AE as ideology may be as significant as actual American deviations from historical patterns.

The long stretch of American hegemony places its stamp on societies the world over and contemporary globalization is the latest installment. The ongoing changes associated with contemporary globalization are partly of a structural nature—technological changes, the information society, flexibilization, individualization—and inflected by, among others, American influence. To probe the question what kind of globalization American hyperpower produces means to reexamine U.S. society.

Other countries are also often referred to as exceptional—such as the German *Sonderweg* and Japanese uniqueness (*Nihonjiron*), the exceptionalism of Britain, France, Scandinavia, Europe, East Asia, China, Australia, and so forth. But in most of these cases exceptionalism is single-issue (such as British labor and French *dirigisme*) rather than multidimensional; it does not also perform as a popular ideology (except in Japan and until recent times Germany); and most important, these nations are not superpowers. Any country would look odd if its historical idiosyncrasies would be amplified on the world stage. This is the real problem and not American exceptionalism per se. Being the sole superpower is exceptional too; Hubert Védrine as French foreign minister used the term hyperpower ("a country

Conflation of the two

that is dominant or preponderant in all categories"). Superpower status is not merely a condition but also a mentality, an outlook, so hyperpower exceptionalism emerges as a theme in its own right.

Major strands of American exceptionalism are free enterprise and laissez-faire ideology, the relative power of business and limited role of government, the ideology of "Americanism," and social inequality. To this familiar profile I add the character of American modernity and the role of the military.

Free Enterprise Capitalism

The usual cornerstones of AE are laissez-faire side by side with a weak state and weak labor organization. But none of these, except the last, is unproblematic in a factual sense. The United States has a lower rate of taxation and many fewer government-owned industries than other industrialized nations.[10] It is "the only industrialized country which does not have a significant socialist movement or labor party."[11] The U.S. federal government behaves like a minimal state but is also strongly regulatory and strong in defence and security. Thus, mixed economy or John Ruggie's "embedded liberalism" is a more apt description than laissez-faire. All along laissez-faire has been embedded in and tempered by government interventions such as Fordism, party machines, the New Deal, military Keynesianism, export credits, local investment incentives, the "war on poverty," and affirmative action. Unlike European social democracy, American Fordism was based more on worker productivity and pay rates than on worker rights, more on corporate designs than government policy. Johnson's Great Society was aborted by the burdens of the Vietnam War. The United States is a residual welfare state and increasingly a workfare state, but still a welfare state.

The implementation of laissez-faire in the United States has been partial, discontinuous and opportunistic; deviations from posture occur anytime political expedience requires. The actual deregulation of business increased sharply in the 1980s. But while practice has been uneven, the *ideology* of free enterprise has been virtually constant. Key features of American capitalism—free enterprise, minimal state, an advanced degree of possessive individualism—are anomalous by international standards, but more anomalous still has been American laissez-faire ideology. Yet this ideology has been consistently upheld as international posture: "Hardly anyone acknowledged or addressed the contradiction between practicing a mixed economy at home and promoting a laissez-faire economy globally."[12] As Paul Krugman observes, "policymakers in Washington and bankers in New York often seem to prescribe for other countries the kind of root canal economics that they would never tolerate here in the USA.... My advice would be to stop listening to those men in suits. Do as we do, not as we say."[13]

Political Conservatism

> That government governs best which governs least
> —Thomas Jefferson.

> Less government is better government
> —Ronald Reagan.

> The era of big government is over
> —William J. Clinton, 1996.

According to Lipset, the enduring values of American exceptionalism—liberty, egalitarianism, individualism, populism, and laissez-faire—have made the United States "the most anti-statist, legalistic and rights-oriented nation," "the most classical liberal polity" and "the great conservative society."[14] A common description of American minimal government is the "night watchman state"; Nettl goes further and refers to the "relative statelessness" of the United States as a society in which only the *law* is sovereign.[15]

Familiar features of the American political system are constitutionalism, checks and balances and the presidential system. Constitutionalism yields a law centered polity and is the foundation of what over time has become an exceptionally litigation prone society[16] and a "legal-rational culture": "In no other industrial society is legal regulation as extensive or coercive as in the United States."[17] The 800,000 American lawyers are one-third of the world total of practicing attorneys. Since the 1970s the law profession has grown three times faster than the economy and litigation has increased at seven times the rate of the growth of population.[18]

The American republic was designed as a weak state with a divided form of government. The antagonism to the state originates in the American fight against a centralized (monarchical) state and derives from the American Revolution. It follows, according to Lipset, that there is no tradition of obedience to the state or law. An example is the failure of the U.S. government to impose the metric system, which is official by law but not being implemented.

> The American separation of powers allows and even encourages members of Congress to vote with their constituents against their president or dominant party view.... American legislators, including Congressional leaders, have voted against and helped to kill bills to carry out major international agreements in response to

small groups of local constituents. . . . As former House speaker Thomas P. (Tip) O'Neill once put it, in Congress, "all politics is local."[19]

The country's large size, federalism, and checks and balances make for a give-and-take system of spoils in Congress: cooperation at a federal level is obtained through regional and special-interest deals and redistribution. This makes it difficult to pass progressive measures in Congress, which in turn holds implications for American world leadership. A result is that what is rightwing in most countries is the political center in the United States.

The exclusion of a third party in framing American political debate is one of the features of American democracy. According to William Greider, "The decayed condition of American democracy is difficult to grasp, not because the facts are secret, but because the facts are visible everywhere."[20] The facts include mass voter absenteeism, campaign financing problems, and sound bite political debate.

Social Inequality: Winner-Takes-All

"As the purest example of a bourgeois nation, America follows the competitive principle of the marketplace in unions, management and other relationships."[21] Relations between management and labor are adversarial and the income spread is the widest among industrialized nations. J. P. Morgan followed the rule that executives in his firms could not earn more than twenty times what blue collar workers earned. In 1998, CEOs at major companies earned 419 times the average pay of blue collar workers and this gap is widening. The bottom fifth of U.S. households receives less than 4 per cent of the national income while the top fifth takes home almost half.[22]

Tying CEO remuneration to stock performance has seen CEO pay rise proportionately to the decimation of full-time jobs as downsizing increases shareholder value.[23] The economists Frank and Cook attribute the emergence of the winner-takes-all system to competitiveness in combination with changes in communication technologies that privilege winners—in corporations, finance, entertainment, sports, and education.[24]

Compared to other advanced countries the United States is marked by greater equality of opportunity and greater inequality of outcome. Robert Merton's classic argument suggests that the differential between opportunity and outcome accounts for the high U.S. crime rate, as aspirations are socially shared but not the means for attaining them.[25] American popular culture reflects this tension.

The United States has greater tolerance for inequality than any advanced society, in terms of political culture and development philosophy (as discussed in Chapter 6). Social inequality has increased markedly since the

1970s. Thirty million Americans live below the poverty line and 43 million are without health insurance. The life expectancy of an African-American male in Harlem is less than that of a male in Bangladesh. That foundations and charities—a "thousand points of light" and faith-based organizations—don't make up for government failure is well-documented.

Americanism

Because of its size, the United States, like some other large countries, tends to be culturally parochial and inward looking. Geographical insularity is another factor. The United States is in many ways self-absorbed and engrossed in collective narcissism. One indicator is the dearth of reporting on foreign affairs. After the end of the cold war foreign reporting declined and foreign correspondents were cutback at a time when the US role in world affairs was increasing, creating the peculiar situation that the people least informed about foreign affairs is the world's most influential. Another indicator is lack of interest in foreign literature and far fewer translations of books in other languages than in other countries.

The United States according to Michael Harrington, is "a country united not by common history but by *ideology*—the American Creed, or Americanism, which also serves as 'substitute socialism.' "26 Americanism combined with exceptionalism yields a fervent nationalism that is exceptional among contemporary societies, huddled around the Constitution, the presidency, an unusual cult of the flag, and a pop culture of America Number One.

In pioneering the use of electronic mass media and mass consumer culture the United States sets standards in commodity fetishism. Its large internal market makes it less dependent on and less sensitive to other countries, so there is little economic incentive to take on foreign horizons.

Shallow Modernity

Through the centuries Europe experienced tribal and peasant cultures, empire, feudalism, monarchy, and absolutism—an Old World indeed. Here modernity is a stratum arising from and interspersed with other historical layers. Continental modernity arises from this historical depth and so the outcome is a complex modernity. Broadly the same applies to social formations in Asia, the Middle East, and Africa. In Europe the central role of the state derives from the combined legacies of imperial history, feudalism, monarchy, and absolutism, while the revolutionary correction of feudalism and absolutism also required a centralized state. Social market capitalism and the continental welfare state bear the imprint of the moral economy and entitlements of feudal times, when lords ruled in exchange for providing economic and military protection to their bondsmen.

In contrast, American modernity is based on the experience of petty commodity production, and slave production in the South, followed by industrialism and Taylorism. In the United States there are "no traditions from before the age of progress," it is a "postrevolutionary new society."[27] Since American independence coincided with the Enlightenment the country was founded on the basis of rational progressivism. Scientism along with religious dissidence and Protestant idealism combined to produce Manifest Destiny and the "Angel of Progress."[28] Gramsci viewed America as "pure rationalism" and Ralf Dahrendorf interprets the United States as the country of the "applied Enlightenment." In the absence of a deep classical tradition, American culture is characterized instead by the "reconciliation of mass and class," which entails the "deradicalization of class."[29]

The absence of dialectics with older strata (neolithic, feudal, absolutist) makes for unmitigated innovation unburdened by history: the unbearable lightness of America. It makes for "rupture" as gospel. Conquest and settler colonialism and immigration too make rupture with history and geography a part of American collective experience. Key features of U.S. capitalism are ramifications of American thin modernity, which in turn shapes America's role in the worldwide interplay of modernities.

Preponderance of the Military

The military apparatus plays a remarkably large role in American politics, economics, and social life. The U.S. government is a minimal state *except* when it comes to law and order and security. The only area in which the government practices industrial policy is in defense; the one area in which the Reagan administration engaged in long-term planning was defense and the space missile defense shield.[30]

The military enjoys broad popular and bipartisan support. The armed forces are the nation's best funded public institution and enjoy the public's greatest trust and confidence—greater than universities, churches, the Supreme Court, corporations, and any other American institution, even in the wake of the Vietnam War.[31] The military serves as an avenue of social mobility for lower classes, which is one of the wheels of military Keynesianism and makes up for a class-biased educational system.[32] Right after the party conventions, presidential candidates first address the Veterans League and invariably propose more resources for the military—making sure that "the American armed forces are the best equipped and best trained in the world." The moral status of the military is popularized and upheld through frequent reiteration of its role in World War II in the media (typically skipping over episodes such as Vietnam and Iran-contra). Military metaphors and desensitization to violence pervade in the entertainment sector. The Pentagon and Hollywood are close; a sizeable share of Hollywood production is devoted to military themes and parallels the phases of the projection of American power.[33] Just to illustrate the pervasiveness of this influence: the choreography of Broadway musicals was originally based on military drill and introduced by James Busby, a drill officer who had made his reputation in World War I.[34]

The role of weapons industries in American industrialization is not exceptional by historical standards; building military strength has been the locomotive of industrialization in advanced countries the world over, particularly in the late nineteenth century. What is exceptional is the enduring role of the military-industrial complex, in line with America's superpower status. Since the late 1940s the Pentagon has consumed $12 trillion in resources and continues to spend $300 to $400 billion yearly.[35] After the end of the cold war, "conversion," and the peace dividend have not paid off. Instead the inclination has been to keep the security apparatus occupied, to upgrade equipment and weapons, provide opportunities for testing and military careers with recurrent budget expansion, and mammoth projects such as Plan Colombia. The conventional war economy thesis may no longer be tenable;[36] the economic rationale of a vast security force may now be overshadowed by political rationales and a regional spoils system that distributes government contracts and military facilities. But the monumental expansion of the military budget of the Bush II administration brings the war economy back.

In FY 2003 military spending makes up 49 percent of the discretionary spending in the budget and education makes up 7 percent.[37] The increase of the military budget by $48 billion as part of the war on terrorism brings the 2003 military budget to $380 billion. This exceeds the total military spending of world's nineteen largest military spenders. Meanwhile deep tax cuts favoring the wealthy go together with cutbacks in spending on infrastructure, education and social services. By 2006 the U.S. military budget would be $450 billion annually.

The constitutional right of citizens to bear arms, the influence of the National Rifle Association, and "gun culture" on the streets and in media, echo American roots as a settler colonial conquest society in which pioneer farmers act as frontier soldiers. A revisionist argument is that the origins of gun culture are not the pioneer West but 1840s industrialization and the civil war.[38] These legacies find expression in a culture in which force and coercion serve as political and economic tools.[39] With over two million citizens behind bars (2.2 million in 2002) the United States achieves the greatest civilian incarceration in history and outranks all nations in the number of prisoners; China is second. The prison population is America's "internal gulag."[40] The United States is alone among wealthy countries in its extensive use of the death sentence. The recourse to force interacts with profit motives. Throughout the United States new prisons are an answer to local economic depression and privatized prisons constitute a prison-industrial complex.[41] Gated communities and video surveillance are part of the privatization of security: "from night watchmen and bodyguards to virtual private armies, the security services industry is booming, while the trade in firearms is breaking all records."[42]

To recapitulate table 8.1 gives an overview of major dimensions of AE.

Globalization as Americanization?

> The whole world should adopt the American system. The American system can survive in America only if it becomes a world system.
>
> —President Harry Truman, 1947

> Americans who wanted to bring the blessings of democracy, capitalism, and stability to everyone meant just what they said—the whole world, in their view, should be a reflection of the United States.
>
> —Stephen Ambrose, 1983

There is no doubt that features of American exceptionalism shape contemporary globalization; yet developing this argument involves several hurdles. First, inherent in "Americanization" is an element of methodological populism. To which unit of analysis does this apply—to *which* America, whose America? The United States is the fourth largest country in size of population, quite heterogeneous and local differences play a significant part. American corporations with decentralized headquarters and offshore tax reporting cannot be simply identified with the United States either. Besides, transnational flows do not just run one way but in multiple directions; there are also trends of Europeanization, Asianization, and Latinization of America, economically and culturally (in foreign ownership, management, style, consumption patterns). Diasporas have changed the character of "America" all along and this bricolage character is part of its make-up. What then is the actual unit at issue; is it a set of "organizing principles" that remain continuous over time, as Lipset would have it or, at another extreme, is America a *site*, a place of transnational synthesis and bricolage? Since waves and layers of diasporas, from the Irish to the Latino, have been shaping "America" it doesn't work to just refer back to the founding fathers in order to diagnose American fundamentals. It would not be productive either to rework the "American challenge" kind of argument (à la Servan-Schreiber); that would place the argument in a setting of national competitiveness à la

Table 8.1 Dimensions of American Exceptionalism

Dimensions	Keynotes	
Free enterprise capitalism	"Business in the U.S. has historically enjoyed an unusual degree of political power."[1] Ideology of reliance on market forces	
Political conservatism	Institutional	Minimal state. Constitutionalism. Extreme separation of powers.
		Weak working class organization. Unusual power of corporations
	Political process	Populism. Voluntary associations. Weak role of parties (state and local, rather than national)
	Values	Individualism. Privatized ethics. Transparency, social engineering
	Ideology	Americanism, patriotism
Minimal state	"the most anti-statist, legalistic and rights-oriented nation" (Lipset)	
Weak working class organization	"increase in the extent of illegal employer resistance to unions"[2]	
Race relations	Race as a substitute for working class solidarity. Whiteness as substitute privilege. Chronic ghetto poverty, incarceration, death penalty	
Voluntary associations	De Tocqueville to Putnam, voluntarism, charity. And gated communities.	
Shallow modernity	The country of the applied Enlightenment	
Americanism	As celebration of the absence of historical burdens. The "meaning of America" served as a surrogate for history.[3]	
Culture	"in the US there is no long-standing traditional establishment of culture on the European model."[4]	

[1] Kammen, "The Problem of AE," 5.
[2] Ibid.
[3] Howe, *25 Years of Dissent*; Kammen, "The Problem of AE."
[4] Mills, *The Sociological Imagination*.

Michael Porter. This kind of national focus is overtaken by accelerated globalization and not appropriate to an analysis of the relationship between AE and globalization.

A second problem is to accommodate historical variation in American politics. AE doesn't neatly match the actual profile of U.S. administrations and is not necessarily intrinsic to American politics; to argue otherwise would be to essentialize American politics. Wilsonian internationalism is also part of U.S. foreign policy and American contributions to world order include the establishment of the UN and Bretton Woods system, the Marshall Plan, support for European unification, and policies in favor of human rights and democracy. While these contributions are disputed, they show there is greater variation to American foreign policy than just the profile of the past decades. In the latter days of the Clinton administration there were changes (mitigation of the embargo on Cuba, settlement of arrears in UN dues, endorsement of the International Criminal Court), some of which were reversed by the next administration.

In situating the transnational role of the United States it helps to distinguish several levels of analysis:

- *Structural dynamics.* This includes scientific and technological changes pioneered by and exported from the United States. Ultimately, these represent an intercivilizational heritage.
- *Fundamental dynamics that are general to industrialized countries.* Here the leading package offered by the country that pioneers these trends affects all; yet these dynamics are not necessarily peculiar to that country. This brings us to the convergence thesis of modernization theory according to which industrial societies would eventually become similar. Trends such as mass production, mass consumption, mass media, suburbanization, and information technology are not "American" per se but since the United States was the first comer they carry an American gloss.
- American corporations and cultural industries seek to draw monopoly rents from their temporary lead "by means fair or foul." This is a common business practice with ample precedent in history. The British destroyed the Indian textile manufactures and trade and sabotaged incipient industrialization in Egypt, Persia, and the Ottoman Empire.[43] Similar contemporary machinations belong to the domain of "Americanization" proper.
- Through international leverage (international financial institutions and WTO) and regional arrangements the US government seeks to institutionalize the advantage of its multinational corporations.
- The war on terrorism and the imperial turn adds a geopolitical agenda.

This suggests that the core questions of global Americanization are the last three points: drawing monopoly rents, their institutionalization through hyperpower leverage, and the geopolitics of "permanent war."

That the line between domestic and international politics is blurring is a familiar point. Often the emphasis falls on the international influencing the domestic; this query asks how the domestic influences the international: how does American politics influence the international domain and the politics of other countries?

Table 8.2 gives a big-picture sample of how AE translates into policies that affect contemporary globalization. Literature on each of these is extensive; this discussion focuses on two themes as faces of AE on the world map: American laissez-faire and its role in shaping capitalism and world politics. The Washington consensus and international development politics are a major part of globalization the American way and have been discussed in Chapter 1.

Table 8.2 American Exceptionalism and International Ramifications

Dimensions of AE	Contemporary international ramifications
Free enterprise capitalism	• US capitalism as the norm of capitalism • Washington consensus, structural adjustment, IMF and World Bank conditionalities • Global model of polarizing growth: growing inequality • Deregulation of international finance • The dollar as international currency; dollarization • The role of American MNCs • Spread of American business standards, law and MBA • Promotion of offshore economies
Free trade	• Trade policy as foreign policy instrument; Section 301 • WTO and neoliberal global trade rules • NAFTA, APEC, and Free Trade Agreements
Minimal state and political conservatism	• Arrears in UN dues • Nonparticipation in international treaties and ICC • Noncompliance with International Court • Double standards in regional affairs (Middle East) • Promotion of procedural form of democracy • Government rollback in development policies
Weak working class organization	• Conservative influence of AFL-CIO (in ICFTU) • Little support for ILO (e.g. labor standards)
Residual welfare/ workfare state	• Rollback of social sectors in development (health, education, social services)
Voluntary associations	• "Fostering democracy by strengthening civil society" • Promotion of NGOs (USAID new policy agenda)
Individualism	• Promotion of NGOs along lines of professionalization, depoliticization, and political fragmentation
Thin modernity	• Transnational social engineering through legal means • Alignment of accounting systems to U.S. standards • One-way transparency (Treasury, IMF, WB) • "Seeing like a hyperpower," global panopticism

Laissez-faire

From the early-twentieth century, a major U.S. export has been its brand of capitalism, as in Taylorism, Fordism, high-mass consumption, free trade, and American corporations and business practices. Since the 1980s under the auspices of the Washington consensus, privatization, liberalization, and deregulation have been added to the repertoire.

American hegemony is part of a series: the rise of U.S. influence followed the era of British hegemony. Manchester liberalism, neoclassical economics from the 1870s and its neoliberal resumption from the late 1970s, form a historical sequence. Its momentum cannot be divorced from the period of approximately 170 years of Anglo-American hegemony (from approximately 1830 onward and interrupted by periods of hegemonic rivalry).[44]

Table 8.2 American Exceptionalism and International Ramifications (continued)

Dimensions of AE	Contemporary international ramifications
Hegemony of military within US	• Cold war spillovers (regional intervention legacies) • Embargoes, sanctions • Militarization of foreign policy • Recurrent war metaphor: war on drugs, war on crime, war on poverty, war on terrorism • Promotion of enemy images (rogue states etc.) • Mammoth projects for military-industrial complex • "Humanitarian militarism" and intervention • Grid of military bases and intelligence surveillance • Redeployment of intelligence monitoring (Echelon) • Covert operations, private military contractors • Nuclear proliferation (nonratification of NTBT 1997) • Health and environmental hazards of military operations (DU in Gulf War, Balkans, Afghanistan, Iraq, and U.S.) • Arms sales, training, and fostering regional arms races • Militarization of borders (U.S.-Mexico model exported to Israel, South Africa)
Americanism	• Unilateralism; acting outside UN mandate • Refusal to serve under UN command • Presenting other states as deviant • Promotion of the "American way"
American culture	• High consumption and resource use • Automobile culture, fossil fuel dependence • Marketing as dominant cultural style • Star and celebrity system • McDonaldization, Disneyfication, Barbiefication • CNN effect and sound bite culture • Internet, Microsoft, dot.com • African American culture (jazz, hiphop) • Abstract expressionism, pop art

By world standards, Anglo-American free enterprise capitalism is an anomaly. Mixed economies and social market capitalism have been the majority practice throughout Europe, Asia, and the developing countries, and central planning prevailed in socialist countries. Also in the British and American experience, free enterprise was part posture and program and only part reality: the self-regulating market was implemented late, partially and intermittently, and the reality was embedded liberalism. Differences between continental European and Anglo-American varieties of embedded liberalism are matters of degree that turn into principle at several junctures; they concern the role of industrial policy, labor regulation, management, banks, venture capital, and stocks. Looking at the U.S., the differences are significant though not quite as large as free enterprise ideology claims them to be. From a European point of view, American influence consists of the ongoing shift from the stakeholder model to the shareholder model of capitalism; or the incorporation of the political economy of social contracts into the political economy of corporations, financial markets, and stock exchanges; and an overall shift from social contracts to legal-rational contractualism. This process is furthest advanced in countries where stock markets are most developed.[45] American laissez-faire economics is being relayed internationally through the workings of stock exchanges, American multinational corporations and their influence on corporate governance, international ratings of creditworthiness and competitiveness, the Washington consensus, foreign investment in the United States and the pull exercised in financial markets when the U.S. economy was dynamic.

American World Leadership

The United States fails to exercise world leadership in environmental, financial, and economic regulation because its political institutions would not permit it to do so (in view of institutional gridlock, special interests, and local politics in Congress) and presumably because its interests, as they are perceived in leading circles, would not benefit from regulation. While in many terrains the United States fails to exercise world leadership, it doesn't permit other institutions to fulfill this role either. Arguably, American interests are a beneficiary of lack of regulation or disarray. The American failure to exercise world leadership then is a matter both of lack of capacity (political institutions) and lack of will (political and economic interest). For instance, the United States is the only developed country that has not ratified the UN Convention on the elimination of all forms of discrimination against women (CEDAW), because doing so would override the authority of state law in family law.[46] Similar constraints apply to the many other treaties in which the United States is the only outsider among advanced countries.

The United States treats the United Nations as a rival for world leadership. For the United States to recognize and strengthen the UN would imply stepping down from its pedestal of world leadership. In the 1980s power in the UN shifted from the General Assembly (one country one vote) to the Security Council and its permanent five members, with the United States as the hegemonic force: the New World Order in brief. The United States defunded critical UN agencies such as Unesco and the UN system generally by chronically withholding its fees; it fails to empower the International Labor Organization, exercises political pressure on the UNDP and other agencies, and bypasses the Security Council when convenient, as in the case of Kosovo and the Iraq war. Instead of empowering the UN, the United States prefers to act through the IMF and World Bank which operate on the basis of financial voting rules. These agencies the United States can control and the outcome has been the Washington consensus.

There are multiple layers and currents to American attitudes toward multilateral institutions. The United States has been in the forefront of the creation of international institutions: the International Court goes back to an American initiative in 1899; the League of Nations and then the United Nations and the ILO have been conceived or pushed by the United States at a time when these institutions served as counterweights to European colonial power. Reisman distinguishes multiple U.S. roles in relation to multilateral institutions (prophetic-reformist, organizational, custodial, and domestic pressure-reactive) which are repeatedly in conflict with one another. This "puts the U.S. among the most avid supporters of multilateral institutions, and yet, in different circumstances, pits it against the members and administration of some of those same institutions."[47]

American reformism reflects "the desire to engage in major international social engineering. . . . The symbol of law is extremely important. Law is to play as large a role in international politics as Americans believe it plays in their own domestic processes, and judicial institutions . . . are deemed central." Accordingly, the "institutional modalities the U.S. helped put into place" are legalistic.[48] This inclination toward international social engineering centered on law reveals America's thin modernity and its Enlightenment complex turned inside out.

To American isolationists, American globalists respond that they want international engagement but *not* under the UN. The UN is perceived as un-American in that it follows a different conception of world order, or as anti-American in view of the Third World majority in the General Assembly and its criticisms of American hegemony. Countries in the South have been the target of stereotyping by American media and political elites who treat the world majority and its concerns as political lowlife. Kissinger saying that the world south of Paris and Bonn has no political relevance doesn't help multipolarity. The Jacksonian or "Joe Six-Pack" approach to international affairs is another strand of American foreign policy.[49]

As a function of American narcissism, American media tend to problematize all countries except the United States. In a casually hostile vision, countries are branded as "loony tunes" or "rogue states," nationalist leaders are deemed "crazy," developing countries or whole religions are backward, the European Union suffers from "rigidities of the labor market," and Japan is guilty of economic nationalism. The absence of self-reflexivity or a sense of humor and irony in viewing America's place in the world seems to be a part of collective habitus.

The U.S. Senate has not ratified the Comprehensive Test Ban Treaty and the Bush II administration develops the national missile defense system and global-reach missiles. Underlying the failure to ratify the nuclear test-ban treaty is the "desire to keep all political and military options open, and, indeed, broaden their scope."[50] The space shield program completely undoes the architecture of arms race control built over many years; the 2002 Congressional Nuclear Posture Review and the idea of using nuclear deterrence against up to forty countries shows what is meant by "keeping options open."

Noteworthy is not AE, but other countries by and large following American leadership without much question. Among OECD countries France is the major exception;[51] other counterweights are Russia and China. Russia has been severely weakened by Washington politics under the guise of the IMF; China has been neutralized through the process of accession to WTO membership. U.S. strength is a function of the weakness or the lack of coherence of other political constellations. European and Asian lack of coherence match American opportunism in international affairs; hence the global stalemate.

Hegemonic stability theory, formulated by Kindleberger and elaborated by Krasner, Keohane, and Ruggie, holds that "in the absence of a world government the global economy can be stabilized when a powerful nation plays the role of flywheel," performing several stabilizing functions.[52] This refers to a policy of carrots rather than sticks. Along the lines of hegemonic compromise, EU countries and Japan grosso modo accept U.S. policies in the context of the G8, OECD, WTO, and IMF because they share overall benefits, such as concessions on trade and agricultural policies in the case of the EU, find shelter under the U.S. military umbrella and benefit from American economic growth. This does not rule out disputes but the differences are not large enough to upset the applecart.

International relations theories may impute more coherence than exists and at times rationalize what may be political improvisation. What of hegemonic stability in view of recurrent crises (Tequila, Asian, Russian, Turkish, Latin American crises, Argentina, Brazil), enduring stalemate in the Middle East and American recession? What of hegemonic stability in view of preventive strike and "permanent war"? By privileging overt politics over covert politics and underplaying strategy and geopolitics, international relations theories may put a systemic gloss on policy processes that, at times, may be better described as absurd.

Beyond American Exceptionalism?

American exceptionalism has affected contemporary globalization in several ways. American laissez-faire transposed globally fosters a worldwide shift from stakeholder capitalism to shareholder capitalism. The American twin, "private wealth and public squalor," is gradually being transferred to the global domain. In three decades of economic management by Washington-based institutions, global inequality has doubled. In world politics, the United States blocks the formation of public goods and international institutions unless they can serve as instruments of American power.

There are various options in assessing AE. One is the view of Timothy Garton Ash: "Contrary to what many Europeans think, the problem with American power is not that it is American. The problem is simply the power. It would be dangerous even for an archangel to wield so much power."[53] This view strips American power from its American imprint, which is unrealistic because the character, scope, and magnitude of American power are not intelligible outside the frame of American dynamics. This option is attractive in that it sidesteps the burden of anti-Americanism. Anti-Americanism is so boring and old-fashioned that one response may be to take American conservatism for granted, like the weather, or appreciate it for the sake of difference and sheer American resilience. The strident conservatism in most American media from CNN to talk radio is so habitual that one hardly notices anymore. But a consequence of this line of thinking is that it means taking the global effects of AE for granted. Besides, if anti-Americanism is old-fashioned, so is Americanism.

Another option is to take AE at face value. This means yielding to essentialism and conservatism in American self-representations, which is the impression one comes away with from Lipset's work. According to Lipset, "the dark side of American exceptionalism" are "developments which, like many of its positive features, derive from the country's organizing principles. These include rising crime rates, increased drug use, the dissolution of the American family, sexual promiscuity, and excessive litigiousness."[54] This essentialism of thinking in terms of principles and values ignores processes and politics. Moreover, this diagnosis is coined in strikingly moral terms, like a neoconservative litany; it overlooks more structural and troubling trends such as the persistence and rise of inequality, the ballooning military and the decline of American democracy.

American exceptionalism is an old-fashioned self-caricature that ignores the other America of the civil rights movement, "1968," social movements from the anti-Vietnam War to the battle of Seattle, and the polls that register majority positions on labor rights, women's rights, the environment, and other issues that are usually far more progressive than those held by media and political elites. This is also a country of vibrant multiculturalism; a country where Michael Moore's *Stupid White Men* goes through nine printings in a week and ends up as the number one bestseller for months on end. Lipset's AE refers to a quasi-existing fantasyland like a Walt Disney model town, ruled by a country club government and Stepford media. The fundamental problem of Lipset's assessment is that it homogenizes American exceptionalism, buys into a narrow version and ignores the political processes through which a *kind* of AE is being produced.

Both extremes of ignoring AE or taking it for granted are simplistic. A middle course is to recognize that AE is a self-caricature that is upheld and reproduced politically and culturally. American fundamentals and dynamics are distinctive, but on this basis, diverse policies, domestic and international, can follow and have followed in the past, such as Wilson's multilateralism, Roosevelt's New Deal, and Jimmy Carter's human rights internationalism (leaving aside the dark sides).

Lipset's assessment is also completely inward-looking and ignores the external ramifications of AE, so it is itself a form of narcissistic Americanism. By world standards, the dark side of the current form of AE is that the *American way is not a replicable and sustainable model of development.* The free market and democracy made in U.S.A are no shining example. American consumption patterns are not replicable—they are not even replicable *within* the United States. Not everyone in this world will or can have a two car family, a suburban home, a college education. Of course, not everyone in the United States does either, but the standard is not in dispute. America's ecological footprint—its excessive use of energy and other resources—is not replicable. The problem with AE is that it drains the world of resources, so Americans suffer from obesity as the national disease, while the rest of the world subsidizes American indulgence and conservatism. Globalization the American way yields winner-takes-all globalization that increasingly mirrors American conditions of glaring inequality, phony marketing culture, and a punitive approach to deviations. This pattern has gone into overdrive in the American permanent war project.

In considering how American institutions affect world politics, what matters is not just what happens but also what doesn't. A prominent discussion concerns the deficit of global public goods;[55] but in fact, "global public goods" itself is a U.S. enforced euphemism for "global governance" is a nonstarter in conservative American circles. What are possible counterpoints to the current scenario of globalization the American way?

There are essentially two options: internal and external change. As to the former, there is "another America" and it is not to be underestimated, but the present rapports de force do not suggest major changes. Another America is possible, but not now. A new American political movement such as a green party is constrained by the institutional features of the American political system. The commercialization of American culture means that public space has been privatized; the media are corporate and the margins of info-tainment are slim. As if in a vast operation of self-colonization, Americans have surrendered their forums of public engagement. The reaction to the Enron episode and corporate scandals and the Iraq war illustrates the power of the status quo. So if there is to be meaningful change in the current direction of globalization, it is to come from outside the United States, which is explored in the next chapter.

CHAPTER **9**

Capitalisms
Asian-European Dialogue after Enron

There are many rooms in capitalism's house.

—Saburo Okita, 1993

This discussion follows four steps. One is to retrieve the varieties of capitalism from the propaganda that claims There Is No Alternative to free market capitalism. Second is to examine the status of American capitalism in light of Enron and related episodes. Third is to consider the tipping points of American capitalism in view of economic trends and military aspirations. Fourth is to probe the scope for alternative capitalisms and the articulation of alternative capitalisms. Looking forward, one option is a substantive dialogue between Asian countries and the European Union with regard to the direction of globalization and contemporary capitalism. This line of argument functions at two levels, as opening up thinking about globalization and probing the scope for choice, and as a broad-brush policy direction.

Continental European welfare states and Asian developmental states, Rhineland capitalism and the state-assisted capitalism of East and Southeast Asia are varieties of coordinated market economies that are characterized by large government intervention and are relatively egalitarian (repeat: relatively). This resembles the type of capitalism in most developing and transitional economies. Together these represent the majority form of capitalism. In contrast, Anglo-American capitalism arose from very particular historical conditions; it is a minority form of capitalism and a global bottleneck when it comes to international reform. Asian and European capitalisms, without essentializing or idealizing them or underestimating the ongoing influence of neoliberal globalization, may share enough chracteristics to represent the potential for a global alternative direction.

Varieties of Capitalism

Now that the confrontation between capitalism and socialism lies behind us, the new pressing issue is the difference between capitalisms. The French economist Michel Albert set the tone with *Le capitalisme contre le capitalisme*. In institutional economics, the varieties of capitalism are variously characterized as liberal market economies (U.S., U.K., Australia, New Zealand) and coordinated market economies (most others). Alternative terminologies are competitive managerial capitalism (U.S.), cooperative managerial capitalism (Germany), and bureaucratic capitalism (Japan); stock market capitalism and welfare capitalism, and so on.[1]

Let's note the disarray of discourses: while varieties of capitalism are an ordinary and widely discussed theme in institutional economics, international political economy, development studies, and analyses of firms and business cultures, it hardly figures in sociology, and most political and policy discourse continues to either preach or target "capitalism." Sources such as *The Economist* and *Wall Street Journal* refer to capitalism in the singular, assuming free markets to be the telos of modern economics. Social activists often use capitalism in the singular, too. Yet the diversity of capitalisms, and whether it is a lasting difference or they are converging, and the scope for reform, are crucial points of dispute.

The diversity of capitalisms is not just a matter of a different set of bullet points; they represent different forms of regulating market relations that are deeply embedded in historical dynamics and particulars of culture and geography. And they represent different modernities with all the intricacies this entails. The way we view and comprehend alternative modernities is shaped by the modernity we are affiliated with politically and epistemologically.[2] Stereotyping self and others, positive and negative imaging, are inherent in the politics of representation of modernities.

Not just the differences among capitalisms and modernities matter but also the ways in which they interrelate (as discussed in Chapter 7). The interaction of capitalisms can be viewed in terms of competition or complementarity among different country capabilities and their specializations in economic sectors or phases of production,[3] and in terms of diversity or growing convergence. Essentially three scenarios are available in relation to multiple capitalisms: lasting diversity, convergence, and mixing.[4]

Diversity. Richard Whitley offers a typical expression of the view that divergence among capitalisms is lasting: "Convergence to a single most effective type of market economy is no more likely in the twenty-first century than it was in the highly internationalized economy of the late nineteenth century."[5] The diversity of institutional settings may be reinforced by foreign investment strategies that have been termed "institutional arbitrage."[6] Accordingly, what matters is not just quantitative data on foreign investment but in which sectors they occur and how they affect corporate organization and governance. For example, leading foreign investors in Brittany in 2002 are Italian, American, and German,[7] but that tells us little about the direction of corporate governance in the region.

Convergence. Susan Strange disputed the idea of lasting difference between capitalisms because it ignores American structural power as both a market force and a political force.[8] The convergence of capitalisms hinges on economic and political dynamics. It involves economic logics in that the most successful form of capitalism exercises the greatest pull in financial markets. One of the forces driving marketization and a dynamic through which capitalisms interact is financialization and the growth of financial services.[9] "The processes of money movement, securities management, corporate reorganization, securitization of assets, derivates trading and other forms of financial packaging are steadily replacing the act of making, growing and transporting things."[10]

Convergence is also politically driven and promoted by relentless propaganda about the superiority of the "free market" which claims that this is the real logic of capitalism in the singular. Particularly since the era of Reagan and Thatcher, American capitalism has been upheld as capitalism tout court, as *the* norm of capitalism, even as American capitalism itself underwent drastic changes (as discussed in Chapter 1). Deregulation created a system characterized by aggressive deal making, high public disclosure (by American accounting standards), CEOs as culture heroes, and winner-takes-all outcomes. The influence of American capitalism occurs at the confluence of several factors. Some are of a general nature: the overall changes associated with accelerated globalization and post-Fordism; some are geopolitical: U.S. hegemony and cold war victory; and some are specific to the United States: low-wage Dixie capitalism and new economy innovation.

The influence of neo-American capitalism over past decades has been characterized as a shift from stakeholder to shareholder capitalism: stakeholder values (of employees, suppliers, creditors, customers, communities) are shortcut in order to increase shareholder value.[11] The rise of Wall Street and the Dow Jones, foreign investment flowing into the U.S. economy (helped by tax incentives accruing to foreign owners), the value of the dollar and the influence of American-style financial services and business practices demonstrate the appeal of this system.

A left-wing version of convergence is the transnational capitalist class argument. This tends to homogenize capitalist interests and essentialize capitalism, to ignore the "biodiversity" of capitalism[12] and the differentiation of the kind presented by microeconomic and institutional comparative analysis. "Crisis of capitalism" theses, likewise, imply convergence and tend to underestimate the extent to which the flexibility of capitalism derives from *capitalisms* and regional variation. The crisis of overproduction—which looms beneath the frailties of American capitalism—while serious enough,[13] does not take adequate account of regional variation; on the wider canvas what matters is not just overproduction but maldistribution. The question is not just whether there is life after capitalism but also whether there is life during capitalism.

In the interaction between capitalisms and modernities, there is no ideologically neutral airspace. Talk about "the West" (in relation to culture, civilization, modernity, history, religion, capitalism, security) glosses over the differences between Europe and North America. On either side of the Atlantic, "the West" is a flag of convenience. In the United States, talk of convergence easily turns to looking down on Europe in terms of economic dynamism (rigid labor markets) or security (weak-kneed). Meanwhile anti-Americanism provides entertainment throughout the world.

Mixing. The third scenario of mixing and institutional hybridization, *in-between* lasting difference and convergence, rarely comes up as such in political economy. This scenario may well be the most plausible, yet it is also vague; for while it's easy to point out instances of institutional blending, it's difficult to assess the relative magnitudes and the terms under which mixing occurs and therefore the overall direction. It is easy to make a case for hybridization but difficult to assess the politics and political economy of hybridity.[14]

Recent signals—the dot.com bust, the collapse of Enron, the burst of the Wall Street bubble, vast expansion of military spending, war, and deep tax cuts—shed a different light on American capitalism and its international standing. How do these signals affect the three scenarios of capitalist futures? If convergence hinges on economic and propaganda appeal, these precisely have been undermined. American military and political clout remains, but is less effective when the U.S. economy is frail and shrinking.

Enron in Wonderland

> If you can't trust the numbers, how can you allocate capital correctly?
>
> —Paul Volcker, former chair of the Federal Reserve Board, 2002

The collapse of Enron and the ensuing corporate scandals reveal more than "a few bad apples."[15] The Enron episode shows the impact of deregulation, financialization and marketization, reveals Washington money culture, and coincides with the failure of the new economy. Enron machinations underlie the California energy crisis and the privatization of energy markets in developing countries. Enron executives created an "accounting hall of mirrors," transferring losses to partnerships that showed profits on investments in Enron stock that was sold to them at a discount. As discussed in Chapter 1, it is a small step from financial engineering to cooking the books.

The previous remedy—manager ownership or stock options for executives—becomes an ailment when executives acting on insider knowledge sell their stocks and disclosure requirements are lax. An analysis of the 1990s Savings and Loan collapse concluded: "Bankruptcy for profit will occur if poor accounting, lax regulation, or low penalties for abuse give owners an incentive to pay themselves more than their firms are worth and then default on their debt obligations."[16] Permissive accounting that does not show the costs until years later and Wall Street's short-term orientation create a system in which it is rational for executives to loot their companies.[17]

This is made possible by institutionalized lack of oversight and accountability on the part of CEOs and chief financial officers, accounting firms (doing double duty as consulting firms from which they derive 90 percent of revenue), banks, lawyers, market analysts, media, and the Securities and Exchange Commission. The failure of oversight institutions yields steep inequity in the distribution of risks. Accountants act as consultants, investment banks recommend the worthless stocks of major client firms, analysts find it easier to talk stocks up than down, media talk up the market, individual investors' savings seep like water through their hands, and insiders walk away with multimillion gains. Between March 2000 and summer 2002, the stock market lost $7.7 trillion in value and retirement plans and savings for college vanished.

If 9/11 was a godsend to the hawks, Enron, the "economic equivalent of Watergate," is "a scandal so good that it hurts."[18] It exposes the stratification of opportunity and risk exposure—"the rich know when to leave"—and institutionalized insider trading. Sixty percent of American households invest in stocks but stock market democratization (people's capitalism) hinges on reliable information. Circles of privilege are networks of information, social insiders in Manhattan and the Hamptons share information; social capital and economic capital overlap, taking on plutocratic and even dynastic forms.[19] That markets are imperfect because information is asymmetric is not an occasional circumstance but a structural condition.

Yet reform in the United States is likely to be limited. The Business Round Table, the Democratic Party (the business-friendly "party of economic growth"), and mainstream economists oppose drastic reform. The key players have all gained their stripes in an ambience of advocating deregulation. The 2002 corporate reform bill imposes stiff penalties and jail sentences for defrauding executives, but fraudulent intent is virtually impossible to prove. Mainstream American economists prefer tweaking deregulation to abandoning it; they opt for combining deregulation with regulation in the form of stiffer monitoring and accounting rules.[20] This glosses over deeper problems. The consequences of the Reagan administration's deregulation of business and finance are now becoming visible—Enron is the tip of an iceberg of corporate malpractice. In the wake of deregulation, corporate malpractice has multiplied while stakeholders have much less legal recourse. Beyond deregulation lies a culture of corporate impunity in which the bottom line matters more than how it is achieved; success matters more than process because arcane accounting rules and lax oversight make the process inscrutable. A culture in which corporations pay no taxes: "taxes are for suckers." Congress itself is tainted because of Washington money politics in "the best democracy that money can buy."[21]

The international ramifications of "Enronitis" may be greater than the domestic spillover. The almost worldwide shift from stakeholder to stockholder capitalism, from worker participation in management to worker participation in stocks (through privatization of social security, pensions, and pension funds) hinges on the reliability of accounting and the compatibility of accounting rules. Contemporary globalization hinges on institutional cohesion and an aura of legality and probity. If it doesn't deliver equity and fairness, at least the winners are real winners. The corporate scandals put an end to this story. While neoliberal ideology proclaims the self-regulating market, real neoliberalism shows the political and insider manipulation of markets, disguised as liberalization and market logic. The logic in growth differs from the logic in contraction: contraction shows the cracks in the mirror.

The Asian crisis of 1997 was blamed on crony capitalism in Thailand, Korea, Malaysia, the Philippines, and Indonesia, made possible by poor financial reporting. Crises in Latin America yielded similar diagnoses. In the Middle East, from Egypt to Turkey, scrutiny shows that neoliberal market gains have actually been the result of financial engineering and political manipulation.[22]

Crisis in the United States means "cracks in the mirror of the future." The Treasury/IMF prescription in times of crisis is fiscal austerity and deflation, but in the wake of 9/11, the Treasury spent billions to bail out airlines and insurance industries. The American way preaches free trade but practices protectionism. The taskmaster of neoliberal orthodoxy is now exposed as crony capitalism USA. The mirror that globalization the neo-American way holds up to the world is CEO enrichment combined with deepening social inequality. IMF jobless, IMF homeless, and IMF riots are bywords in many countries; now homelessness in the United States is on the increase.

What remained of the new international financial architecture that was discussed in the wake of recurrent crises was "transparency," advocated by the Treasury and IMF and included in the World Bank's good governance package. All along it really meant the alignment of accounting systems to American standards, so Wall Street and the Treasury could read the books; a one-way transparency. American accounting standards are now exposed as "standards of greed" and "accounting reports are worth no more than the paper they are written on,"[23] so the United States has lost the high ground of legal probity. If its own rules are bogus, can it serve as the international rule maker? "Around the world, the architects of the global economy are rethinking the idea that the United States should be the undisputed standard-setter for everything from executive compensation to accounting. They point to the dark side of a Western-style capitalist system that rewarded greed and short-term gain and turned high-flying chief executives into celebrities."[24] The foundation of transnational neoliberalism is a hegemonic compromise that increasingly operates by default rather than conviction in the absence of a cohesive enough alternative coalition.

The Enron episode may turn out to be a tipping point. Is this what awaits at the end of the road of deregulation? Is swindle capitalism the next chapter after casino capitalism? The tipping point occurs if deregulation and no-nonsense capitalism drive the U.S. economy down. No-nonsense capitalism has gradually removed so many safeguards—accountability, transparency, legal recourse against malpractice by corporations, accounting firms, and market analysts—that eventually the economy and its infrastructure itself may decline.

Tipping Points

What are the points of vulnerability of current U.S. policies? A major undertow is the lack of legitimacy of the present policies. But in the theater that matters for practical purposes in the short term, the United States, the public institutions, from media to political parties, hardly function. The media are corporate and serve as cheerleaders. So a legitimacy crisis does not manifest and rarely translates into political consequences. In the Enron episode, the losses were colossal but the consequences minor and the corrections cosmetic. With docile media, even if more scandals erupt the administration is practically buffered from their political consequences. Public uproar abroad can be dismissed as "anti-Americanism."

The main arena in which the U.S. administration is *not* sheltered from adverse publicity and its consequences is the economy. Southern conservatives may have political capital to spare, but Southern economics does not travel well even in the United States and now comes with rising unemployment, Wall Street decline, and receding foreign investment. The military-industrial complex is no longer the growth engine it was in the past. At the same time as adopting deep tax cuts in 2003, Congress raised the national debt limit to $7.4 trillion. This allows the federal government more deficit spending, but states and cities are required by law to balance their budgets. Given Wall Street losses, recession and the cost of counterterrorism measures, states (indebted by $78 billion in 2003) and cities will further cut social and education spending (by $75 billion in 2002 and 2003), and while services are declining federal tax cuts will have to be compensated for by raising state and local taxes. The shift from social and entrepreneurial government to law-and-order government that is being effected at the federal level is thus being reproduced at the state and local level.

In addition, the reach of Southern economics is not global. Enron and Washington's belligerence have ruptured the American aura of growth, dynamism and innovation on which foreign investment, the status of the dollar and the appeal of American cultural exports depend. Since early 2003, China has overtaken the United States as the prime place for foreign investment.

The American current account deficit—what the United States owes the rest of the world because of trade and financial imbalances—is the largest in world history. It consists for about 80 percent of the trade deficit, the excess of imports over exports. Catherine Mann, a former U.S. chief economist, asks: "The U.S. current account deficit, driven by the United States' widening trade deficit, is the largest it has ever been, both as a share of the U.S. economy and in dollar terms. How much longer can the United States continue to spend more than it earns and support the resumption of global growth?"[25] In the early 1980s, the United States was a net creditor to the rest of the world; it is now the largest net debtor. According to the congressional budget office, the current account deficit is anticipated to rise from $420 billion in 2002 (4.1 percent of GDP) to $480 billion in 2003 and $730 billion in 2006 (5.9 percent of GDP), bringing the deficit over 2004–13 to $1.4 trillion. Financing the present deficit requires a capital inflow of $1.9 billion each trading day.[26] "On a flow basis, the U.S. is now attracting more net capital than all the developing countries combined."[27]

A *Financial Times* report observes that "the U.S. is protected by its ability to borrow in its own currency and to attract inward direct investment and equity purchases." Yet it concludes, "What makes the claims relatively safe for the U.S. also makes them risky for foreign investors. As U.S. assets become a bigger component of their wealth, they must become nervous about the currency and valuation risks."[28] The growing deficit and increasing debt service weaken the dollar, which stimulates U.S. exports, but also makes U.S. securities and dollar assets less lucrative for foreign investors. In 2002, Europeans were net sellers of U.S. securities and Asians became the largest overseas investors in U.S. assets.[29] Japan alone holds $386.6 billion in U.S. Treasury bonds (per April 2003) and China has become one of the world's five largest holders of Treasury securities.[30] Asian central banks own more than $1 trillion of U.S. Treasury bonds. "Asian investors are in into the dollar so deep, in fact, that they would have trouble bailing out, even if they wanted to. Their own dollar sales would drive the currency's value into a tailspin before they could liquidate their holdings." Yet they could distribute more of their reserves at home to spur domestic consumer spending and reduce their reliance on exports.[31]

When foreigners cease to supply the $500 billion that the U.S. economy needs each year, the U.S. government will borrow on the domestic financial market and compete with private borrowers, which according to textbook economics will drive up interest rates and slow down economic growth.

What is in the cards is a profound reordering of the world economy, which is difficult because of the high degree of transnational financial and economic interconnectedness. Asia and Europe have such large dollar holdings that liquidating them would endanger their financial position and an American economic crisis would damage their exports. The Federal Reserve reckons that a "steep cliff" for the dollar is not in the international economic interest; so the U.S. government continues on its path of deficit spending. Washington's preoccupation with American primacy and permanent war is not only provincialism turned inside out but also out of step with economic realities. As Will Hutton notes, "The multilateralism that Bush scorns is, in truth, an economic necessity." American military might "is a strategic position built on economic sand."[32] Anatol Lieven observes,

> Given its immense wealth, the United States can afford a military capable of dominating the earth; or it can afford a stable, secure system of social and medical entitlements for a majority of its aging population; or it can afford massive tax cuts for its wealthiest citizens and no tax raises for the rest. But it cannot afford all three, unless it can indefinitely sustain them through a combination of massive trade deficits and international borrowing. This seems most unlikely, especially in the midst of a global economic downturn.[33]

Given the structural weaknesses of the American economy, relying on the military-industrial complex and permanent war are like adding to the *Titanic* rather than changing its course; as a large-scale pyramid scheme, they postpone the day of reckoning. U.S. military might is Goliath with feet of clay. Part of the Goliath complex is the repeated assertion of being number one.

Essentially, American military might and permanent war are made possible and paid for by the flow of dollars from the world's surplus countries, especially in Asia and Europe.

An Alternative Rapport

In this light, it is important to recover the ground that European and Asian capitalisms represent, analytically and politically. What is at stake is the shape and direction of globalization at a time when the American way has become a global bottleneck. Asian-European and intercontinental dialogue may probe the scope for an alternative rapport—not always looking at Washington but following an alternative course.

Major international agreements have come about without American cooperation—such as the Kyoto protocol, the International Criminal Court, the ban on anti-personnel mines, the cleaner energy plan, the UN agreement to curb the international flow of illicit small arms, the UN biological and toxic weapons convention, the UN convention on the rights of the child, and the UN covenant on economic, social, and cultural rights. These agreements have not been anti-American; they don't exclude the United States, the U.S. excludes itself. Economies and technologies are now so interwoven and America's military lead is so dominant that an anti-hegemonic coalition is neither feasible nor desirable; but there is scope for an alternative coalition that the United States is welcome to join but that operates independent of the American orbit.

It would be important to extend these forms of multilateral cooperation to international finance, development, and trade policies. Substantive dialogue and rapport between Asian countries and the European Union can contribute to setting a new agenda. Newly industrialized countries in Asia and Latin America and developing and transitional countries share a common interest in stable multilateral institutions, regulation of international finance and, arguably, reorientation towards a social and democratic capitalism. Global justice movements such as the World Social Forum and international labor organizations make essential contributions to shaping the transnational reform agenda. A coalition of Asian, African, European, American, and Latin American progressive forces could redirect and reshape the course of globalization. Rather than complain about neoliberalism and Washington policies, let's turn the picture around and consider the resources and resilience of alternative capitalisms. Let's consider some of the issues at stake in a European-Asian dialogue, mixing pros and cons along the way.

Economies and multinational corporations are now so interwoven across regions that delineating European, Asian, and American spheres, each with their autonomous room of maneuver, no longer makes sense. The notion of regional blocs and interregional rivalry is not a valid description of contemporary dynamics. Yet, the next step along this logic, that states are powerless in an increasingly borderless world, takes matters too far. So the present argument pertains to the in-between zone of public policy where state (and local government) and regional policy (such as by the EU) do matter. Some time ago, Ronald Dore outlined the possible ramifications of a Wall Street decline:

> ... just as the 1930s depression prompted the postwar attempts at the social regulation of capitalism, so, if the coming bursting of the Wall Street bubble is more cataclysmic than a "correction" and real depression in the dominant economy gives enough backing to "global capitalism in crisis' talk, things could change. There could, once again, with Japan and a German-led Europe in the vanguard, be various attempts to reassert the nation-state's power in the name of society, to "embed" the economic activity within its borders in norms and social structures that amount to something more than mere monitoring of free and fair markets.[34]

Clearly, however, this kind of reconstruction cannot be confined within national borders.

But is there sufficient internal and regional cohesion that can serve as a basis for interregional cooperation? Varieties of capitalism should not be essentialized; they are ever in flux and internally contested and international links do double duty as domestic props. The interaction between capitalisms and modernities is a minefield of ideologies and stereotypes, which prompts caution when it comes to Asian-European dialogue. Which Asia, which Europe? Internal diversity is too extensive for "Asia" and "Europe" to serve as meaningful units. The idea of an East Asian or Tiger "model" is disputed. Diversity in Europe is likewise profound. The United Kingdom is part of the European Union but follows Anglo-American rather than Rhineland capitalism. Yet in each sphere, the spectrum of debate is typically wider than in the United States and this pluralism is a major resource in Asian-European and intercontinental dialogue. America's weakness is that it is dominated by single orthodoxy, while pluralism elsewhere retains the biodiversity of capitalism.

Indicators and accounting standards define the way firms and economies are rated. There are large gaps between, say, the Human Development Index of the UNDP and the Competitiveness Index and the ratings used by market analysts to assess country creditworthiness. Stock market capitalism, according to Ronald Dore, "means an economy centred on the stock market as the measure of corporate success and on the stock market index as a measure of national well-being, as opposed to an economy which has other, better, more pluralistic criteria of human welfare for measuring progress towards the good society."[35] A dialogue between Asian and European countries can contribute to setting more meaningful and pluralistic international standards.

In European accounting principles, "substance prevails over form" while in American accounting "form prevails over substance." American accounting rule books are twice as thick as European ones, but since what matters is the letter rather than the spirit of the law, lawyers can always find new loopholes. Cultural differences underlie the difference in systems, which are ultimately a matter of different modernities: American applied Enlightenment and shallow modernity underlie its legalistic culture, in contrast to the complex and historically textured modernities of other civilizations. So what underlies the present contestation over accounting rules is so to speak a clash of modernities—by way of a tongue in cheek variation on the clash of civilizations. The European Commission decided in 2000 that by 2005 all companies in the EU must report according to International Accounting Standards Board; it now urges the United States to internationalize its accounting standards and adopt the European rules.[36]

In 1997, the IMF blocked the formation of an Asian Emergency Regional Fund proposed by Japan. Thailand has recently proposed an Asian Bond Fund.[37] Asian-European dialogue could discuss redirecting Asian and European development funds from Washington-based institutions to regional institutions, such as an Asian Fund, regional development banks, or UN institutions.

Concerns in Asia are that Asian capitalisms need to become more democratic, less patriarchal, more ecologically sustainable, and socially responsive. Reconstruction in the wake of the Asian crisis is an opportunity for renewal in this direction.[38]

In Asia, memories of European colonialism still linger. If American influence has shown mixed results, would it now make sense to lean over to European perspectives? Why not just go it alone? The options include an Asian renaissance, Pacific Century, or a global century. A rejoinder is that transnational interaction takes place anyway and radio silence is not an option. The same applies to Europe. The Maastricht Treaty positions the EU amid competing capitalisms, transnational financialization, and stock market capitalism, which all affect transnational capital flows. Absent alternatives, the EU goes along with standards of neoliberal capitalism in the OECD and international forums; in WTO negotiations, European demands for lifting trade barriers have often been more draconic than American ones. The present argument favors Europe changing its course internally by strengthening its social charter, and externally, by being less self-absorbed and engrossed in the EU process of integration and enlargement, and more outward looking.

The "East Asian Miracle" was appropriated by the World Bank as a demonstration of free market, export-oriented economic growth, in Sinic Asia as a success story of Confucian ethics, and in Japan as a demonstration of the importance of education and human capital.[39] European conservatives, British Tories, and American neoconservatives held up the East Asian mirror to put pressure on trade unions and welfare state claims. European conservatives and social democrats alike bestowed praise on East Asian welfare systems as models of lean and effective government. In this view, East Asian welfare systems subordinate welfare to economic efficiency, are low cost, create incentives for hard work and use available social resources rather than state dependency. But their downsides have not been as widely considered: Asian welfare systems burden the family and especially women; they reproduce inequalities, lack of institutional integration, and authoritarian political legacies.[40] Likewise, the Asian crisis has been hijacked by parties of all ideological stripes to prove their various points.

The European Union leads the way in regional institutional integration and there is no Asian equivalent.[41] At any rate, both Asia and Europe suffer from democratic deficits in governance. The new people's regionalism in Asia can play an important part in transregional dialogue; social movements and transnational NGOs such as Third World Network, Focus on the Global South, Arena, and others play a major role in articulating criticisms of the WTO, APEC, bio-engineering, Genetically Modified Food, and ecological concerns.

Interregionalism can serve as a clearinghouse for global multilateral forums, in the sense that multilateral negotiation becomes a staggered process.[42] In the WTO, it can mean Asian and European pressure for internationally equitable trade rules. In international development, it can mean redirecting development efforts outside the orbit of the IMF and World Bank and strengthening regional development institutions instead. In international finance, it can mean backing for a Tobin tax accord.

A familiar hurdle is Asian resistance to Western or European insistence on human rights. The emphasis on *human security* in Asian perspectives places social concerns above individual rights, unlike human rights.[43] This offers a basis for dialogue with European social democracy more than with American individualist leanings. The human development approach has been inspired by East Asian experiences and resembles some forms of European social democracy, so it offers a further Eurasian meeting ground.[44]

Most Asian economies are deeply entangled in American technology, investments, markets, security cooperation, and culture. China's room of maneuver is limited by its WTO membership. From the viewpoint of Asian countries, diversifying external relations may provide room of maneuver in relation to the United States. Preemptive transregionalism has been in the air for some time. APEC owes its existence to keeping Europe's role in Asia restricted and the Asia-Europe Meetings (ASEM) have been a response to this maneuver.[45] From European viewpoints, there may be as much to gain from strengthening relations with Asia as there is from American points of view. If in the American case, the bottom line is market access and geopolitics, the spectrum of interests and engagement in the case of Europe is likely to be wider.

A European concern, besides integration, is the renewal of social democracy. The welfare state cannot be rebuilt on a national basis but must be rebuilt on a European and possibly on a transnational scale.[46] Keynesian demand management as the basis of the welfare state may lead to welfare dependency (and the familiar neoconservative allegations) and should be redirected toward social distribution with an emphasis on skills and capabilities, on education, health care, and housing, as in the Scandinavian and human development approaches. American economic dynamism led to the allegation of Europe's "rigidities of the labor market," but many new jobs in the United States don't come with a living wage and social inequality is rising. The renewal of social democracy is essential, in turn, for reshaping European identity and addressing the crisis of multiculturalism. Rolling back the welfare state at a time when immigration is increasing and more investments in education, housing, health, and social services are needed to accommodate growing social demand, has contributed to a right-wing swing in many European countries. The stalemate of the European welfare state and the crisis of multiculturalism interact.[47]

The Rhine tortoise may yet overtake the American hare, to follow the metaphor of Michel Albert. It would be ironic if two targets of American disdain because of their deviation from free market norms, Asia and Europe, would converge and set an alternative social market standard.

Eurasia

Europe, according to Paul Valéry, is the "cap d'Asie." Ancient routes over land and sea such as the Silk Roads connect the two. Eurasia dreaming is too poetic a theme for our times of earnest political economy discussion. Nevertheless, Eurasia has inspired many dreams, claimed in turn by the Persian Empire, Alexander, the Mongol Empire, the Ottomans, Napoleon, and the Russian empire. Eurasia resonates with undercurrents of Russian populism—Russian soul bridging Asia and Europe—and plays a part in Turkish imaginaries. The idea of a "new Silk Road" goes back some time.[48] A recent Eurasian dream was an anti-hegemonic coalition of Russia and

China, which never materialized because for both it would have meant exclusion from American investments and technology.

The latest claimant to Eurasia is the United States. In American geopolitics, Eurasia ranks as the world's heartland: "he who controls Eurasia controls the world."[49] In Zbigniew Brzezinski's panorama of American geopolitical objectives, Europe figures as America's "democratic bridgehead" and Japan, Korea, and Taiwan as American protectorates. Today's most coveted stretch of real estate is Central Asia, whose oil and gas reserves dwarf those of the Middle East. Andre Gunder Frank reminds us of the latent theme of the "centrality of Central Asia," "truly the missing link in Eurasian and world history."[50]

A familiar account of the international order is a global triangle with North America, West Europe, and East Asia as its poles and governed in the spirit of multilateralism.[51] Washington's permanent war weakens this triad. In addition the United States has long been a bottleneck in reform towards a more equitable, accountable and sustainable global order. A Eurasian rapport might help to strengthen moderate forces within the United States.

U.S. policy has long aimed to forestall a coalition between France, Germany and Russia, which the Iraq war is bringing about. The logical American countermove is to build an alternative coalition with Japan and China.[52] But China also opposes the Iraq war. Russia, China, and the five Central Asian states now cooperate in the Shanghai Cooperation Organization. This is part of the geopolitical and geo-economic setting of Eurasian dialogue.

If Eurasian dialogue focuses primarily on economic and social policy, what about defense and security? American military spending is at such a level that no country or region can or would conceivably wish to compete. American strategic investments represent a global lead that is not recoverable; they suggest an inhospitable world that increasingly reflects American alienation. Here the objective of Eurasian dialogue is to promote international stability through multilateralism and to strengthen international law and multilateral institutions that circumscribe the impact of American geopolitics.

Over past decades, the world majority has been gradually moving towards strengthening international law and developing constructive multilateral norms and institutions. In many instances, the United States is virtually the only country or the only developed country that has not joined the new accords. For decades, the United States has concentrated on building the free market regime of the Washington consensus, which is now crumbling, and military power, while withholding cooperation from other international agreements, particularly those that would restrict its exercise of power or legal system. The American refusal to take part in multilateral agreements

158 · Globalization or Empire?

is no incidental stubbornness but embedded in hyperpower exceptionalism. For some time the United States has been marching to a different drummer than the rest of the world. This "city on the hill" is "a place apart, protected by its oceans,"[53] so indifference to the consequences of military interventions other than those that significantly affect the balance of power, is not a farfetched assumption. This is why at this stage correction has to come from outside the United States.

Coda

As discussed in the first chapter, American capitalism has played a large part in shaping contemporary globalization in its own image, as neoliberal globalization. The global shift from stakeholder to shareholder capitalism looks risky when the American model itself is at risk, as the Enron episode illustrates. By over-rewarding upper strata and underpaying lower and middle strata, neoliberalism undermines its own foundations. Dixie capitalism has not been merciful to Americans (30 percent of the American workforce does not earn a living wage; 43 million go without medical insurance; "the rich get richer and the poor get prison"). Wal-Mart, the country's largest company and the world's largest retailer, doesn't pay a living wage. Most goods sold in Wal-Mart are cheap imports, particularly from China. Over the years the United States has been deindustrializing, deskilling and consuming to such an extent that its trade deficit and job loss are structural.[54]

A fundamental part of American neoliberalism is the military industrial complex, which has deep roots, as discussed in several chapters, and major ramifications—such as the economic shift from the Frost Belt to the Sunbelt, the rise of the Southern conservatives and their right-wing Christianity and culture of militarism. This America undertakes neoliberal empire, a project that is not sustainable militarily, politically or economically. If neoliberal globalization was a theater of the absurd in which global inequality has grown steeply, neoliberal empire is a theater of the grotesque. The worldwide concern and antagonism that the United States now elicits consists of several layers. It consists of anger over neoliberal globalization and its consequences for the livelihood of the world majority, over "McDonaldization" or the influence of American consumer and marketing culture, its opting out of multilateral cooperation and reform, and American regional policies, particularly in the Middle East. The United States harvests accumulated disaffection. The most recent anger concerns the Iraq war. But the Iraq war is but an expression of a deeper problem, part of which is the Pentagon's planning for permanent war. War is not the answer to the world's problems, but 5 percent of the world's population that spends 40 percent of world military spending, probably has no other answers to give.

With so much of the national treasure spent on the military, why is there no serious, sustained national conversation and public debate in the United States about this spending and its purpose, and its consequences for the American economy and society? Privileging military contracts means that the U.S. economy has become uncompetitive. Reflecting on the situation deeply, perhaps the essential problem is that the United States has been spoiled by several generations of economic success. This underlies the fundamental weakness of American institutions. Empowerment for Americans would mean a return to a New Deal type of economic regulation. The New Deal took shape in response to economic crisis, and short of economic crisis a return to New Deal politics is unlikely. The United States has long been marked by a greater preponderance of business over labor than any advanced country. The Southern conservatives are adamantly opposed to New Deal politics and are also strongly invested in the military-industrial complex and the authoritarian culture of threat inflation and stereotyping of the "rest" of the world that comes with it. Liberals who buy into threat inflation and endorse empire also endorse, knowingly or not, American authoritarianism and the disempowerment of Americans, for that is the price of primacy. For fear of global instability, they legitimate and unleash an American militarism that is itself globally perceived as a destabilizing force.

For Americans the cost of pursuing primacy is that the United States has become an authoritarian, conservative society. Overinvestment in the military has incapacitated the country in many other spheres. The country is undereducated, culturally backward and inward-looking, and economically on its knees and dependent on foreign borrowing. The continually reiterated drone of the world's wealthiest, richest, most powerful country in fact refers to the world's largest debtor nation with unsustainable levels of debt. The exercise of unrestrained power will have the usual unanticipated consequences. Its foundations are growing economic weakness, reduced manufacturing capacity and an external deficit so large that it is unsustainable. The grand strategy of permanent war signals the beginning of the end of American power.

Notes

1. Tickell and Peck, "Making Global Rules," 2003.
2. Quotes are from Wood, "The Rise of the Prison-Industrial Complex," 2003, 24.
3. Cummings, *Dixiefication*, x.
4. Ibid., 6. Cummings notes, "it is the traditional Southern conservative economic policies and their infusion and combination with national conservative economic policies of the Republican party, starting in the 1960s—a process which I call Dixiefication—that has dominated the economic agenda of the country the past three decades . . ." (7).
5. Ibid., 10.
6. Wood, "The Rise of the Prison-Industrial Complex," 27.
7. Hutton, *The World We're In*, 106.
8. Ibid. and Chapter 9 below.
9. Lind, *Made in Texas*, 77 and 80.
10. Ibid., 47.
11. Applebome, *Dixie Rising*, 10.
12. See Jansson, "Internal Orientalism," 2003. Zinn, *The Southern Mystique*.
13. Lind, *Made in Texas*, 70.
14. Ibid., 84.
15. Ibid., 81–2. Cf. Applebome, *Dixie Rising*, 13.
16. Cummings, *Dixiefication*, 117.
17. Lind, *Made in Texas*, 94.
18. Cummings, *Dixiefication*, 75.
19. A transitional figure is Robert Reich (e.g., *The Next American Frontier*).
20. See Hutton, *The State We're In*, and Chapter 9 below.
21. Cummings, *Dixiefication*, 21.
22. According to Michael Porter (*Competitiveness of Nations*, 508–9), in 1990 the U.S. has lost competitive edge in transportation-related goods, machinery and machine tools, office products, consumer electronics and durables, apparel, steel, and telecommunications equipment. Cf. Cummings, *Dixiefication*, 157; Hutton, *The World We're In*.
23. Halliday, *The Second Cold War*.
24. Johnson, "American Militarism and Blowback," 2002.

25. Nederveen Pieterse, *Development Theory*.
26. Thacker, "The High Politics of IMF Lending," 1999, 70.
27. Kindleberger, "International Public Goods," 1986, 10.
28. The term is used by Gilpin, *The Challenge of Global Capitalism*.
29. Hutton and Giddens, *Global Capitalism*.
30. Bello et al., *Siamese Tragedy*, 52; and Bello, *Deglobalization*.
31. Cf. Manzo, "The "New" Developmentalism," 1999.
32. Beck, "The Chernobyl of Globalization," *FT*, November 6, 2001. Klein, *GW*, November 1–7, 2001.
33. R. W. Stevenson, "Government Fiddles and the Economy Burns," *NYT*, December 16, 2001.
34. Williamson, "What Washington Means by Policy Reform," 1990.
35. E.g., George Soros, *The Crisis of Global Capitalism* and *On Globalization*.
36. J. Cassidy, "Master of Disaster," *The New Yorker*, July 15, 2002.
37. GAO Report, "International Financial Crises: Challenges Remain in IMF's Ability to Anticipate, Prevent and Resolve Financial Crises," Washington, DC, 2003. M. Crutsinger, "IMF Reforms Fall Short—Auditors," *Bangkok Post*, June 18, 2003.
38. Bello, *Deglobalization*.
39. On the dismissal of Joseph Stiglitz and the resignation of Ravi Kanbur, see Wade, "The USA and the World Bank," 2002.
40. Stiglitz, *Globalization and its Discontents*. Cf. Nederveen Pieterse, *Development Theory*, ch. 11.
41. Carrier, *Meanings of the Market*, "Introduction."

Chapter 2

1. Priest, *The Mission*. Bacevich, *American Empire*. The influence of the military of course goes way back; e.g., in the 1960s Juan Bosch in the Dominican Republic introduced the term *Pentagonism*.
2. Nye, *The Paradox of American Power*, 143.
3. Bhagwati and Patrick, *Aggressive Unilateralism*.
4. Mastanduno, "Preserving the Unipolar Moment," 1997, 66.
5. Huntington, "The Lonely Superpower," 1999, 36.
6. Gruber, *Ruling the World*.
7. Brooks and Wohlforth, "American Primacy," 2002, 21.
8. Ibid., 30 and 31.
9. Ibid., 31.
10. The increase of $48 billion for FY 2003 equals the entire military budget of Japan. It brings military spending for 2003 to a total of $380 billion, which exceeds the combined military spending of the next 19 largest military spenders. The U.S. intelligence community's roughly $30 billion budget is greater than the national defense budgets of all but six countries in the world. This budget exceeds cold war military spending by more than 15 percent. Defense spending would rise to $405 billion in 2005.
11. R. Ratnesar, "In Defense of Hegemony," *Time*, June 18, 2001.
12. E.g., Drury, *Leo Strauss*. Elizabeth Drew, "The Neocons in Power," *New York Review of Books*, June 12, 2003. Hersh, "Selective Intelligence," 2003. P. Escobar, "This War is Brought to You by . . ." *Asia Times Online*, March 20, 2003.
13. According to Reagan, "Government is the problem, not the solution." "Government involvement in the economy was to be restricted. But Reagan was perfectly happy to get the government involved in social issues such as abortion and school prayer. Reagan also wanted the government expanded when it came to national defense, which he wanted to increase. . . . The Reagan administration was staffed by a variety of people, including supply-siders, monetarists, neoconservative intellectuals and front men for the concentration of corporate economic power." Cummings, *Dixiefication*, 79.
14. Stockman, *Triumph of Politics*, 402.
15. "Extensive tax cuts will require Congress to limit the growth of social programs and public

investment and undermine other programs altogether. . . . Rising deficits will inevitably force Congress to starve those "wasteful" social programs. The prospective high deficits may even make it imperative to privatize Social Security and Medicare eventually." Jeff Madrick, "The Iraqi Time Bomb," *NYT Magazine*, April 6, 2003.

16. Even without new tax cuts the Committee for Economic Development, an organization of leading CEOs, predicts a decade of "annual deficits of $300 billion to $400 billion, increasing as far as the eye can see," and opposes new tax cuts. D. Broder, "CEOs Fear Projected Budget Deficits," *News Gazette* (Champaign, IL), March 6, 2003.

17. Cockburn, *Out of Control*.

18. Hersh, "Selective Intelligence," 2003.

19. Cf. Lieven, "The Push for War," 2002. On Christian Zionism see Nederveen Pieterse, "The History of a Metaphor," 1992.

20. The National Security Doctrine shares the assumptions of the PNAC report written for the incoming administration in September 2000. D. Kagan et al., *Rebuilding America's Defenses*.

21. Kagan, *Paradise and Power*.

22. Beinin, "Pro-Israel Hawks," 2003. Lind, "The Israel Lobby," 2002.

23. See "America and the IMF/World Bank: What leadership?" *The Economist*, April 20, 2002.

24. E.g., Denzin and Lincoln (eds.), *9/11 in American Culture*.

25. Halabi, "Orientalism," 1999.

26. "While neoconservative intellectuals provided the rationalizations, Southern fundamentalists provided the agenda for George W. Bush in social policy" (this refers to "faith-based institutions"). Lind, *Made in Texas*, 141–2 and 118.

27. A critique of American unilateralism from a conservative viewpoint is Prestowitz, *Rogue Nation*.

28. Wallerstein, *Decline of American Power*, 26.

29. Harvey, "The 'New' Imperialism," 2004.

30. " . . . under the Bush administration the Treasury takes its marching orders from White House political operatives. As the New Republic reports, when John Snow meets with Karl Rove, the meetings take place in Mr Rove's office." P. Krugman, "Everything is Political," *NYT*, August 5, 2003.

31. Shimshon Bichler and Jonathan Nitzan, *Dominant Capital and the New Wars* (www.bnarchives.net).

32. Rubin, "Stumbling into War," 2003.

33. Johnson, "American Militarism and Blowback," 2002, 22.

34. J. Habermas, "The Fall of the Monument," *The Hindu*, June 5, 2003.

35. Sardar and Davis, *Why Do People Hate America?*

Chapter 3

1. Mallaby, "The Reluctant Imperialist," 2002.

2. Kaplan, *Warrior Politics*. M. Ignatieff, "Nation-Building Lite," *NYT Magazine*, July 28, 2002. R. A. Cooper, "Why We Still Need Empires," *The Observer*, April 7, 2002. M. Boot, "The Case for American Empire," *Weekly Standard*, October 15, 2001.

3. Thus, a headline reads "The Imperial Presidency vs. the Imperial Judiciary" (L. Greenhouse, *NYT*, September 8, 2002).

4. E.g., Ferguson, *Empire*.

5. C. Asquith, "Righting Iraq's Universities," *NYT Education Life*, August 3, 2003.

6. E.g., Barnet and Cavanagh, *Global Dreams*. Korten, *When Corporations Rule*.

7. Examples are the role of ITT with the CIA in the overthrow of the Allende government in Chile, the United Fruit Company, and U.S. exploits in Central America, and so forth (cf. Horowitz, *Corporations and the Cold War*).

8. George, *How the Other Half Dies*.

9. Walter, "Do They Really Rule the World?" 1998.

10. An example is Mohammadi and Absan, *Globalisation or Recolonization?* Some would consider "development" recolonization since it is externally imposed. According to Edward

Goldsmith, what Marxists refer to as "imperialism" and what western governments today call "development" amount to much the same thing ("Development as Colonialism," 2002). A rejoinder is that development is not merely externally imposed but owned as much by the global South.

11. Johnson, *Blowback*, 19–20. Parenti, *Against Empire*, 1. Cf. Petras and Morley, *Republic or Empire?*; Petras and Veltmeyer, *Imperialism Unmasked*; Furedi, *The New Ideology of Imperialism*.

12. Williams, *Tragedy of American Diplomacy* and *Empire as a Way of Life*. Chomsky, *Year 501*. Lefever, *America's Imperial Burden*.

13. Zinn, *On War*, 153.

14. E.g., Said, *Culture and Imperialism*.

15. Nye, "U.S. Power and Strategy after Iraq," 2003, 70.

16. Fine, "Economics Imperialism," 2002.

17. Henderson, "Fighting Economism," 1996, 581 and 582. Teivanen (*Enter Economism, Exit Politics*) gives a detailed account of economism as politics in disguise in the case of Peru.

18. Hardt and Negri, *Empire*, xiv–xv.

19. "This 'smoothing' of the world is convenient since it effectively exonerates any single country—including the United States—from any responsibility for the ills of the world" (Bichler and Nitzan, "Dominant Capital and the New Wars," 2003, 7).

20. A detailed discussion is Nederveen Pieterse, *Empire and Emancipation*, ch. 1.

21. E.g., Fieldhouse, *Economics and Empire*.

22. If we add radical antidevelopment perspectives, the equation widens and reads modernization = Westernization = capitalism = globalization = imperialism.

23. Doyle, *Empires*.

24. Haass, "What to Do with American Primacy?" 2001.

25. Brzezinski, *Grand Chess Game*, 213; and Chapter 5 below.

26. Thomas, "Globalisation as Paradigm Shift," 2000. This kind of literature is much more common (e.g., Falk, Chossudovsky, MacEwan and many others).

27. Tomlinson, *Cultural Imperialism*.

28. Giddens, *Consequences of Modernity*, 64.

29. Fieldhouse, *Colonial Empires*.

30. This discussion contrasts *contemporary* globalization (not globalization tout court) and empire. A wider discussion is in Nederveen Pieterse, *Globalization and Culture*.

31. McMichael, *Development and Social Change*; Friedman, *Lexus and Olive Tree*; Wallerstein, *Decline of American Power*.

Chapter 4

1. I. H. Daalder and J. M. Lindsay, *NYT*, May 10 2003.

2. Finnegan, "The Economics of Empire," 2003, 50.

3. Quoted in Rhodes, "The Imperial Logic of Bush's Liberal Agenda," 2003, 133. Cf. Mandelbaum, *The Ideas that Conquered the World*.

4. Rice, "Promoting the National Interest," 2000, 47, 49.

5. F. Zakaria, "Our Way," *The New Yorker*, October 14–21, 2002. Rhodes, "The Imperial Logic," 2003.

6. Quoted in Mearsheimer, *The Tragedy of Great Power Politics*.

7. Kagan, *Paradise and Power*. Kaplan, *Warrior Politics*.

8. See Glennon, "Why the Security Council Failed," 2003.

9. Spruyt, "Empires and Imperialism," 2001, 239. A further clause of universalistic empire is "The ultimate objective is to incorporate all other territories within the empire. The areas not subjected simply mark the limits of practical expansion" (ibid.).

10. Boyle, *Criminality of Nuclear Deterrence*. Blum, *Rogue State*.

11. When NATO for the first time in its existence invoked Article V, declaring 9/11 an attack on all allies, Rumsfeld's dismissive reaction was "the mission will define the coalition" (Hirsh, "Bush and the World," 2002).

12. D. H. Rumsfeld, "A New Kind of War," *NYT*, September 27, 2001.

13. Boot, *Small Wars.*
14. In the pericentric theory of empire the turbulent frontier drives metropolitan policy (Fieldhouse, *The Colonial Empires*).
15. This is widely reported; e.g., Confessore, "G.I. Woe," 2003.
16. Quoted in T. Turnpiseed, "The Iraq War Could Become the Greatest Defeat in United States' History," www.CommonDreams.org, August 14, 2003.
17. Rhodes, "The Imperial Logic," 2003, 142.
18. T. Shanker, "Rumsfeld Urges Reshaping of Pentagon Employee System," *NYT*, June 5, 2003.
19. A NYT editorial speaks of "detax-and-spend policies" and quotes the Concord Coalition ("The Deficit Floats Up and Away," July 16, 2003).
20. Dumbrell, "Unilateralism," 2002, 281. Begala, *It's Still the Economy.*
21. Tim Shorrock, "Crony Capitalism goes Global," *The Nation*, April 1, 2002 and "Selling (off) Iraq," *The Nation*, June 23, 2003.
22. D. Baum, "Nation Builders for Hire," *NYT Magazine*, June 22, 2003.
23. This is called "objective analysis—meaning I provide the objective, you supply the analysis." Kurt Campbell quoted in P. E. Tyler, "Spy Wars Begin at Home," *NYT*, November 3, 2002.
24. Singer, *Corporate Warriors.* L. Wayne, "America's For-Profit Secret Army," *NYT*, October 13, 2002.
25. Dyer, *The Perpetual Prisoner Machine.* M. Reiss, "The Correctional-Industrial Complex." *NYT*, August 2, 1998. Cf. Chapter 8 below.
26. Hoffman, "Lessons of 9/11," 2002, 13.
27. T. Shanker, "Officials Debate Whether to Seek a Bigger Military," *NYT*, July 21, 2003. P. W. Singer, "Have Guns, Will Travel," *NYT*, July 21, 2003.
28. Nye, "U.S. Power and Strategy after Iraq," 2003, 71.
29. N. Ferguson, "The Empire Slinks Back," *NYT Magazine*, April 27, 2003.
30. E. Becker and E. L Andrews, "Performing a Free Trade Juggling Act, Offstage." *NYT*, February 8, 2003.
31. K. Watkins, "The main development from WTO talks is a fine line in hypocrisy," *GW*, 5–11 September, 2002.
32. E. Becker, "U.S. Unilateralism Worries Trade Officials," *NYT*, 17 March, 2003.
33. Becker and Andrews, "Performing a Free Trade Juggling Act," 2003.
34. Finnegan, "Economics of Empire," 2003, 42.
35. E. Iritani, "Singapore Trade Deal Gives U.S. 'Full Access,'" *LAT*, May 7, 2003.
36. D. Altman, "Global Trade Looking Glass: Can U.S. Have It Both Ways?" *NYT*, November 9, 2002.
37. Lewis, "Bush and Iraq," 2002.
38. N. Klein, "America is not a Hamburger," *GW*, March 21–27, 2002.
39. Rampton and Stauber, *Weapons of Mass Deception.* E. Bumiller, "Even critics of the war say the White House spun it with skill," *NYT*, April 20, 2003.
40. W. P. Strobel and J. S. Landay, "Pentagon Hires Image Firm to Explain Airstrikes to World," *San Jose Mercury News*, October 19, 2001; Rampton and Stauber, *Weapons of Mass Deception.*
41. E.g., Johnson, "American Militarism and Blowback," 2003.
42. Friedman, "Power and Peril," *NYT*, August 13, 2003.
43. An alternative reading, and unconfirmed reports, hold that to forestall urban warfare one of Iraq's top generals had been bought off (for $25 million and passage out of the country) to withdraw Republican Guards from Baghdad before American forces arrived. "Why Baghdad fell without a fight," *Hindustan Times*, June 3, 2003. The general is identified as General Maher Sufian al-Tikriti, a Republican Guard commander.
44. Executive Order 1303, "Protecting the Development Fund for Iraq and Certain Other Property in Which Iraq has an Interest." See S. Kretzmann and J. Valette, "Operation Oil Immunity," www.*AlterNet.org*, 2003 and www.*EarthRights International*, July 28, 2003.
45. M. Sieff, "Soaring Cost of 'Rescuing' Iraq," United Press International, July 31, 2003.
46. Gresh, "Crimes and Lies," 2003. "The US Master Plan," *Middle East Economic Digest*, London, March 14, 2003.
47. J. S. Herrington, "Make Iraq Our New Strategic Oil Reserve," *LAT*, March 23, 2003.

48. W. Vieth, "A Fund Could Spread Iraq's Oil Wealth to its Citizens," *LAT*, May 1, 2003.
49. Rumsfeld, "A New Kind of War," 2001.
50. M. Klare, "Endless Military Superiority," *The Nation*, July 14, 2002.
51. "Constant Conflict," *Parameters*, 2003;*http://carlisle-www.army.mil/usawc/Parameters/ 97summer/peters.htm*. Cf. Peters, *Fighting for the Future*.
52. J. Borger, "US planning global-reach missiles: Allies not required," *GW*, July 3–9, 2003.
53. Krishna, "An Inarticulate Imperialism," 2002. Cf. F. Rich, "The Waco Road to Baghdad," *NYT*, August 17, 2002.
54. Drury, *Leo Strauss*.
55. Kaplan, "Supremacy by Stealth," 2003.
56. Campbell and Ward, "New Battle Stations?" 2003.
57. Johnson, *Blowback*, 19.
58. S. Fidler and M. Husband, "Bush foreign policy is 'creating risks for US companies'," *FT*, November 11, 2003.

Chapter 5

1. Walton, "Will Global Advance Include the World's Poor?" 1997, 2.
2. UNDP, *HDR* 1996, 13.
3. Franklin, *Equality*.
4. Cohen and Rogers, "Can Egalitarianism Survive Internationalization?" 1997.
5. Hinsch, "Global Distributive Justice," 2001, 59.
6. Hurrell, "Global Inequality," 2001, 35.
7. According to UNDP, *HDR* 1999, 3. "At the global level, the ratio of average income of the richest country in the world to that of the poorest has risen from about 9 to 1 at the end of the nineteenth century to at least 60 to 1 today. That is, the average family in the United States is 60 times richer than the average family in Ethiopia" (Birdsall, "Life is Unfair," 1998; cf. Sutcliffe, *100 Ways of Seeing an Unequal World*, 83). ". . . the top 10 percent of the US population receives an aggregate income equal to the income of the poorest 43% of people in the world, or differently stated, the total income of the richest 25 million Americans is equal to the total income accruing to almost two billion people" (Thorbecke and Charumilind, "Economic Inequality and its Socioeconomic Impact," 2002, 1479).
8. Novak, "Concepts of Poverty," 1996, 53.
9. The Human Poverty Index is related to the Human Development Index (UNDP, *HDR* 1997, 17).
10. UNDP, *HDR* 1996, 27.
11. Ibid., 13.
12. L. Elliott and C. Denny, "Top 1% Earn as Much as the Poorest 57%," *GW*, January 18, 2002.
13. Samad, "The Present Situation in Poverty Research," 1996, 36.
14. Pogge ("Priorities of Global Justice," 2001, 7, no. 4) argues that the World Bank in its *World Development Report 2000* newly specified the international poverty line by replacing the purchasing power of one U.S. dollar in 1985 with the purchasing power of 1.08 U.S. dollar in 1993, without adequately factoring in US inflation between 1985 and 1993. "This revision thus lowers the international poverty line by 19.6 percent and thereby conveniently reduces the widely publicized number of global poor without cost to anyone."
15. "Up-to-date data are necessary to ensure that the poor and the intensity of poverty are kept visible to the public eye, but it may still be wise to put somewhat less energy into sheer measurement research, and instead turn to issues that yield more in poverty understanding" (Øyen, "Poverty Research Rethought," 1996, 10).
16. "From the United States comes the observation that, for all its usefulness, the poverty line has two major economic weaknesses: (1) it relies too heavily on annual money income, which is extremely difficult to obtain accurately from the households surveyed, and (2) the monetary income itself is an inadequate indicator of command over resources" (Wilson, "Drawing Together Some Regional Perspectives on Poverty," 1996, 21). On difficulties of measurement, see e.g., Firebaugh, "Empirics of World Income Inequality," 1999. Sutcliffe,

100 Ways of Seeing. Babones, "Population and Sample Selection Effects," 2002. Ravallion, "The Debate on Globalization, Poverty and Inequality," 2003.
17. Mishra, "North America: Poverty amidst Plenty," 1996, 482.
18. W. Sachs, *Planet Dialectics.*
19. "Poverty itself is a highly political issue where power and interest groups have had a significant (some would say overwhelming) influence on patterns of distribution and the existence of poverty" (Wilson, "Drawing Together Some Regional Perspectives on Poverty," 1996, 24).
20. R. Wade, "Winners and Losers," *The Economist,* April 28–May 4, 2001.
21. Øyen, "Poverty Research Rethought," 1996, 11.
22. Sutcliffe, *100 Ways of Seeing,* 10, 13.
23. UNDP, *HDR* 1996, 13.
24. Atkinson, "Is Rising Inequality Inevitable?" 1999, 3.
25. On the U.S., see Mishra, "North America," 1996; Burtless, "Growing American Inequality," 1999; and recent reports, e.g., R. W. Stevenson, "Income Gap Widens between Rich and Poor in 5 States and Narrows in 1," *NYT,* April 24, 2002. "In the United Kingdom ... the richest 20 percent earned seven times as much as the poorest 20 percent in 1991, compared with only four times as much in 1977. The British gap between males with the highest wage rates and those with the lowest is larger now than at any time since the 1880s, when UK statistics on wages were first gathered systematically." (Frank and Cook, *The Winner-Take-All Society,* 5). Bornschier, "Changing Income Inequality," 2002.
26. Cornia, "Liberalization, Globalization and Income Distribution," 1999, 1–2. Sarkar, "Are Poor Countries Coming Closer to the Rich?" 1999.
27. UNDP, *HDR* 1997, 3.
28. World Bank, *Knowledge for Development,* 25.
29. Wade, "Winners and Losers."
30. Walton, "Will Global Advance Include the World's Poor?" 1997, 4. Wade, "Winners and Losers."
31. "Number of Millionaires Grows in 2002," *Bangkok Post,* June 13, 2003. "Social science and politics have defined poverty as a pathological symptom of society but, illogically, not riches" (Sutcliffe, *100 Ways of Seeing,* 12).
32. World Bank, *A Better World for All.*
33. Enron fits neatly into this equation. "The company embodied the get-obscenely-rich-quick culture that grew up around the intersection of digital technology, deregulation and globalization. It rode the zeitgeist of speed, hype, novelty and swagger. Petroleum was hopelessly uncool; derivatives were hot. Companies were advised to unload the baggage of hard assets, like factories or oilfields, which hold you back in the digital long jump, and concentrate on buzz and brand" (Bill Keller, "Enron for Dummies," *NYT,* January 26, 2002).
34. Bergesen and Bata, "Global and National Inequality," 2002.
35. Atkinson, "Is Rising Inequality Inevitable?" 1999, 1.
36. Mishra, "The Welfare of Nations," 1996, 324.
37. Street, "The International Dimension," 1994.
38. Sachs, "The Strategic Significance of Global Inequality," 2001, 187, 189.
39. Wade, "Winners and Losers".
40. On new containment see Duffield, *Global Governance and the New Wars* and Chapter 6.
41. Birdsall, "Life is Unfair," 1998.
42. Gray, "After Social Democracy," 1996, 42.
43. Thorbecke and Charumilind, "Economic Inequality and its Socioeconomic Impact," 2002: 1480.
44. Park and Brat, "A Global Kuznets Curve?" 1995, 106.
45. Ibid., 128. World Bank, *The State in a Changing World.*
46. Atkinson, "Is Rising Inequality Inevitable?" 1999.
47. Smith, "Technology and the Modern World-System," 1993.
48. Smith, "Technology, Commodity Chains and Global Inequality," 1997.
49. Burkett, "Beyond the 'Information Rich and Poor,'" 2000.
50. Bhagwati, "Poverty and Reforms," 1998, 45.
51. The chapter on Macroeconomic Issues in the World Bank's *Poverty Reduction Strategy*

Sourcebook notes that "Economic growth is the single most important factor influencing poverty, and macroeconomic stability is essential for high and sustainable rates of growth." The revised version of April 2001 adds: "Moreover, growth alone is not sufficient for poverty reduction. Growth associated with progressive distributional changes will have a greater impact on poverty than growth which leaves distribution unchanged." Yet this is subject to overall macroeconomic stability and market friendly policies (http://www.worldbank.org/poverty/strategies/sourctoc.htm).

52. Ehrenreich, *Fear of Falling* and *Nickel and Dimed.*
53. Wade, "Winners and Losers"; Atkinson, "Is Rising Inequality Inevitable?" 1999.
54. Cornia, "Liberalization, Globalization and Income Distribution," 1999.
55. Mishra, "North America," 1996, 403 and 404.
56. Karlyn Bowman ("The Declining Political Potency of Economic Inequality," 2000) refers to the declining interest in economic inequality in the U.S. "Today, Democratic politicians talk about the digital divide, often as a surrogate for the old discussions of income inequality. This new formulation is less likely to irritate allies and funders on Wall Street than criticism of salaries and stock options."
57. Johnson and Schaefer, "Congress Should Slash—or Kill—Foreign Welfare," 1998. In Senator Jesse Helms's terminology foreign aid goes down "foreign rat-holes" (D. Bandow, "Shaping a New Foreign Aid Policy for Today's World," *USA Today*, 124 (2612), May 1996). On U.S. domestic and globalization policies see Chapter 8 below.
58. Nederveen Pieterse, *Development Theory.*
59. UNDP, *HDR* 1996, 17.
60. Mishra, "North America," 1996, 485.
61. Sen, *Inequality Reexamined.*
62. Wilson, "Drawing Together Some Regional Perspectives on Poverty," 1996, 30.
63. Bairoch, "Le bilan economique du colonialisme," 1980. Stavrianos (*Global Rift*) discusses several episodes of destruction and sabotage of industrial capabilities in the Third World during colonialism.
64. World Bank, *The World Bank Participation Sourcebook* and UNDP 2000.
65. On financial practices in the World Bank see e.g., Adams, "The World Bank's Finances," 1997.
66. Pogge observes that in sub-Saharan Africa a transition to democracy has only been achieved in resource-poor countries (with South Africa as an exception) ("Introduction," 2001, 19–21).
67. E.g., Connell, "Class Formation on a World Scale," 1984.
68. Sklair, *The Transnational Capitalist Class;* Cox, "Perspective on Globalization," 1996.
69. See Symposium on the Transnational Ruling Class Formation Thesis, *Science & Society*, 2001–2002. Embong, "Globalization and Transnational Class Relations," 2000.
70. Wallerstein, *World Inequality.*
71. Arrighi and Drangel, "The Stratification of the World Economy," 1996.
72. Miller, "Poverty as a Cause of War," 2000.
73. This research agenda is too large to develop here and since on most of these themes there is extensive literature indicative references must suffice. In the order of the points listed, see e.g., (1) Hurrell and Woods, *Inequality, Globalization, and World Politics*; Harrod, "Global Realism," 2001; Beitz, "Does Global Inequality Matter?" 2001. (2) Wade and Veneroso, "The Asian Crisis," 1998. (3) Wade, "The United States and the World Bank," 2002. (4) McMichael, *Development and Social Change*; Chossudovsky, "Global Poverty in the Late 20th Century," 1998. (5) Chossudovsky, *The Globalization of Poverty.*
74. Ruggie, "Globalization and the Embedded Liberalism Compromise," 1997.
75. See Kapstein, "A Global Third Way," 1998–99; Deacon et al., *Global Social Policy*; Nederveen Pieterse, *Global Futures.*
76. This and the quotes below are from a table in Rowe, "Strategies for Change," 1979, 224.
77. Rocamora, "Third World Revolutionary Projects," 1992. Cf. Foran, *Future of Revolutions.*
78. Both are quoted in Buchanan, "Center and Periphery," 1985, 92.
79. Lundgren, "When I Grow Up I Want a Trans Am," 1988.
80. "In South Africa it was 'separate development'; in Australia, 'border protection and mandatory detention'" (Adele Horin, "Ruddock's Ugly World of Barbed Words and Wire,"

2002, http://www.smh.com.au/news/specials/natl/woomera/index.html). Thanks to Fazal Rizvi for this reference.

81. Sachs, "The Strategic Significance of Global Inequality," 2001, 197.
82. Linklater, "The Evolving Spheres of International Justice," 1999.
83. Pogge, "Priorities of Global Justice," 2001.
84. Pogge, "Introduction: Global Justice," 2001, 14.
85. Pogge, "Priorities," 2001, 9.
86. Pogge, "Introduction," 2001, 3.
87. UNDP, *HDR* 2003. Thorbecke and Charumilind, "Economic Inequality," 2002, 1479. Edwards, "Poverty Reduction Strategies," 2001.
88. In Hedley, "The Information Age," 1999, 86.
89. Gray, "After Social Democracy," 1996, 45.

Chapter 6

1. Friedman, *Lexus and Olive Tree*, 248.
2. "Envirowar" may be "the Great War of the 21st century": "Equating environmental violations to international aggression will become a major foreign policy issue in the twenty-first century" (Celente, *Trends 2000*, 266, 268). Cf. Barnett, *Environmental Security*. Klare, *Resource Wars*.
3. E.g., D. Campbell, "Breaking the Law is Big Business," *GW*, April 18, 1999.
4. Celente, *Trends 2000*, 291, 292.
5. Special issues of *International Sociology* (14, 4, 1999) and the *European Journal of Social Theory* (4, 1, 2001) are devoted to war and social theory.
6. Chomsky, *The New Military Humanism*.
7. McNeill, *Pursuit of Power*.
8. Gray, *Postmodern War*, 7.
9. In procurement for US military equipment the maximum weight of vehicles is now set at nineteen tons, down from seventy tons, as in the M-1A2 Abrams tank. (T. Ricks and R. Suro, "U.S. Army to Cut Reliance on Big Tanks: Flexibility demands that heavy armor give way to wheeled vehicles," *IHT*, November 17, 2000.)
10. Toffler, *War and Anti-War*, 172.
11. Toffler, *War*, 171.
12. Carter, "Adapting US Defense to Future Needs," 1999–2000, 110.
13. Rumsfeld, "Transforming the Military," 2002.
14. Laird and Mey, "The Revolution in Military Affairs," 1999.
15. T. Shanker, "New Top General Tells Legislators U.S. Will Probably Need a Larger Army," *NYT*, July 30, 2003.
16. Quoted in Toffler, *War*, 190.
17. Roles and Missions Commission, *Joint Vision 2020*.
18. Rathmell, "Mind Warriors at the Ready," 1998, 290. In Iraq, "An information grand strategy would identify the key nodes in the Iraqi political system and select from a range of tools to disrupt them" (ibid.). Key nodes identified include media and the educational system, the intelligence services, elite military units, and the ruling elite.
19. Toffler, *War*, 102, 177.
20. Myerly, *British Military Spectacle*.
21. Andrew S. Grove, CEO of Intel, wrote *Only the Paranoid Survive* (1996). In an interview he remarks that "Competition is warfare," speaks of security and "strategic inflection points" (K. Auletta, "Only the Fast Survive," *New Yorker*, October 20–27, 1997).
22. Hirsh, "Bush and the World," 2002.
23. Thus an Israeli general in the West Bank finds himself in-between Security Council criticism of Israel's "disproportionate use of force" and Israeli right-wing criticism of insufficient use of force. "If I were to use all my force I could probably wipe out Beit Jalla in a matter of hours," General Gantz said. "Should I do that? I definitely don't want to do it." His concern is Israel's lack of nonlethal weapons. (W. A. Orme, Jr., "In West Bank, an Israeli General Faces the Paradox of Military Superiority," *IHT*, November 18–19, 2000.)
24. Pfc. I. Kindblade, "We Don't Feel Like Heroes Anymore," *The Oregonian*, August 5, 2003.
25. E.g., Galbraith, *Anatomy of Power*; Mann, *Sources of Social Power*.
26. Castells, *The Information Age*.

27. Dufffield, "Network War," 2001.
28. Mulgan, *Politics* and *Connexity.*
29. Laclau and Mouffe, *Hegemony and Socialist Strategy.*
30. This is argued in Nederveen Pieterse, *Empire and Emancipation,* Ch. 14.
31. Toffler, *War,* 178.
32. Stuart Slade quoted in Toffler, *War,* 177–78 and 185.
33. Arquilla and Ronfeldt, *Networks and Netwars.*
34. Brzezinski, *The Grand Chess Game,* 210.
35. Cf. McLaughlin et al., "Evolution in Democracy-War Dynamics," 1999.
36. Toffler, *War,* 181.
37. Beeley, "Islam as a Global Political Force," 1992.
38. Schaeffer, *Understanding Globalization.*
39. Sheptycki, "The Global Cops Cometh," 1998.
40. Ohmae, *Borderless World.* Geographers in particular dissent and refer to the spatial dimensions of re-localization and re-territorialization (e.g., Brenner, "Globalisation as Reterritorialisation," 1999).
41. Freedman, "The Changing Forms of Military Conflict," 1998–99, 48.
42. Cf. e.g., Chaliand and Rageau, *Strategic Atlas* and Keegan and Wheatcroft, *Zones of Conflict.*
43. Augé, *The War of Dreams*; Foster, *Fighting Fictions.*
44. Ben-Eliezer, *The Making of Israeli Militarism*; Margalit, *Views in Review.*
45. Nandy, "The fantastic India-Pakistan Battle," 1997; Silva, *Political Violence.*
46. Booth, *Strategy and Ethnocentrism.* Farrell, "Culture and Military Power," 1998.
47. Gray, "Strategic Culture as Context," 1999, 62–9.
48. Dessler, "Constructivism," 1999, 124; Katzenstein, *The Culture of National Security.*
49. Johnston, *Cultural Realism*; Der Derian and Shapiro, *International/Intertextual Relations.*
50. Guéhenno, "The Impact of Globalization on Strategy," 1998–99, 14.
51. F. Zakaria, "The Arrogant Empire," *Newsweek,* March 24, 2003.
52. In evolutionary biology it is argued that susceptibility to ideological persuasion or "indoctrinability" is rooted in humanity's past (Eibl-Eibesfeldt and Salter, *Indoctrinability, Warfare and Ideology*). The role of cerebral and ideological influences is often overestimated and that of signs and images underrated; according to semiotic and Lacanian perspectives, ideology and language may themselves be conditioned by and stand in for deeper strata of imageries, symbols, and signs. One view holds that images and stereotypes acquire meaning by being embedded in discourse (Ryan, *Race and Ethnicity,* 98–100). A Lacanian view is that discourses and narratives arise from and cluster around images that serve as anchors and attractors at deeper strata of consciousness.
53. E.g., Allen, *The Media of Conflict*; Carruthers, *The Media of War.*
54. Freedman, "The Changing Forms of Military Conflict," 1998–99, 52.
55. Myerly, *British Military Spectacle.*
56. Lash and Urry, *Economies of Signs.*
57. Julier, *The Culture of Design.*
58. Latour, "Technology is Society Made Durable," 1991. Goonatilake, *Aborted Discovery.*
59. M. Danner, "The Battlefield in the American Mind," *NYT,* October 16, 2001.
60. Hitler, *Mein Kampf,* 459–60, quoted in Earle, *Makers of Modern Strategy,* 510–11.
61. Taylor, *War and Media*; Hammond and Herman, *Degraded Capability*; Thussu, "Media Wars," 2000.
62. Cf. Lane, *Profits from Power.*
63. Arguably what mattered was not simply technological advantage (because often technological differentials between colonial armies and local forces were not so large) but rather political and military organization (Nederveen Pieterse, *Empire and Emancipation*).
64. "Mass violence is not inevitable," *UN Chronicle,* 1998, 1, 36–7. "Low-tech weapons like assault rifles, machine guns, pistols and hand grenades have been responsible for as much as 90 percent of the world's conflict-related killings in the decade since the end of the Cold War." ("A Plague of Small Arms," *IHT,* April 11, 2001).
65. Jentleson et al., "Foreign Military Intervention," 1992.
66. Freedman, "The Changing Forms of Military Conflict," 1998–99, 52.

67. Ibid., 52.
68. In the words of Adam Roberts, "Willing the End but Not the Means," 1999.
69. Summers, *On Strategy*. Both the Korean and Vietnam wars were undeclared wars.
70. Freedman, "The Changing Forms of Military Conflict," 1998–99, 47.
71. Falk, *Predatory Globalization*, 163. Ignatieff, *Virtual War*.
72. Mike Davis ("LA: The Fire this Time," 1992) compares Los Angeles to Belfast and the West Bank.
73. The "Srebrenica syndrome" in the Netherlands is discussed in Both, *From Indifference to Entrapment*.
74. Scott, *Seeing like a State*.
75. Virilio, *War and Cinema* and *The Vision Machine*.
76. See Brown, *The Illusion of Control*.
77. A case in point is the Palestinian Authority in the West Bank and Gaza, discussed in Sayigh, "Palestinian Security Capabilities," 2000.
78. "Deterrence is mounted along borders; compellence is undertaken within borders. Deterrence is a military task; compellence is a police function" (Maynes, "Squandering Triumph," 1999, 21).
79. Ikenberry ("The Myth of Post-Cold War Chaos," 1996) views policies of dual containment of rogue states and terrorism as a continuation of the cold war order.
80. Carter, "Adapting US Defense to Future Needs," 1999–2000.
81. R. Khalaf, "Gaza's Residents Dig In as Israel Tightens Noose," *FT*, February 8, 2001.
82. The National Security Strategy of the United States of America, 2002, ii.
83. Remote sensing capabilities have been traditionally attributed to the gods. Ample theological disputes have sought to address the dilemmas arising from these capabilities; now humans enter this pantheon.
84. The West's three permanent members of the Security Council, the U.S., Britain, and France, account for 80 percent of the world's weapons sales (R. Norton-Taylor, "US Sells Half the World's Arms Exports," *GW*, October 20–27, 2000).
85. Taking constructivism into the future, these views represent applied constructivism: a combination of patterns of hegemony and collective imagination, and the reconstructive potential of social constructivism (Unger, *Social Theory*; Hajer, "Ökologische Modernisierung," 1997).
86. See "The Business of Peace—The Private Sector as a Partner in Conflict Prevention and Resolution." Report by International Alert, the Prince of Wales International Business Leaders Forum and the Council on Economic Priorities; *www.international-alert.org*. Cf. Alao, "Business and Conflict," 2001.
87. Rivero, *The Myth of Development*.
88. This follows from the wider interpretation of Chapter VII of the UN Charter. See Taylor, "Reform of the International System," 1995 and Nederveen Pieterse, *World Orders in the Making*, which also discusses reforms of humanitarian intervention.
89. Oberschall, "Shared Sovereignty," 1999.
90. Sakamoto, "An Alternative to Global Marketization," 2000. Beck, "The Terrorist Threat," 2003. Hirsh, *Law against Genocide*.
91. Ferencz, "Make Law not War," 1998.
92. Sanchez, *The Arms Bazaar*.
93. Fisher et al., *Working with Conflict*. Santa Barbara, "Preventing War," 1998.
94. Rupesinghe, *Conflict Transformation*.

Chapter 7

1. E.g., Gopal, "Images of World Society,"1998.
2. Cf. Nederveen Pieterse, *Globalization and Culture*, 30.
3. Pipes, *The Hidden Hand*.
4. Goudge, *The Whiteness of Power*.
5. Nandy, "Shamans, Savages and the Wilderness," 1989.
6. Kaplan, *The Ends of the Earth* and *The Coming Anarchy*.

7. Mandelbaum, "Is Major War Obsolete?" 1998–99, 20.
8. Mandelbaum, "Learning to Be Warless," 1999, 151.
9. Weart, *Never at War*, 22.
10. Schwartz, *Century's End*, 192.
11. Boulding, *The Future*, 199.
12. Stockton, "Defensive Development?" 1996, 147.
13. E.g., Berke et al., *Even Paranoids Have Enemies*; Spencer, "Microcybernetics as the Meta-Technology of Pure Control," 1996.
14. Pearson, *Total War 2006*.
15. Chua, *World on Fire*.
16. O'Hagan and Fry, "The Future of World Politics," 2000. Dessouki, "Globalization and the Two Spheres of Security," 1993.
17. Cf. Adelman and Suhrke, *Early Warning and Conflict Management*; Uvin, "Ethnicity and Power in Burundi and Rwanda," 1999.
18. Maynes, "Squandering Triumph," 1999.
19. Gilbert, "Soundtrack for an Uncivil Society," 1996, 6.
20. A recent version is Kagarlitsky, *New Barbarism*. Cf. Hobsbawm, "Barbarism: A User's Guide," 1994. The reification of ethnicity also resonates with American conservatives; see Ashbee, "Politics of Paleoconservatism," 2000.
21. A wider discussion is Nederveen Pieterse, "Deconstructing/ Reconstructing Ethnicity," 1997.
22. Maynes, "Squandering Triumph," 1999, 19.
23. Rajasingham, "Militarization, Population Displacement, and the Hidden Economies of Armed Conflicts," 1997.
24. Abrahamanian, "The US Media, Huntington and September 11," 2003.
25. Mitchell, "McJihad," 2002.
26. Even in critical accounts, the matrix of interpretation remains binary, as in Tariq Ali's *Clash of Fundamentalisms* and Achcar's *Clash of Barbarisms*.
27. Bodansky, *Bin Laden*. Orbach, "Usama Bin Laden and Al-Qaida," 2001; Cooley *Unholy Wars*. A general account is Johnson, *Blowback*.
28. Applebaum and Henderson, "The hinge of history," 1995, 3.
29. Peck and Tickell, "Searching for a New Institutional Fix," 1994, 286–7.

Chapter 8

1. An example of articulation is the discussion of American cold war politics and cultural policies by Saunders, *Who Paid the Piper*.
2. "The Peril of Too Much Power," *NYT*, April 9, 2002.
3. Galtung, "A structural theory of imperialism," 1971.
4. Tyrell, "American Exceptionalism in an Age of International History," 1991, 1031. Hereafter American Exceptionalism in titles is abbreviated as AE, as in the text.
5. Kammen, "The Problem of AE," 1993, 3; cf. Appleby, "Recovering America's Historic Diversity," 1992.
6. On history, see Tyrell, "AE." On labor, Davis, *Prisoners of the American Dream*; Voss, *The making of AE*. On race, Frederickson, *The black Image*; Jones, *American Work*. And in political science, Lipset, *American Exceptionalism*.
7. Lipset, *AE*, 98.
8. Kammen, "The Problem of AE." R. Fantasia and K. Voss, "US: State of the Unions," *Le Monde Diplomatique*, June 2003.
9. Quoted in Kammen, "The problem of AE," p. 7.
10. Kammen, "The problem of AE," pp. 38–9.
11. Lipset, *AE*, 33.
12. Kuttner, *The End of Laissez-Faire*, 10–1.
13. "Do As We Do, and Not As We Say," *NYT*, July 20, 2001.
14. Lipset, *AE*, 35.
15. Nettl, "The State as a Conceptual Variable," 1968, quoted in Lipset, *AE*, 40.
16. "Constitutionalism, the idea that a written constitution spells out the "supreme law of the land" and sets limits on the ruling authorities—including the legislatures elected by the

people—must be seen ... as one of the most important elements of American modernity.... In the US, the Constitution became the locus and symbol of the 'general will' " (Heideking, "The Pattern of American Modernity," 2000, 225).

17. Haley in Lipset, *AE*, 228.
18. Lipset, *AE*, 227 and Hutton, *The World We're In*, 160.
19. Lipset, *AE*, 42.
20. Greider, *Who Will Tell the People*, 11. Cf. Kuttner, *Everything for Sale*; Patterson, *The Vanishing Voter*.
21. Lipset, *AE*, 225.
22. Henwood, "Booming, Borrowing, and Consuming," 1999; cf. Henderson et al., *Calvert-Henderson Quality of Life Indicators*.
23. Klein, *No Logo*.
24. Frank and Cook, *The Winner-Take-All Society*.
25. Merton, *Social Theory and Social Structure*.
26. Quoted in Lipset, *AE*, 84, 88.
27. Ibid., 37, 228.
28. Drinnon, *Facing West*.
29. Zunz, *Why the American Century?*
30. Albert, *Capitalism against Capitalism*, 29.
31. Karsten, *The Military in America*, 457.
32. In education, "We rank 19th among the 29 nations of the OECD. Twenty-eight million Americans cannot identify the United States on a world map! ... The salaries of United States teachers are the lowest as a percentage of national income on earth" (Croose Parry, "Our World," 2000: 13).
33. Sharp, "Reel Geographies of the New World Order," 1998.
34. J. Voeten, "De militaire musical-choreografie van "42nd Street"," *NRC Handelsblad*, August 25, 2000.
35. Boggs, "Overview," 2002, 17.
36. Melman, *The Permanent War Economy*.
37. Caldicott, *The New Nuclear Danger*.
38. Bellesiles, *Arming America*.
39. Duclos, *The Werewolf Complex*.
40. T. Egan, "Hard Time: Less Crime, More Criminals," *NYT*, March 7, 1999.
41. Hallinan, *Travels in a Prison Nation*.
42. Albert, *Capitalism against Capitalism*, 47.
43. Stavrianos, *Global Rift*.
44. Cf. Nederveen Pieterse, "Continuities of Empire," in *Empire and Emancipation*.
45. Aguilera and Jackson, "The Cross-National Diversity of Corporate Governance," 2003.
46. Cf. *http://www.cwfa.org/library/nation/2000–09* and Hirsen, *The Coming Collision*.
47. Reisman, "The United States and International Institutions," 1999–2000, 65, 63.
48. Ibid., 65 and 75. "The Cold War paradigm was the United States as global policeman ... the post-Cold War paradigm is the United States as global attorney" (G.J. Wallance quoted in W. Glaberson, "U.S. Legal System becomes Global Arbiter," *NYT*, June 21, 2001). Yet its own legal standing is questionable (Scheuerman, "The Twilight of Legality?" 2000).
49. Mead, *Special Providence*.
50. Andréani, "The Disarray of US Non-Proliferation Policy," 1999–2000, 59.
51. Mamère and Warin, *Non Merci, Oncle Sam*. Meunier, "The French Exception," 2000.
52. Kuttner, *The End of Laissez-Faire*, 12.
53. "The Peril of Too Much Power," *NYT*, April 9, 2002.
54. Lipset, *AE*, 267.
55. Kaul et al., *Global Public Goods*.

Chapter 9

1. E.g., Hampdon-Turner and Trompenaars, *Seven Cultures of Capitalism*; Crouch and Streeck, *Political Economy of Modern Capitalism*; Boyer, "The Seven Paradoxes of Capitalism," 1996. Groenewegen, "Institutions of Capitalisms," 1997. Dore, *Stock Market Capitalism*; Hall and Soskice, *Varieties of Capitalism*; Hodgson et al., *Capitalism in Evolution*.

2. Galtung, "Structure, Culture and Intellectual Style," 1981.
3. Whitley, *Divergent Capitalisms*; Dore, *Stock Market Capitalism*.
4. Similar scenarios apply to cultural change and modernities (as argued in Nederveen Pieterse, *Globalization and Culture*).
5. Whitley, *Divergent Capitalisms*, 3.
6. "... companies may shift particular activities to other nations in order to secure the advantages that the institutional frameworks of their political economies offer for pursuing those activities. Thus, companies may move some of their activities to liberal market economies, not simply to lower labor costs, but to secure access to institutional support for radical innovation. This helps to explain why Nissan locates design facilities in California, Deutsche Bank acquires subsidiaries in Chicago and London, and German pharmaceutical firms open research labs in the United States. Conversely, companies may locate other activities in coordinated market economies in order to secure access to quality control, skill levels, and capacities for incremental innovation that their institutional frameworks offer. General Motors locates its engine plants in Düsseldorf rather than in Spain. Over time, corporate movements of this sort should reinforce differences in national institutional frameworks, as firms that have shifted their operations to benefit from particular institutions seek to retain them" (Hall and Soskice, *Varieties of Capitalism*, 57).
7. Sansoucy, "La Bretagne et l'Investissement étranger," 2002.
8. According to Susan Strange, "the very sources of US hegemonic power—its unrivalled military capabilities, its capacity through the acceptability of the dollar to borrow abroad but in its own currency, its guardianship of the world's largest single, rich market—have insulated it from the degrees of vulnerability experienced by others." She notes "a growing asymmetry of regulatory power among the governments of capitalist countries. The government of the USA exercises a global reach over enterprises and markets in other countries" ("The Future of Global Capitalism," 1997, 189).
9. Financial services "have replaced traditional branches of manufacturing as a major focus of international competitiveness (today you could buy the whole American steel industry with 5 percent of the shares of America Online)" (Dore, *Stock Market Capitalism*, 3). That is, until AOL restated its earnings.
10. K. Phillips, "The Cycles of Financial Scandal," *NYT*, July 17, 2002.
11. Stakeholder capitalism is a critical counterpoint, but has been watered down by New Labour (Dore, *Stock Market Capitalism*).
12. Pagano, "Information Technology," 2001.
13. See Brenner, *The Boom and the Bubble*.
14. Nederveen Pieterse, *Globalization and Culture*.
15. By late 2003 this includes energy companies (Enron, Dynegy, Halliburton, First Energy), communications (Tyco, Global Crossing, WorldCom, Adelphia, AOL TimeWarner, Qwest), accounting firms (Andersen, KPMG), banks (Merrill Lynch, City Group, CS First Boston, JP Morgan Chase, Salomon), mutual funds and firms such as ImClone, Cisco, Xerox, K-Mart, Martha Stewart Living Omnimedia, HealthSouth, Rite Aid, Tenet, etc. While more and more firms restate their earnings, now facing financial turmoil are states and local governments.
16. Akerlof and Romer, "Looting," 1993, 2.
17. J. Madrick, "Economic Scene," *NYT*, July 11, 2002.
18. J. Balzar, "Enron: A Scandal So Good that it Hurts," *LAT*, January 18, 2002.
19. Phillips, *Wealth and Democracy*.
20. L. Uchitelle, "Looking for Ways to Make Deregulation Keep its Promises," *NYT*, July 28, 2002.
21. Palast, *The Best Democracy Money Can Buy*.
22. E.g., Mitchell, "No Factories, No Problems," 1999.
23. These are quotes from *New York Times* reports.
24. E. Iritani, "After Scandals, US Economic Model is Hard to Sell Abroad," *IHT*, July 8, 2002. Cf. "Pourquoi le capitalisme doit changer," 2002.
25. Mann, "Is the U.S. Current Account Deficit Sustainable?" 2000.
26. Spannaus, "First Casualty of an Iraq War Will Be the U.S. Dollar," 2003.
27. McKinnon, "The International Dollar Standard," 2001.

28. M. Wolf, "An Unsustainable Black Hole," *FT*, February 26, 2002. Foreign investors own 36 percent of American government debt and 18 percent of corporate debt.

29. According to *Forbes* magazine, smart money in America now goes short on the dollar and long on the euro. "In a postbubble world 'Buy America' is suddenly seen as a risky alternative" (R. Lenzner, "Greenback on its Back," *Forbes*, August 12, 2002).

30. "Sliding Dollar's Fate May Be Decided in Asia," *WSJ*, January 20, 2003. In 2003 Asian central bankers began to move into other currencies, especially the euro, and gold (whose price has jumped by 31 percent since 9/11). The Russian Central Bank (with reserves of almost $50 billion) and the Bank of China (with $400 billion in assets) sounded similar warnings. Spannaus, "First Casualty of an Iraq War," 2003.

31. "Asia Could Shape Fate of the Dollar," *Asian WSJ*, June 23, 2003.

32. *Observer*, January 26, 2003, quoted in Spannaus, "First Casualty of an Iraq War," 2003.

33. A. Lieven, "The Empire strikes Back," *The Nation*, July 7, 2003.

34. Dore, *Stock Market Capitalism*, 221.

35. Ibid., 10.

36. This involves shifting from the American GAAP to IAS. P. Meller, "International Accounting Rules Urged on U.S.," *NYT*, February 22, 2002.

37. Cf. Bello et al., *Siamese Tragedy*, 248.

38. Ibid. and Cuperus, "Social Justice and Globalization," 2001.

39. Wade, "Japan, the World Bank and the Art of Paradigm Maintenance," 1996.

40. White et al., "Welfare Orientalism," 1997, 17–8. Kristof and WuDunn, *Thunder from the East*.

41. Institutional dimensions of Asian-European relations have been extensively discussed in the context of the Asia-Europe meetings. (Chirathivat et al., *Asia-Europe on the Eve of the 21st Century*; Manivannan, *Social Justice, Democracy and Alternative Politics*; Brennan et al., *ASEM Trading New Silk Routes*.)

42. Rüland, "The EU as Inter-regional Actor," 2001, 47–8.

43. "Human Security in a New World Disorder," 2002. Tow et al., *Asia's Emerging Regional Order*.

44. Discussed in Nederveen Pieterse, *Development Theory*, Ch. 8.

45. Rocamora, "Asia-Europe Economic Relations," 1995, 38.

46. " . . . what is badly missing thus far is a comprehensive strategy for an effective transnational cooperation that can cope with economic globalization through setting and enforcing worldwide social, financial and ecological standards for its functioning" (Meyer, "Success and Limitations of Western Social Democracy," 2001, 57). On transnational social policy, see Deacon et al., *Global Social Policy*.

47. A wider discussion is Nederveen Pieterse, "Many Doors to Multiculturalism," 2003.

48. Abdel-Malek, "Historical Initiative: the New 'Silk Road'," 1994.

49. Brzezinski, *The Grand Chess Game*, xiv.

50. Frank, "The Centrality of Central Asia," 1992, 51.

51. Dosch, "ASEAN-EU Relations," 2001.

52. I. Wallerstein, "The Righteous War," Commentary 107, February 15, 2003, *http://fbc.binghamton.edu/commentr.htm*

53. Hirsh, "Bush and the World," 2002, 30.

54. E.g., Todd, *Après l'Empire*; Wallerstein, *Decline of American Power*.

Bibliography

Abdel-Malek, A. "Historical Initiative: The New 'Silk Road'." *Review* 17, 4 (1994): 451–99.

Abrahamanian, Ervand. "The US Media, Huntington and September 11." *Third World Quarterly* 24, 3 (2003): 529–44.

Achcar, G. *The Clash of Barbarisms: Sept 11 and the Making of the New World Disorder*. New York: Monthly Review Press, 2003.

Adams, Patricia. "The World Bank's Finances: An International Debt Crisis." In *Globalization and the South*, edited by C. Thomas and P. Wilkin. London: Macmillan, 1997, 163–83.

Adelman, H. and A. Suhrke. *Early Warning and Conflict Management*, study 2. *The International Response to Conflict and Genocide: Lessons from the Rwanda Experience*. Copenhagen: Steering Committee of the Joint Evaluation of Emergency Assistance to Rwanda, 1996.

Aguilera, R., and G. Jackson. "The Cross-National Diversity of Corporate Governance: Dimensions and Determinants." *Academy of Management Review* 28 (3) (2003).

Ahmed, Nafeez Mossadeq. *The War on Freedom: US Complicity in 9–11 and the New Imperialism*. Joshua Tree, CA: Tree of Life Books, 2003.

Akerlof, G. A. and P. M. Romer. "Looting: The Economic Underworld of Bankruptcy for Profit." *Brookings Papers on Economic Activity* 2 (1993): 1–74.

Alao, A. "Business and Conflict." *Conflict, Security & Development Group Bulletin* 11 (2001): 8–11.

Albert, M. *Capitalism against Capitalism*. London: Whurr, 1993.

Ali, Tariq. *A Clash of Fundamentalisms*. London: Verso, 2002.

Allen, T. (ed.). *The Media of Conflict: War Reporting and Representations of Ethnic Violence*. London: Zed, 1999.

Ambrose, S. E. *Rise to Globalism: American Foreign Policy since 1938*. 3rd rev. edn., Harmondsworth: Pelican, 1983.

Anderla, G., A. Dunning, and S. Forge. *Chaotics: An Agenda for Business and Society for the 21st Century*. London: Adamantine Press, 1997.

Andréani, G. "The Disarray of US Non-Proliferation Policy." *Survival* 41, 4 (1999–2000): 42–61.

Anonymous, "Mass Violence is not Inevitable." *UN Chronicle* 1 (1998): 36–7.

Applebaum, R. P. and J. Henderson. "The Hinge of History: Turbulence and Transformation in the World Economy." *Competition & Change* 1, 1 (1995): 1–12.

Applebome, Peter. *Dixie Rising: How the South Is Shaping American Values, Politics and Culture*. New York: Times Books, 1996.

Appleby, Joyce. "Recovering America's Historic Diversity: Beyond Exceptionalism." *Journal of American History* 79 (1992): 419–31.

Arquilla, J. and D. Ronfeldt. *Networks and Netwars: The Future of Terror, Crime and Militancy.* Santa Monica, CA: Rand and National Defense Research Institute, 2001.

Arrighi, G. and J. Drangel. "The Stratification of the World Economy: An Exploration of the Semi-Peripheral Zone." *Review* 10 (1996): 9–74.

Atkinson, A. B. "Is Rising Inequality Inevitable? A Critique of the Transatlantic Consensus." Helsinki, UNU WIDER Annual Lectures #3, 1999.

Augé, M. *The War of Dreams: Studies in Ethno Fiction.* London: Pluto, 1999.

Babones, S. J. "Population and Sample Selection Effects in Measuring Internal Income Inequality." *Journal of World-Systems Research* 8, 1 (2002): 8–29.

Bacevich, A. J. *American Empire: The Realities and Consequences of US Diplomacy.* Cambridge, MA: Harvard University Press, 2002.

Bairoch, P. "Le bilan économique du colonialisme: mythes et réalités." In *History and Underdevelopment,* edited by L. Blussé, H. L Wesseling, and G. D. Winius. Leiden: Leiden University, 1980, 29–41.

Baran, P. *The Political Economy of Growth.* Harmondsworth: Penguin, 1973.

Barber, B. J. *Jihad vs. McWorld.* New York: Ballantine Books, 1996.

Barnet, R. J., and J. Cavanagh. *Global Dreams: Imperial Corporations and the New World Order.* New York: Simon & Schuster, 1994.

Beck, U. "The Terrorist Threat: World Risk Society Revisited." *Theory, Culture & Society* 19, 4 (2003): 39–55.

Beeley, B. "Islam as a Global Political Force." In *Global Politics,* edited by A. G. McGrew, et al. Cambridge: Polity, 1992, 293–311.

Begala, P. *It's Still the Economy, Stupid: George W. Bush, the GOP's CEO.* New York: Simon & Schuster, 2002.

Beinin, Joel. "Pro-Israel Hawks and the Second Gulf War." *Middle East Report* April 6 (2003).

Beitz, C. R. "Does Global Inequality Matter?" *Metaphilosophy* 32, 1 (2001): 95–112.

Bellesiles, M. A. *Arming America: The Origins of a National Gun Culture.* New York: Random House, 2000.

Bello, W. *Deglobalization: Ideas for a New World Economy.* London: Zed, 2003.

Bello, W., S. Cunningham, and Li Kheng Po. *A Siamese Tragedy: Development and Disintegration in Modern Thailand.* London and Bangkok: Zed and Focus on the Global South, 1998.

Ben-Eliezer, U. *The Making of Israeli Militarism.* Bloomington: Indiana University Press, 1998.

Bergesen, A. J., and M. Bata. "Global and National Inequality: Are They Connected?" *Journal of World-Systems Research* 8, 1 (2002): 130–44.

Berke, J. H., S. Pierides, A. Sabbadini, and S. Schneider. *Even Paranoids Have Enemies: New Perspectives on Paranoia and Persecution.* London: Routledge, 1998.

Berkowitz, Bruce. *The New Face of War.* New York: Free Press, 2003.

Berman, Paul. *Terror and Liberalism.* New York: Norton, 2003.

Bhagwati, Jagdish. "Poverty and Reforms: Friends or Foes?" *Journal of International Affairs* 52, 1 (1998): 33–45.

Birdsall, Nancy "Life is Unfair: Inequality in the World." *Foreign Policy* 111 (summer 1998): 73–94.

Blum, W. *Rogue State: A Guide to the World's Only Superpower.* London: Zed, 2001.

Bodansky, Y. *Bin Laden.* New York: Forum, 2001.

Boggs, Carl. "Overview: Globalization and the New Militarism." *New Political Science* 24 (2002): 9–20.

Boot, M. *The Savage Wars of Peace: Small Wars and the Rise of American Power.* New York: Basic Books, 2002.

Booth, K. *Strategy and Ethnocentrism.* London: Croom Helm, 1979.

Bornschier, V. "Changing Income Inequality in the Second Half of the 20th Century." *Journal of World-Systems Research* 8, 1 (2002): 100–29.

Bosch, Juan. *Pentagonism: A Substitute for Imperialism.* New York: Grove, 1968.

Both, N. *From Indifference to Entrapment: the Netherlands and the Yugoslav Crisis, 1990–1995.* Amsterdam: Amsterdam University Press, 2000.

Boulding, K. E. and E. Boulding. *The Future.* London: Sage, 1995.

Boyer, Robert. The Seven Paradoxes of Capitalism. Paris: CEPREMAP # 9620, 1996.

Boyle, Francis A. The Criminality of Nuclear Deterrence. Atlanta, GA: Clarity Press, 2002.

Brennan, B., E. Heijmans, and P. Vervest (eds.). ASEM Trading New Silk Routes, beyond Geopolitics and Geo-economics: Towards a New Relationship between Asia and Europe. Amsterdam and Bangkok: Transnational Institute and Focus on the Global South, 1997.

Brenner, N. "Globalisation as Reterritorialisation: The Re-scaling of Urban Governance in the European Union." Urban Studies 36, 3 (1999): 431–51.

Brenner, Robert. The Boom and the Bubble: The US in the World Economy. London: Verso, 2002.

Brooks, S., and W. Wohlforth. "American Primacy in Perspective." Foreign Affairs 81, 4 (2002): 20–33.

Brown, Seyom. The Illusion of Control: Force and Foreign Policy in the 21st Century. Washington, DC: The Brookings Institution, 2003.

Brzezinski, Zbigniew K. The Grand Chess Game: American Primacy and Its Geostrategic Imperatives. New York: Basic Books, 1997.

Buchanan, Keith. "Center and Periphery: Reflections on the Irrelevance of a Billion Human Beings." Monthly Review 37 (July–August, 1985): 86–97.

Burkett, I. "Beyond the 'Information Rich and Poor': Understandings of Inequality in Globalising Informational Economies." Futures 32, 7 (2000): 679–94.

Burtless, G. "Growing American Inequality: Sources and Remedies." In Setting National Priorities: The 2000 Election and Beyond, edited by H. J. Aaron and R. D. Reischauer. Washington, DC: Brookings Institution Press, 1999, 137–66.

Caldicott, Helen. The New Nuclear Danger: George W. Bush's Military Industrial Complex. New York: New Press, 2002.

Campbell, K. M., and C. J. Ward. "New Battle Stations?" Foreign Affairs 82, 5 (2003): 95–103.

Carrier, James G. "Introduction." In Meanings of the Market: The Free Market in Western Culture, edited by James G. Carrier. Oxford: Berg, 1997, 1–67.

Carruthers, S. L. The Media at War: Communication and Conflict in the 20th Century. London: Macmillan, 1999.

Carter, A. B. "Adapting US Defence to Future Needs." Survival 41, 4 (1999–2000): 101–22.

Castells, M. The Information Age: Economy, Society and Culture. Oxford: Blackwell, 1996.

Celente, G. Trends 2000. New York: Warner Books, 1997.

Chaliand, G., and J-P. Rageau. Strategic Atlas: World Geopolitics. Harmondsworth: Penguin, 1985.

Chalk, P. Non-Military Security and Global Order: The Impact of Extremism, Violence and Chaos on National and International Security. London: Macmillan, 2000.

Chirathivat, S., F. Knipping, P. H. Lassen, and Chia Siow Yue (eds.). Asia-Europe on the Eve of the 21st Century. Bangkok: Centre for European Studies at Chulalongkorn University, and Singapore: Institute of Southeast Asian Studies, 2001.

Chomsky, Noam. The New Military Humanism. Cambridge, MA: South End Press, 1999.

———. Year 501: The Conquest Continues. Cambridge, MA: South End Press, 1993.

Chossudovsky, M. "Global Poverty in the Late 20th Century." Journal of International Affairs 52, 1 (1998): 293–311.

Chossudovsky, M. The Globalization of Poverty: Impacts of IMF and World Bank Reforms. London: Zed, 1997.

Chua, Amy. World on Fire. New York: Doubleday, 2003.

Cockburn, Leslie. Out of Control. New York: Atlantic Monthly Press, 1987.

Cohen, J. and J. Rogers. "Can Egalitarianism Survive Internationalization?" Bonn: Max Planck Institute for the Study of Societies. Working Paper 97/2, 1997.

Confessore, N. "G.I. Woe." The Washington Monthly (March 2003): 35–42.

Connell, R.W. "Class Formation on a World Scale." Review 7 (3) (1984): 407–40.

Conniff, R. The Natural History of the Rich: A Field Guide. New York: Norton, 2002.

Connors, M. The Race to the Intelligent State: Charting the Global Information Economy in the 21st Century. Oxford: Capstone, 1997.

Cooley, J. Unholy Wars: Afghanistan, America and International Terrorism. London: Pluto, 1999.

Cornia, G. A. Liberalization, Globalization and Income Distribution. Helsinki: UNU Wider Working Paper 157, 1999.

Cox, R. W. "A Perspective on Globalization." In *Globalization: Critical Reflections*, edited by J. Mittelman. Boulder, CO: Lynne Rienner, 1996, 21–30.

Croose Parry, R-M. "Our World on the Threshold of the New Millennium." *WFSF Futures Bulletin* 26, 1 (2000): 12–5.

Crouch, Colin and Wolfgang Streeck (eds.). *Political Economy of Modern Capitalism: Mapping Convergence and Diversity.* London: Sage, 1997.

Cummings, S. D. *The Dixiefication of America: The American Odyssey into the Conservative Economic Trap.* Westport, CT: Praeger, 1998.

Cuperus, R. "Social Justice and Globalization." In *Social Justice, Democracy and Alternative Politics,* edited by Manivannan, 2001, 91–106.

Davis, Mike. "LA: The Fire this Time." *Covert Action Information Bulletin* 41 (1992): 12–21.

———. *Prisoners of the American Dream.* London: Verso, 1986.

Deacon, B., M. Hulse, and P. Stubbs. *Global Social Policy.* London: Sage, 1998.

Denzin, N. K., and Y. S. Lincoln (eds.). *9/11 in American Culture.* Walnut Creek, CA: Altamira Press, 2003.

Der Derian, J. and M. J. Shapiro (eds.). *International/Intertextual Relations: Postmodern Readings of World Politics.* New York: Maxwell Macmillan International, 1989.

Dessler, D. "Constructivism within a Positivist Social Science." *Review of International Studies* 25, 1 (1999): 123–37.

Dessouki, A. E. H. "Globalization and the Two Spheres of Security." *Washington Quarterly* 16, 4 (1993): 109–17.

Dore, R. P. *Stock Market Capitalism/Welfare Capitalism: Japan and Germany versus the Anglo-Saxons.* Oxford: Oxford University Press, 2000.

Dosch, J. "The ASEAN-EU Relations: An Emerging Pillar of the New International Order?" In *Asia-Europe on the Eve of the 21st Century,* edited by Chirathivat et al. 2001, 57–72.

Doyle, M. *Empires.* Ithaca, NY: Cornell University Press, 1986.

Drinnon, R. *Facing West: The Metaphysics of Indian-Hating and Empire-Building.* Minneapolis: University of Minnesota Press, 1980.

Drury, Shadia B. *Leo Strauss and the American Right.* Houndmills: Macmillan, 1997.

Duclos, D. *The Werewolf Complex: America's Fascination with Violence.* Oxford: Berg, 1998.

Duffield, M. "Network War." *Conflict, Security & Development Group Bulletin* 11 (2001): 5–7.

———. *Global Governance and the New Wars: The Merging of Development and Security.* London: Zed, 2001.

Dumbrell, John. "Unilateralism and 'America First'? President George W. Bush's Foreign Policy." *The Political Quarterly* 73 (2002): 279–87.

Dyer, Joel. *The Perpetual Prisoner Machine: How America Profits from Crime.* Boulder, CO: Westview Press, 1999.

Earle, E. M. (ed.). *Makers of Modern Strategy.* Princeton, NJ: Princeton University Press (orig. edn. 1943), 1971.

Editors. "More Security for Less Money." *The Bulletin of the Atomic Scientists* (Sep/Oct 1995): 34–9.

Edwards, Chris. "Poverty Reduction Strategies: Reality or Rhetoric?" The Hague, Institute of Social Studies seminar paper, 2001.

Ehrenreich, B. *Nickel and Dimed: On (Not) Getting by in America.* New York: Henry Holt, 2001.

———. *Fear of Falling: The Inner Life of the Middle Class.* New York: Harper Perennial, 1990.

Eibl-Eibesfeldt, I., and F. K. Salter (eds.). *Indoctrinability, Warfare and Ideology.* Oxford: Berg, 1999.

Embong, Abdul R. "Globalization and Transnational Class Relations: Some Problems of Conceptualization." *Third World Quarterly* 21, 6 (2000): 989–1000.

Falk, Richard. *Predatory Globalization.* Cambridge: Polity, 1999.

Farrell, T. "Culture and Military Power." *Review of International Studies* 24 (1998): 407–16.

Ferencz, B. B. "Make Law not War." *The World Today* 54, 6 (1998): 152–53.

Ferguson, N. *Empire: The Rise and Demise of the British World Order and the Lessons for Global Power.* New York: Basic Books, 2002.

Fieldhouse, D. K. *Economics and Empire 1830–1914.* London: Weidenfeld and Nicolson, 1973.

———. *The Theory of Capitalist Imperialism.* London: Longman, 1967.

———. *The Colonial Empires.* New York: Delacorte, 1965.

Fine, Ben. "Economics Imperialism and the New Development Economics as Kuhnian Paradigm Shift?" *World Development* 30, 12 (2002): 2057–70.

Finnegan, William. "The Economics of Empire: Notes on the Washington Consensus, *Harper's Magazine* 306 (May 2003): 41–54.

Firebaugh, G. "Empirics of World Income Inequality." *American Journal of Sociology* 104 (1999): 1597–630.

Fisher, S., D. I. Abdi, J. Ludin, R. Smith, and S. Williams. *Working with Conflict: Skills and Strategies for Action.* London: Zed, 2000.

Foran, J. (ed.). *The Future of Revolutions: Rethinking Radical Change in the Age of Globalization.* London: Zed, 2003.

Foster, K. *Fighting Fictions: War, Narrative and National Identity.* London: Pluto, 1999.

Frank, A. G. "The Centrality of Central Asia." *Bulletin of Concerned Asian Scholars* 24, 2 (1992): 50–74.

Frank, R. H., and P. J. Cook *The Winner-Take-All Society.* New York: Free Press, 1995.

Frank, Tom. *One Market under God: Extreme Capitalism, Market Populism and the End of Economic Democracy.* New York: Doubleday, 2000.

Franklin, Jane (ed.). *Equality.* London: Institute for Public Policy Research, 1997.

Frederickson, G. M. *The Black Image in the White Mind: The Debate on African-American Character and Destiny, 1817–1914.* Middletown, CT: Wesleyan University Press, 1971.

Freedman, L. "The Changing Forms of Military Conflict." *Survival* 40, 4 (1998–99): 39–56.

Friedman, T. L. *The Lexus and the Olive Tree: Understanding Globalization.* 2nd edn. New York: Anchor Books, 2000.

Fukuyama, F. *The End of History and the Last Man.* New York: Free Press, 1992.

Furedi, F. *The New Ideology of Imperialism.* London: Pluto, 1994.

Galbraith, J. K. *The Anatomy of Power.* Boston: Houghton Mifflin, 1983.

———. *Annals of an Abiding Liberal.* New York: New American Library, 1979.

Galtung, J. "A Structural Theory of Imperialism." *Journal of Peace Research* 9, 2 (1971).

———. "Structure, Culture and Intellectual Style." *Social Science Information* 206, 6 (1981): 816–56.

Gaonkar, Dilip P. "On Alternative Modernities." *Public Culture* 11, 1 (1999): 1–18.

George, Susan. *How the Other Half Dies: The Real Reasons for World Hunger.* 2nd edn. Harmondsworth: Penguin, 1977.

Giddens, A. *The Consequences of Modernity.* Stanford, CA: Stanford University Press, 1990.

Gilbert, J. "Soundtrack for an Uncivil Society: Rave Culture, the Criminal Justice Act and the Politics of Modernity." *New Formations* 31 (1996): 5–22.

Gilpin, R. *The Challenge of Global Capitalism: The World Economy in the 21st Century.* Princeton, NJ: Princeton University Press, 2000.

Glennon, M. J. "Why the Security Council Failed." *Foreign Affairs* 82, 3 (2003): 16–35.

Goldsmith, E. "Development as Colonialism." *World Affairs* 6, 2 (2002): 18–37.

Goonatilake, S. *Aborted Discovery: Science and Creativity in the Third World.* London: Zed, 1984.

Gopal, Sarvepalli. "Images of World Society: A Third World View," *Social Science Information Journal* 50, 3 (1998): 375–380 (reprint of 1982).

Goudge, P. *The Whiteness of Power: Racism in Third World Development and Aid.* London: Lawrence & Wishart, 2003.

Gray, C. H. *Postmodern War: The New Politics of Conflict.* New York: Guilford Press, 1997.

Gray, C. S. "Strategic Culture as Context: The First Generation of Theory Strikes Back." *Review of International Studies* 25, 1 (1999): 49–69.

Gray, John. "After Social Democracy and beyond Anglo-Saxon Capitalism." *New Perspectives Quarterly* 13, 4 (1996): 40–6.

Greider, W. *Who Will Tell the People? The Betrayal of American Democracy.* New York: Simon & Schuster, 1992.

Gresh, A. "Crimes and Lies in 'Liberated' Iraq." *Le Monde Diplomatique,* May 2003.

Groenewegen, J. "Institutions of Capitalisms: American, European, and Japanese Systems Compared." *Journal of Economic Issues* 31, 2 (1997): 333–47.

Grossman, Lt. Col. D. *On Killing: The Psychological Cost of Learning to Kill in War and Society.* New York: Little, Brown, 1996.

Grove, D. John (ed.). *Global Inequality: Political and Socioeconomic Perspectives.* Boulder, CO: Westview Press, 1979.

Gruber, L. *Ruling the World: Power Politics and the Rise of Supranational Institutions.* Princeton, NJ: Princeton University Press, 2000.

Guéhenno, J-M. "The Impact of Globalisation on Strategy." *Survival* 40, 4 (1998–99): 5–19.

Guyatt, N. *Another American Century? The United States and the World after 2000.* London: Zed, 2000.

Haass, R. N. "What to Do with American Primacy?" In *The Global Agenda: Issues and Perspectives,* edited by C. W. Kegley Jr and E. R. Wittkopf. 6th edn. New York: McGraw-Hill, 2001, 147–57.

Hajer, M. A. "Okologische Modernisierung als Sprachspiel." *Soziale Welt* 48 (1997): 107–32.

Halabi, Yakub. "Orientalism and US Democratization Policy in the Middle East." *International Studies,* 36, 4 (1999): 375–92.

Hall, P.A. and D. Soskice (eds.). *Varieties of Capitalism: The Institutional Foundations of Comparative Advantage.* Oxford: Oxford University Press, 2001.

Halliday, F. *The Second Cold War.* London: Verso, 1986.

Hallinan, J. T. *Travels in a Prison Nation.* New York: Random House, 2000.

Hammond, P. and E. S. Herman (eds.). *Degraded Capability: The Media and the Kosovo Crisis.* London: Pluto, 2000.

Hampdon-Turner, C. and F. Trompenaars. *Seven Cultures of Capitalism.* New York: Doubleday, 1993.

Hardt, M. and A. Negri. *Empire.* Cambridge, MA: Harvard University Press, 2000.

Harrod, J. "Global Realism: Unmasking Power in the International Political Economy." In *Critical Theory and World Politics,* edited by R. Wyn Jones. Boulder, CO: Lynne Rienner, 2001.

Harvey, D. "The 'New' Imperialism: Accumulation by Dispossession." In *Socialist Register: The New Imperial Challenge,* edited by L. Panitch and Colin Leys. London: Merlin Press, 2004, 63–87.

———. *The Condition of Postmodernity.* Oxford: Blackwell, 1989.

Hedley, R. A. "The Information Age: Apartheid, Cultural Imperialism, or Global Village?" *Social Science Computer Review* 17, 1 (2002): 78–87.

Heideking, J. "The Pattern of American Modernity from the Revolution to the Civil War." *Daedalus* 129, 1 (2000): 219–48.

Henderson, H. "Changing Paradigms and Indicators: Implementing Equitable, Sustainable and Participatory Development." In *Development: New Paradigms and Principles for the 21st Century,* edited by M. J. Griesgraber and B. G. Gunter. London: Pluto, 1996, 103–36.

Henderson, H. "Fighting Economism." *Futures,* 28, 6–7 (1996): 580–83.

Henderson, H., J. Lickerman, and P. Flynn (eds.). *Calvert-Henderson Quality of Life Indicators.* Bethesda, MD: Calvert Group, 2000.

Henwood, D. "Booming, Borrowing, and Consuming: The US Economy in 1999." *Monthly Review* 51, 3 (1999).

Hersh, Seymour M. "Selective Intelligence." *New Yorker,* May 6, 2003.

Hervey, J. L. and L. S. Merkel. "A Record Current Account Deficit: Causes and Implications." *Economic Perspectives* 24, 4 (2000): 3–12.

Hinsch, W. "Global distributive justice." *Metaphilosophy* 32, 1–2 (2001): 58–78.

Hirsen, J. L. *The Coming Collision: Global Law vs. US Liberties.* Lafayette, LA: Huntington House, 1999.

Hirsh, D. *Law against Genocide: Cosmopolitan Trials.* London: Glasshouse Press, 2003.

Hirsh, M. "Bush and the World." *Foreign Affairs* 81, 5 (2002): 18–43.

Hitler, A. *Mein Kampf.* Translated by R. Manheim. Boston: Houghton Mifflin (orig. edn. 1925), 1971.

Hobsbawm, E. J. "Barbarism: A User's Guide." *New Left Review* 206 (1994): 44–54.

Hodgson, G. M., M. Itoh, and N. Yokokawa (eds.). *Capitalism in Evolution: Global Contentions, East and West.* Cheltenham and Northampton, MA: Elgar, 2001.

Hoffman, Bruce. "Lessons of 9/11." Santa Monica, CA: RAND Corporation, 2002.

Hoffman, S. *World Disorders: Troubled Peace in the Post-Cold War Era.* Lanham, MD: Rowman & Littlefield, 1998.

Howe, I. (ed.). *25 Years of Dissent: An American Tradition.* New York: Methuen, 1979.

Human Security in a New World Disorder, *Asian Exchange,* 17–18, 2–1 (2002).

Huntington, S. P. "The Lonely Superpower." *Foreign Affairs* 78, 2 (1999): 35–49.

———. *The Clash of Civilizations.* New York: Simon and Schuster, 1996.

Hurrell, A. "Global Inequality and International Institutions." *Metaphilosophy* 32, 1–2 (2001): 34–57.

Hurrell, A. and N. Woods. "Globalisation and Inequality." *Millennium* 24, 3 (1995): 447–70.

———— (eds.). *Inequality, Globalization, and World Politics.* Oxford: Oxford University Press, 1999.

Hutton, W. and A. Giddens (eds.). *Global Capitalism.* New York: New Press, 2000.

Hutton, Will. *The World We're In.* London: Little, Brown, 2002.

————. *The State We're In.* London: Jonathan Cape, 1995.

Ignatieff, M. *Virtual War.* London: Chatto & Windus, 2000.

Ikenberry, G. J. "The Myth of Post-Cold War Chaos." *Foreign Affairs* 75, 3 (1996): 79–91.

————. "America's Imperial Ambition." *Foreign Affairs* 81, 5 (2002): 44–60.

Jansson, David R. "Internal Orientalism in America: W. J. Cash's *The Mind of the South* and the Spatial Construction of American National Identity." *Political Geography* 22 (2003): 293–316.

Jentleson, B. W., A. E. Levite, and L. Berman. "Foreign Military Intervention in Perspective." In *Foreign Military Intervention: the Dynamics of Protracted Conflict*, edited by B. W. Jentleson, A. E. Levite, and L. Berman. New York: Columbia University Press, 1992.

Johnson, B. T., and B. D. Schaefer. "Congress Should Slash—or Kill—Foreign Welfare." *Human Events* 54, 22 (1998): 24–7.

Johnson, Chalmers. "American Militarism and Blowback: The Costs of Letting the Pentagon Dominate Foreign Policy." *New Political Science* 24, 1 (2002): 21–38.

————. *Blowback: The Costs and Consequences of American Empire.* New York: Henry Holt, 2000.

Johnston, A. *Cultural Realism: Strategic Culture and Grand Strategy in Chinese History.* Princeton, NJ: Princeton University Press, 1995.

Jones, J. *American Work: Four Centuries of Black and White Labor.* New York: Norton, 1998.

Julier, Guy. *The Culture of Design.* London: Sage, 2000.

Kagan, D., G. Schmitt, and T. Donnelly. *Rebuilding America's Defenses: Strategies, Forces and Resources for a New Century.* Washington, DC: PNAC, 2000.

Kagan, R. *Of Paradise and Power: America and Europe in the New World Order.* New York: Knopf, 2003.

Kagarlitsky, B. *New Realism, New Barbarism: Socialist Theory in the Era of Globalization.* London: Pluto, 1999.

Kammen, M. "The Problem of American Exceptionalism: A Reconsideration." *American Quarterly* 45, 1 (1993): 1–43.

Kaplan, R. D. "Supremacy by Stealth: Ten Rules for Managing the World." *Atlantic Monthly*, July/August, 2003.

————. *Warrior Politics: Why Leadership Demands a Pagan Ethos.* New York: Random House, 2002.

————. *The Coming Anarchy: Shattering the Dreams of the Post Cold War.* New York: Random House, 2000.

————. *The Ends of the Earth.* New York: Random House, 1996.

Kapstein, E. B. "A Global Third Way." *World Policy Journal* 15, 4 (1998–99).

Karsten, P. (ed.). *The Military in America: From the Colonial Era to the Present.* 2nd edn. New York: Free Press, 1986.

Katzenstein, P. J. (ed.). *The Culture of National Security: Norms and Identity in World Politics.* New York: Columbia University Press, 1996.

Kaul, I., I. Grunberg, and M. A. Stern (eds.). *Global Public Goods: International Cooperation in the 21st Century.* New York: Oxford University Press, 1999.

Keegan, J. and A. Wheatcroft. *Zones of Conflict: An Atlas of Future Wars.* New York: Simon & Schuster, 1986.

Keohane, R. O. and H. V. Milner (eds.). *International and Domestic Politics.* Cambridge: Cambridge University Press, 1996.

Kindleberger, C. P. "International Public Goods without International Government." *American Economic Review* 76 (1) (1986): 1–13.

Klare, M. *Resource Wars.* New York: Henry Holt, 2001.

Klein, Naomi. *No Logo.* London: Flamingo, 2000.

Kobrin, S. J. "The MAI and the Clash of Globalization." *Foreign Policy* 97–109 (Fall 1998).

Korten, David C. *When Corporations Rule the World.* London: Earthscan, 1995.

Krishna, S. "An Inarticulate Imperialism: Dubya, Afghanistan and the American Century." *Alternatives: Turkish Journal of International Relations* 1, 2 (2002).

Kristof, N. D. and S. WuDunn. *Thunder from the East: Portrait of a Rising Asia.* New York: Knopf, 2000.

Kuttner, R. *Everything for Sale.* New York: Alfred Knopf, 1998.

Kuttner, R. *The End of Laissez-Faire: National Purpose and the Global Economy after the Cold War.* New York: Alfred Knopf, 1991.

Laclau, E. and C. Mouffe. *Hegemony and Socialist Strategy.* London: Verso, 1985.

Laird, R. F., and H. M. Mey. *The Revolution in Military Affairs: Allied Perspectives.* Washington, DC: National Defense University, McNair Paper 60, 1999.

Lane, F. C. *Profits from Power: Readings in Protection Rent and Violence Controlling Enterprises.* Albany: State University of New York Press, 1979.

Lash, S. and J. Urry. *Economies of Signs and Space.* London: Sage, 1994.

Latour, B. "Technology is Society Made Durable." In *A Sociology of Monsters: Essays on Power, Technology and Domination,* edited by J. Law. London: Routledge, 1991, 103–31.

Lefever, E. W. *America's Imperial Burden: Is the Past Prologue?* Boulder, CO: Westview, 1999.

Lewis, Anthony. "Bush and Iraq." *New York Review of Books,* November 7, 2002.

Lieven, Anatol. "The Push for War." *London Review of Books* 24, 19 (October 3, 2002).

Lind, M. *Made in Texas: George W. Bush and the Southern Takeover of American Politics.* New York: Basic Books, 2003.

———. "The Israel Lobby." *Prospect,* April 2002.

Linklater, A. "The Evolving Spheres of International Justice." *International Affairs* 75, 3 (1999): 473–82.

Lipset, S. M. *American Exceptionalism: A Double-Edged Sword.* New York: Norton, 1996.

Lundgren, Nancy. "When I Grow Up I Want a Trans Am: Children in Belize Talk about Themselves and the Impact of the World Capitalist System." *Dialectical Anthropology* 13, 3 (1988): 269–76.

Mallaby, S. "The Reluctant Imperialist." *Foreign Affairs* 81, 2 (2002): 2–7.

Mamère, Noël and O. Warin. *Non merci, Oncle Sam.* Paris: Ramsay, 1999.

Mandelbaum, M. "Is Major War Obsolete?" *Survival* 40, 4 (1998–99): 20–38.

———. "Learning to be Warless." *Survival* 41, 2 (1999): 149–52.

———. *The Ideas that Conquered the World: Peace, Democracy, and Free Markets in the Twenty-First Century.* New York: Public Affairs, 2002

Manivannan, Ramu (ed.). *Social Justice, Democracy and Alternative Politics: An Asian-European Dialogue.* Bangkok: Spirit in Education Movement and Friedrich Ebert Stiftung, 2001.

Mann, Catherine L. "Is the U.S. Current Account Deficit Sustainable?" *Finance and Development,* 37, 1 (2000).

———. *Is the US Trade Deficit Sustainable?* Washington DC: Institute for International Economics, 1999.

Mann, M. *The Sources of Social Power.* Cambridge: Cambridge University Press, 1986.

Manza, Jeff. "Race and the Underdevelopment of the American Welfare State." *Theory and Society* 29, 6 (2000): 819–32.

Manzo, Kate. "The 'New' Developmentalism: Political Liberalism and the Washington Consensus." In *The American Century: Consensus and Coercion in the Projection of American Power,* edited by D. Slater and P. Taylor. Oxford: Blackwell, 1999, 98–114.

Margalit, A. *Views in Review: Politics and Culture in the State of Israel.* New York: Farrar, Straus & Giroux, 1998.

Mastanduno, Michael. "Preserving the Unipolar Moment: Realist Theories and U.S. Grand Strategy after the Cold War." *International Security* 21, 4 (1997): 49–88.

Maynes, C. W. "Squandering Triumph." *Foreign Affairs* 78, 1 (1999): 15–22.

McKinnon, R. "The International Dollar Standard and Sustainability of the U.S. Current Account Deficit." *Brookings Panel on Economic Activity: Symposium on the U.S. Current Account,* 2001.

McLaughlin, S., S. G. Mitchell, and H. Hegre. "Evolution in Democracy-War Dynamics." *The Journal of Conflict Resolution* 43, 6 (1999): 771–92.

McMichael, P. *Development and Social Change: A Global Perspective.* Thousand Oaks, CA: Pine Forge Press, 1996.

McNeill, W. *The Pursuit of Power.* Chicago: University of Chicago Press, 1982.

Mead, W. R. *Special Providence: American Foreign Policy and How It Changed the World.* New York: Knopf, 2001.

Mearsheimer, John. *The Tragedy of Great Power Politics.* New York: Norton, 2002.

Melman, S. *The Permanent War Economy: American Capitalism in Decline.* New York: Simon and Schuster, 1974.

Merton, R. K. *Social Theory and Social Structure.* Glencoe, IL: Free Press, 1957.

Meunier, Sophie. "The French Exception." *Foreign Affairs* 79, 4 (2000): 104–16.

Meyer, T. "Success and Limitations of Western Social Democracy." In *Social Justice, Democracy and Alternative Politics,* edited by Manivannan. Bangkok, 2001, 48–58.

Miller, M. "Poverty as a Cause of War." Cambridge: 50th Pugwash Conference on Science and World Affairs, 3–8 August, 2000.

Mills, C. Wright. *The Sociological Imagination.* Harmondsworth: Penguin (orig. edn. 1959), 1970.

Mishra, R. "North America: Poverty amidst Plenty." In *Poverty,* edited by E. Øyen, et al. Oslo: Scandinavian University Press, 1996, 453–93.

Mishra, R. "The Welfare of Nations." In *States against Markets: The Limits of Globalization,* edited by R. Boyer and D. Drache. London: Routledge, 1996, 316–33.

Mitchel, T. "McJihad: Islam in the US Global Order." *Social Text* 20, 4 (2002): 1–18.

———. "No Factories, No Problems: The Logic of Neo-liberalism in Egypt." *Review of African Political Economy* 82 (1999): 455–68.

Mohammadi, Ali, and Muhammad Absan. *Globalisation or Recolonization? The Muslim World in the 21st Century.* London: Ta-Ha Publishers, 2002.

Moore, Michael. *Stupid White Men and Other Sorry Excuses for the State of the Nation.* New York: HarperCollins, 2002.

Mulgan, G. *Connexity.* (Rev. edn.) London: Vintage, 1998.

———. *Politics in an Antipolitical Age.* Cambridge: Polity, 1994.

Myerly, S. H. *British Military Spectacle.* Cambridge, MA: Harvard University Press, 1996.

Nandy, A. "The Fantastic India-Pakistan Battle." *Futures* 29, 10 (1997): 909–18.

———. "Shamans, Savages and the Wilderness: On the Audibility of Dissent and the Future of Civilizations." *Alternatives* 14 (1989): 263–77.

Nederveen Pieterse, Jan. *Empire and Emancipation: Power and Liberation on a World Scale.* New York: Praeger, 1989.

———. "The History of a Metaphor: Christian Zionism and the Politics of Apocalypse." In *Christianity and Hegemony: Religion and Politics on the Frontiers of Social Change,* edited by J. Nederveen Pieterse. Oxford: Berg, 1992, 191–233.

———. "Deconstructing/Reconstructing Ethnicity." *Nations and Nationalism* 3, 3 (1997): 1–31.

———. "Hybrid Modernities: Mélange Modernities in Asia." *Sociological Analysis* 1, 3 (1998): 75–86.

———. "Collective Action and Globalization." In *Globalization and Social Movements,* edited by P. Hamel, H. Lustiger-Thaler, J. Nederveen Pieterse, and S. Roseneil. London: Palgrave, 2001, 21–40.

———. *Development Theory: Deconstructions/Reconstructions.* London: Sage, 2001.

———. "Many Doors to Multiculturalism." In *Whither Multiculturalism? A Politics of Dissensus,* edited by B. Saunders and D. Haljan. Leuven: Leuven University Press, 2003, 21–34.

———. *Globalization and Culture: Global Mélange.* Boulder, CO: Rowman & Littlefield, 2004

———. (ed.). *World Orders in the Making: Humanitarian Intervention and Beyond.* London: Macmillan, 1998.

———. (ed.). *Global Futures: Shaping Globalization.* London: Zed, 2000.

Nettl, J. P. "The State as a Conceptual Variable." *World Politics* 20, 4 (1968): 559–92.

Novak, Mojca. "Concepts of Poverty." In *Poverty,* edited by Øyen, et al., 1996, 47–61.

Nye, Joseph S., Jr. "U.S. Power and Strategy after Iraq." *Foreign Affairs,* 82, 4 (2003): 60–73.

———. *The Paradox of American Power: Why the World's Only Superpower Can't Go It Alone.* New York: Oxford University Press, 2002.

O'Hagan, J. and G. Fry. "The Future of World Politics." In *Contending Images of World Politics,* edited by G. Fry and J. O'Hagan. London: Macmillan, 245–61.

Oberschall, A. "Shared Sovereignty: Cooperative Institutions for Deeply Divided Societies." *Sociological Analysis* 2, 5 (1999): 71–7.

186 · Bibliography

Bibliography

Ohmae, K. *The Borderless World: Power and Strategy in the Global Marketplace.* London: Harper Collins, 1992.
Okita, Saburo. "Many Paths to Development." In *Facing the Challenge: Responses to the Report of the South Commission,* The South Centre. London: Zed, 1993, 272–81.
Orbach, B. "Usama Bin Ladin and Al-Qaida: Origins and Doctrines." *Middle East Review of International Affairs Journal* 5, 4 (2001): 1–7.
Øyen, E. "Poverty Research Rethought." In *Poverty,* edited by Øyen, et al., 1996, 3–17.
Øyen, E., S. M. Miller, and S. A. Samad (eds.). *Poverty: A Global Review: Handbook on International Poverty Research.* Oslo: Scandinavian University Press, 1996.
Pagano, U. 2001 "Information technology and the "biodiversity" of capitalism." In *Capitalism in Evolution,* edited by Hodgson, et al., 2001.
Palast, G. *The Best Democracy Money Can Buy.* London: Pluto, 2002.
Pape, R. A. *Bombing to Win: Air Power and Coercion in War.* Ithaca, NY: Cornell University Press, 1996.
Parenti, Michael. *Against Empire.* San Francisco: City Lights Books, 1995.
Park, W. G., and D. A. Brat. "A Global Kuznets Curve?" *Kyklos* 48, 1 (1995): 105–31.
Patterson, T. E. *The Vanishing Voter: Public Involvement in an Age of Uncertainty.* New York: Alfred Knopf, 2002.
Peacewatch, *UN Chronicle* 1 (1998): 64–6.
Pearson, S. *Total War 2006: the Future History of Global Conflict.* London: Hodder and Stoughton, 1999.
Peck, J. and A. Tickell. "Searching for a New Institutional Fix: The *After*-Fordist Crisis and the Global-Local Disorder." In *Post-Fordism,* edited by A. Amin. Oxford: Blackwell, 1994, 280–315.
Peters, R. *Fighting for the Future: Will America Triumph?* Mechanicsburg, PA: Stackpole Books, 1999.
Petras, J., and H. Veltmeyer. *Globalization Unmasked: Imperialism in the 21st Century.* London: Zed, 2001.
Petras, J. and M. H. Morley. *Empire or Republic? American Global Power and Domestic Decay.* New York: Routledge, 1995.
Phillips, K. *Wealth and Democracy: A Political History of the American Rich.* New York: Broadway, 2002.
Pipes, D. *The Hidden Hand: Middle East Fears of Conspiracy.* London: Macmillan, 1996.
Pogge, T. "Introduction: Global Justice." *Metaphilosophy* 32, 1–2 (2001): 1–5.
Pogge, T. "Priorities of Global Justice." *Metaphilosophy* 32, 1–2 (2001): 6–24.
Porter, M. E. *The Competitive Advantage of Nations.* New York: Free Press, 1990.
"Pourquoi le capitalisme doit changer," *Alternatives Economiques,* 206, September 2002.
Prestowitz, Clyde. *Rogue Nation.* New York: Basic Books, 2003.
Priest, Dana. *The Mission: Waging War and Keeping Peace with America's Military.* New York: Norton, 2003.
Rajasingham, D. "Militarization, Population Displacement, and the Hidden Economies of Armed Conflicts: The Challenge to Peace Building." Colombo: unpublished paper, 1997.
Rampton, S. and J. Stauber. *Weapons of Mass Deception: The Uses of Propaganda in Bush's War on Iraq.* Los Angeles: J.P. Tarcher, 2003.
Rathmell, A. "Mind Warriors at the Ready." *The World Today* 54, 11 (1998): 289–91.
Ravallion, M. "The Debate on Globalization, Poverty and Inequality: Why Measurement Matters." World Bank Policy Research Working Paper 3038, 2003.
Reich, R. B. *The Next American Frontier.* Harmondsworth: Penguin, 1983.
Reisman, W. M. "The United States and International Institutions." *Survival* 41, 4 (1999–2000): 62–80.
Rhodes, E. "The Imperial Logic of Bush's Liberal Agenda." *Survival* 45, 1 (2003): 131–54.
Rice, C. "Promoting the National Interest." *Foreign Affairs* 79, 1 (2000): 45–62.
Rich, P. B. (ed.). *Warlords in International Relations.* London: Macmillan, 1999.
Rivero, O. de. *The Myth of Development: The Non-Viable Economies of the 21st Century.* London: Zed, 2001.
Roberts, A. "Willing the End but not the Means." *The World Today* 55, 5 (1999): 8–12.
Rocamora, J. "Asia-Europe Economic Relations: Challenges to Progressive Solidarity." In *ASEM Trading,* edited by Brennan, et al., 1997, 37–47.
Rocamora, J. "Third World Revolutionary Projects and the End of the Cold War." In *Paradigms*

Lost: The Post-Cold War Era, edited by C. Hartman and P. Villanova. London: Pluto, 1992, 75–86.

Roles and Missions Commission 2000. *Joint Vision 2020.* Washington, DC: Government Printing Office.

Rowe, E. Thomas. "Strategies for Change: A Classification of Proposals for Ending Inequality." In *Global Inequality,* edited by Grove, 1979, 221–36.

Rubin, James P. "Stumbling into War." *Foreign Affairs* 82, 5 (2003): 46–66.

Ruggie, J. G. "Globalization and the Embedded Liberalism Compromise: The End of an Era?" Bonn: Max Planck Institute for the Study of Societies. Working Paper 97/1, 1997.

Ruiz, P. O. and R. Minguez. "Global Inequality and the Need for Compassion: Issues in Moral and Political Education." *Journal of Moral Education* 30, 2 (2001).

Rüland, J. "The EU as Inter-regional Actor: The Asia-Europe Meeting." In *Asia-Europe on the Eve of the 21st Century,* edited by Chirathivat, et al. 2001, 43–56.

Rumsfeld, Donald H. "Transforming the Military." *Foreign Affairs* 81, 3 (2002): 20–32.

Rupert, M. *Producing Hegemony: The Politics of Mass Production and American Global Power.* Cambridge: Cambridge University Press, 1995.

Rupesinghe, K. (ed.). *Conflict Transformation.* New York: St Martin's Press, 1995.

Ryan, J. *Race and Ethnicity in Multi-Ethnic Schools.* Clevedon: Multilingual Matters, 1999.

Sachs, J. D. "The Strategic Significance of Global Inequality." *Washington Quarterly* 24, 3 (2001): 187–98.

Sachs, W. *Planet Dialectics: Explorations in Environment and Development.* London: Zed, 1999.

Safarian, A. E. and W. Dobson (eds.). *East Asian Capitalism: Diversity and Dynamism.* Toronto: University of Toronto Press, 1996.

Said, E. W. *Culture and Imperialism.* New York: Knopf, 1993.

Saighal, V. *Third Millennium Equipoise.* New Delhi: Lancer, 1998.

Sakamoto, Y. "An Alternative to Global Marketization: East Asian Regional Cooperation and the Civic State." In *Global Futures,* edited by Nederveen Pieterse, 2000, 98–117.

Samad, Syed Abdus. "The Present Situation in Poverty Research." In *Poverty,* edited by Øyen, et al. 1996, 33–46.

Sanchez, O. A. *The Arms Bazaar.* New York: UNDP Office of Development Studies, 1995.

Sansoucy, L. "La Bretagne et l'Investissement étranger." Quimper: *Quest Atlantique,* 2002.

Santa Barbara, J. "Preventing War: The Role of the Global Citizen." *Peace Research Reviews* 14, 5 (1998): 1–13.

Sarkar, Prabirjit. "Are Poor Countries Coming Closer to the Rich?" *Review* 22, 4 (1999): 387–406.

Saunders, Frances S. *Who Paid the Piper: The CIA and the Cultural Cold War.* London: Granta Books, 1998.

Sayigh, Yezid. "Palestinian Security Capabilities." *Bulletin of the Conflict, Security & Development Group* 8 (2000): 1–5.

Schaeffer, R. K. *Understanding Globalization.* Lanham, MD: Rowman & Littlefield, 1997.

Scheuerman, W. E. "The Twilight of Legality? Globalisation and American Democracy." *Global Society* 14, 1 (2000).

Schwartz, H. *Century's End: An Orientation Manual toward the Year 2000.* Rev. edn. New York: Doubleday, 1996.

Scott, J. C. *Seeing like a State.* New Haven, CT: Yale University Press, 1998.

Sen, A. *Inequality Reexamined.* Cambridge, MA: Harvard University Press, 1992.

Sen, G. *The Military Origins of Industrialisation and International Trade Rivalry.* London: Pinter (orig. edn. 1984), 1995.

Servan-Schreiber, J-J. *Le Défi Américain.* Paris, 1967.

Sharp, Joanne P. "Reel Geographies of the New World Order: Patriotism, Masculinity, and Geopolitics in Post-Cold War American Movies." In *Rethinking Geopolitics,* edited by G. O. Tuathail and S. Dalby. London: Routledge, 1998, 152–69.

Sheptycki, J. W. E. "The Global Cops Cometh: Reflections on Transnationalization, Knowledge Work and Policing Subculture." *British Journal of Sociology* 49, 1 (1998): 57–74.

Siegel, F. F. *Troubled Journey: From Pearl Harbor to Ronald Reagan.* New York: Hill and Wang, 1984.

Silva, P. L. de. *Political Violence and Its Cultural Constructions: Representation and Narration in Times of War.* London: Macmillan, 2001.

Singer, P. W. *Corporate Warriors: The Rise of the Privatized Military Industry.* Ithaca, NY: Cornell University Press, 2003.

Sklair, L. *The Transnational Capitalist Class.* Oxford: Blackwell, 2001.

Smith, D. A. "Technology and the Modern World-System: Some Reflections." *Science, Technology & Human Values* 18, 2 (1993): 186–96.

Smith, D. A. "Technology, Commodity Chains and Global Inequality: South Korea in the 1990s." *Review of International Political Economy* 4, 4 (1997): 734–62.

Soros, G. *On Globalization.* New York: Public Affairs, 2002.

———. *The Crisis of Global Capitalism.* New York: Public Affairs, 1998.

Spannaus, E. "First Casualty of an Iraq War Will Be the U.S. Dollar." *Executive Intelligence Review,* February 7 (2003).

Spencer, G. "Microcybernetics as the Meta-Technology of Pure Control." In *Cyberfutures,* edited by Z. Sardar and J. Ravetz. London: Pluto, 1996, 61–76.

Spruyt, Hendrik. "Empires and Imperialism." In *Encyclopedia of Nationalism,* Vol. 1. New York: Academic Press, 2001, 237–49.

Stavrianos, L. S. *Global Rift: The Third World Comes of Age.* New York: Morrow, 1981.

Stiglitz, J. E. *Globalization and Its Discontents.* New York: Norton, 2002.

Stockman, D. A. *The Triumph of Politics: How the Reagan Revolution Failed.* New York: Harper & Row, 1986.

Stockton, N. "Defensive Development? Re-examining the Role of the Military in Complex Political Emergencies." *Disasters: Journal of Disaster Studies and Management* 20, 2 (1996): 144–48.

Strange, S. "The Future of Global Capitalism; or, Will Divergence Persist Forever?" In *Political Economy of Modern Capitalism,* edited by Crouch and Streeck, 1997, 182–91.

Street, Brian. "The International Dimension." In *Text, Discourse and Context: Representations of Poverty in Britain,* edited by U. H. Meinhof and K. Richardson. London: Longman, 1994, 47–66.

Summers, H. G., Jr. *On Strategy: The Vietnam War in Context.* Carlisle Barracks, PA: Strategic Studies Institute U.S. Army War College, 1981.

Sutcliffe, Bob. *100 Ways of Seeing an Unequal World.* London: Zed, 2001.

Taylor, P. "Options for the Reform of the International System for Humanitarian Assistance." In *The Politics of Humanitarian Intervention,* edited by J. Harriss. London: Pinter, 1995, 91–144.

Taylor, P. M. *War and Media: Propaganda and Persuasion in the Gulf War.* Manchester: Manchester University Press, 1992.

Thacker, S. C. "The High Politics of IMF Lending." *World Politics* 52 (1999): 38–75.

The Transnational Ruling Class Formation Thesis: A Symposium, *Science & Society* 65, 4 (2001–2002).

Thérien, J-P. "Reinterpreting the Global Poverty Debate." New Orleans: International Studies Association conference paper, 2002.

Thomas, Clive. "Globalisation as Paradigm Shift: Response from the South." In *Globalisation, a Calculus of Inequality: Perspectives from the South,* edited by D. Benn and K. Hall. Kingston, Jamaica: Ian Randle, 2000, 8–22.

Thorbecke, E., and C. Charumilind. "Economic Inequality and its Socioeconomic Impact." *World Development* 30, 9 (2002): 1477–95.

Thussu, Daya K. "Media Wars and Public Diplomacy." *Javnost/The Public,* 7, 3 (2000): 5–17.

Tickell, A. and J. Peck. "Making Global Rules: Globalisation or Neoliberalisation?" In *Remaking the Global Economy: Economic-Geographical Perspectives,* edited by J. Peck and H. W-C Cheung. London: Sage, 2003.

Todd, Emmanuel. *Après l'Empire: Essai sur la decomposition du système américain.* Paris: Gallimard, 2002.

Toffler, A. and H. Toffler. *War and Anti-War.* New York: Warner Books, 1993.

Tomlinson, J. *Cultural Imperialism.* Baltimore, MD: Johns Hopkins University Press, 1991.

Tow, W. T., R. Thakur, and In-Taek Hyun (eds.). *Asia's Emerging Regional Order: Reconciling Traditional and Human Security.* Tokyo and New York: United Nations University Press, 2000.

Tyrell, I. "American Exceptionalism in an Age of International History." *The American Historical Review* 96 (1991): 1031–55.

UNDP. *Human Development Report.* New York: Oxford University Press, 1996, 1997, 1999, 2003.

UNDP. *Poverty Report 2000: Overcoming Human Poverty.* New York: UNDP, 2000.

Unger, R. M. *Social Theory.* Cambridge: Cambridge University Press, 1987.

Uvin, Peter. "Ethnicity and Power in Burundi and Rwanda: Different Paths to Mass Violence." *Comparative Politics* 31, 3 (1999): 253–72.

Virilio, P. *The Vision Machine.* Bloomington, IN: Indiana University Press, 1994.

Virilio, P. *War and Cinema: The Logistics of Perception.* London: Verso, 1989.

Voss, Kim. *The Making of American Exceptionalism: The Knights of Labor and Class Formation in the Nineteenth Century.* Ithaca, NY: Cornell University Press, 1993.

Wade, R. "The United States and the World Bank: The Fight over People and Ideas." *Review of International Political Economy* 9, 2 (2002), 201–29.

———. "Japan, the World Bank and the Art of Paradigm Maintenance: The East Asian Miracle in Political Perspective." *New Left Review* 217 (1996): 3-36.

Wade, R. and F. Veneroso. "The Asian Crisis: The High Debt Model versus the Wall Street-Treasury-IMF Complex." *New Left Review* 228 (1998): 3–24.

Wallace, W. "Europe, the Necessary Partner." *Foreign Affairs* 80, 3 (2001): 16–34.

Wallerstein, I. *The Decline of American Power.* New York: New Press, 2003.

———. (ed.). *World Inequality: Origins and Perspectives on the World System.* Montréal: Black Rose Books, 1975.

Walter, A. "Do They Really Rule the World?" *New Political Economy* 3, 2 (1998): 288–92.

Walton, M. "Will Global Advance Include the World's Poor?" Broadway, England: Aspen Institute, International Peace and Security Program, 1997.

Weart, S. R. *Never at War: Why Democracies Will not Fight One Another.* New Haven, CT: Yale University Press, 1998.

White, Gordon and Roger Goodman. "Welfare Orientalism and the Search for an East Asian Welfare Model." In *The East Asian Welfare Model,* edited by R. Goodman, G. White, and Huck-ju Kwon. London: Routledge, 3–24.

Whitley, R. *Divergent Capitalisms: The Social Structuring and Change of Business Systems.* Oxford: Oxford University Press, 1999.

Williams, W. A. *Empire as a Way of Life.* New York: Oxford University Press, 1980.

———. *The Tragedy of American Diplomacy.* New York: Delta, 1962.

Williamson, J. "What Washington Means by Policy Reform." In *Latin American Adjustment: How Much Has Happened?* edited by J. Williamson. Washington, DC: Institute for International Economics, 1990.

Wilson, F. "Drawing Together Some Regional Perspectives on Poverty." In *Poverty,* edited by Øyen, et al. 1996, 18–32.

Wood, Philip J. "The Rise of the Prison-Industrial Complex in the United States." In *Capitalist Punishment: Prison Privatization and Human Rights,* edited by A. Coyle, A. Campbell, and R. Neufeld. Atlanta, GA and London: Clarity Press and Zed, 2003, 16–29.

Woodward, Bob. *Bush at War.* New York: Simon & Schuster, 2002.

World Bank. *A Better World for All.* Washington, DC: World Bank, 2000.

———. *Knowledge for Development: World Development Report 1999.* New York: Oxford University Press, 1999.

———. *The State in a Changing World: World Development Report 1997.* New York: Oxford University Press, 1997.

———. *The World Bank Participation Sourcebook.* Washington, DC: World Bank, 1996.

Zinn, Howard. *On War.* New York: Seven Stories Press, 2001.

———. *The Southern Mystique.* New York: Knopf, 1964.

Zoellick, R.B. "Congress and the Making of US Foreign Policy." *Survival* 41, 4 (1999–2000): 20–41.

Zunz, Olivier. *Why the American Century?* Chicago: University of Chicago Press, 1998.

Index